President Lincoln's Recruiter

ALSO BY MICHAEL A. EGGLESTON

The Tenth Minnesota Volunteers, 1862–1865: A History of Action in the Sioux Uprising and the Civil War, with a Regimental Roster (McFarland, 2012)

President Lincoln's Recruiter

General Lorenzo Thomas and the United States Colored Troops in the Civil War

MICHAEL A. EGGLESTON

McFarland & Company, Inc., Publishers
Jefferson, North Carolina, and London

LIBRARY OF CONGRESS CATALOGUING-IN-PUBLICATION DATA

Eggleston, Michael A., 1937–
   President Lincoln's recruiter : General Lorenzo Thomas and the United States Colored Troops in the Civil War / Michael A. Eggleston.
      p.   cm.
   Includes bibliographical references and index.

   ISBN 978-0-7864-7217-8
   softcover : acid free paper ∞

   1. Thomas, Lorenzo, 1804–1875. 2. Generals — United States — Biography. 3. United States — History — Civil War, 1861–1865 — Biography. 4. United States — History — Civil War, 1861–1865 — Participation, African American. 5. United States. Army — African American troops — History — 19th century. 6. United States. Colored Troops — History. 7. Johnson, Andrew, 1808–1875 — Impeachment. I. Title. II. Title: General Lorenzo Thomas and the United States Colored Troops in the Civil War.
   E467.1.T43E35 2013
   973.7092 — dc23   [B]   2013006040

BRITISH LIBRARY CATALOGUING DATA ARE AVAILABLE

© 2013 Michael A. Eggleston. All rights reserved

No part of this book may be reproduced or transmitted in any form or by any means, electronic or mechanical, including photocopying or recording, or by any information storage and retrieval system, without permission in writing from the publisher.

Cover photograph: General Lorenzo Thomas, President Lincoln's recruiter (Library of Congress)

Manufactured in the United States of America

McFarland & Company, Inc., Publishers
  Box 611, Jefferson, North Carolina 28640
    www.mcfarlandpub.com

To my wife Margaret, for her hard work reviewing this book.
Her infinite patience made it a reality.

Acknowledgments

This history relies upon the records, letters, diaries, and reminiscences of many of the participants mentioned in this book. In this regard, I am indebted to the staff at the library of the U.S. Military Academy for providing me with access to documents within their archives.

The Library of Congress has an excellent online resource from which people can download photographs, many of which appear in this book. Documents can also be downloaded. The National Achieves also has online resources that will help researchers.

Many excellent histories of African American involvement in the Civil War are available, but two stand out as superior works. James M. McPherson's *The Negro's Civil War* was written nearly fifty years ago and shattered the myth that African Americans were passive about the war and their freedom. Since then, most scholars and historians have followed McPherson's view of the Civil War. Perhaps the best history was written by Dudley Taylor Cornish more than fifty years ago, titled *The Sable Arm: Negro Troops in the Union Army, 1861–1865*. It is an immense resource of background and supporting documentation.

I am deeply indebted to Al Andreoni in Virginia; Professor Sheri David at the Northern Virginia Community College; Mark and Mary Holmes in Minnesota; Jack Harrigan in Arizona; and Frances Rogers in New York for the time that they took to review this book and the valuable comments they offered that helped improve my work.

Table of Contents

Acknowledgments	vii
Preface	1
Introduction	7
1. The River and the Rock	13
2. Life in the Fourth U.S. Infantry Regiment	19
3. President Lincoln's Recruiter	31
4. The Impeachment of President Andrew Johnson	83
Biographical Dictionary	101
Appendix A. Family History of Lorenzo Thomas	119
Appendix B. Early Recruiting Efforts	121
Appendix C. The Impeachment Articles	136
Appendix D. The Senate Votes	147
Appendix E. The Thomas Papers	148
Appendix F. Significant Battles Fought by U.S. Colored Troops	157
Appendix G. Medal of Honor	166
Chapter Notes	177
Bibliography	189
Index	197

Preface

A year or so ago I wrote the history of a Civil War regiment, the 10th Minnesota Volunteers.[1] In writing this book, I was impressed by the performance of African American soldiers at the Battle of Nashville in 1864. They may have been the key factor in winning this battle and perhaps the war.

Checking further, I found that one man seemed to have been instrumental in organizing African American troops to fight for the Union. His name was Lorenzo Thomas, and he was a 1823 graduate of the United States Military Academy (USMA) at West Point. As I pieced together his story, I realized that no one had published a biography of this unique individual. His name appears in larger histories of the Seminole Wars, the Mexican War and, of course, the Civil War. He was also a key participant in the impeachment trial of President Andrew Johnson after the Civil War. Lorenzo Thomas was a consummate bureaucrat, but at the same time he was an experienced officer who had fought in three wars and had been cited for gallantry. Most important, he had a fierce dedication to performing his duty to the best of his ability.

The fact that Lorenzo Thomas left no memoirs makes writing a complete biography difficult. However, he did leave a vast paper trail behind in his letters and telegrams, many of which are available at the National Archives and the Library of Congress. Records include dispatches sent by telegraph or courier that provide insight into what was happening. Reading his correspondence, I was struck by the fact that Thomas was always very respectful but very candid in his letters. In a letter answering Lincoln, he summarized his thoughts by simply stating, "This man should not be trusted."[2] For years he feuded with the secretary of war, Edwin Stanton. Stanton disliked Thomas, although Thomas did not let their mutual dislike interfere with his duty. He kept Stanton constantly informed (perhaps over-informed) of his progress in the West. After the war, the conflict between Stanton and Thomas came to a head in the impeachment hearings of President Andrew Johnson (Chapter 4), for it appears that Thomas was a key figure in winning acquittal for Andrew Johnson. The life of Lorenzo Thomas is thus, in a sense, a cold case reaching back more than two hundred years to New Castle, Delaware, in 1804, the year of Thomas' birth. During his lifetime, Thomas crossed paths and clashed with many people more familiar to us today than Thomas himself.

This book focuses on the records compiled at the time of the war, such as *The War of Rebellion: A Compilation of the Official Records of the Union and Confederate Armies*.[3] These records provide valuable information, including thousands of firsthand reports by commanders engaged in the fighting. A word of caution, though. I have tried to inject some realism into the reports of the time based upon facts. For example, many losing generals downplayed their defeats. Confederate General John Bell Hood declared victory at the Battle of Franklin when a sizable part of his command had been destroyed by the Yankees, and he ultimately lost the West for the Confederacy through his incompetence. The end for Hood followed at the Battle of Nashville.

Also, I have attempted to simplify flag officer ranks because some were brigadier generals and later major generals and so forth. These ranks changed over time and mean little compared to their positions and what they did. I simply refer to these as "general." I have likewise quoted statements made at the time, but have not attempted to explain their meaning. For example, "a lady of the town" was not intended to describe a leading citizen. I leave that and other statements to the reader's conclusion.

Research also concentrated on newspaper articles written at that time. A number of books have been published that provide African American accounts of their participation in the war. I have quoted these as much as I can. These sources provide insight into what these soldiers saw as well as their reactions to the war.

I have included photographs and other illustrations to help the reader visualize this narrative. Soldiers always have had an exquisite way of expressing themselves. This has not changed since the time of Julius Caesar. A good example is a quote from the diary of Private Lord of the 72nd Illinois that I had to read twice before I realized what he was saying. He wrote:

> I went back to get some more water, and about twenty feet above where I got the water (last night) a man shot through the head lay with his head in the little stream. I called George. We didn't say much ... I can't say that I was really sick but I felt queer, and George said he did. George looked sick, and he said I did. We didn't have any coffee that morning and we didn't drink any water.[4]

As a U.S. Military Academy graduate, Class of 1961, I was also interested in how well the members of West Point's "Long Gray Line" performed in the Civil War. Of course they did well. They were among the few leaders with any military training (at government expense) when this war started. "At government expense" was an important factor during the 19th century (and perhaps today). It made the difference between a college education or none. Given his family's circumstances when he was growing up, Robert E. Lee could not afford higher education. Had he not received an appointment to West Point, he probably would not have attended college. I chose to review the Civil War records of many of the West Point graduates. Many on opposing sides were classmates, such as John Bell Hood and John Schofield at the battles of Franklin and Nashville.

What is more interesting is how well those with no military background performed. These include General James Steedman, who commanded the U.S. Colored Troops (USCT) at Nashville, and also General Nathan Bedford Forrest, and General John McArthur, who served at Nashville. These men were among thousands of leaders who, without military training, stepped up to key responsibilities and made major contributions. There were also tens of thousands of African Americans who fought exceptionally well on both sides, but nearly all of their officers were white, which hurt recruiting. There were few African American officers in the Civil War other than the Louisiana regiments, which Lincoln attempted to justify as necessary to the war effort, as seen in Appendix 3. Appendix F provides a record of significant battles fought by African Americans for the Union.

I have tried to summarize how, especially in the South, slavery motivated African Americans to fight either for or against the Union and how African Americans were one of the decisive factors in the Civil War. My sources can be found in the chapter notes and the bibliography. In the South, millions of African Americans remained on farms and plantations, in urban labor or in government service and their very presence supported the Confederate war effort. Some mention of Confederate activities and the slaves in this book was necessary since these factors affected the recruiting efforts of Lorenzo Thomas.

Rosters allow readers to connect with their ancestors. Unfortunately, rosters of African Americans who served are incomplete, especially for the South. There are more than 200,000 names of African Americans who fought for the North, and space does not permit listing all those who served, but the National Park Service website can be searched for the names of all blacks who fought in the Civil War. It is the best resource that one can use to find ancestors.⁵ The African American Civil War Memorial in Washington, D.C., includes tablets with a list of 200,000 African American soldiers who fought for the North. Important information about blacks who won the Medal of Honor and photographs of some of them are provided in Appendix G. But the problem with numbers is that they depend on who is counting and when. In addition, Confederate numbers are sketchy and very often contradictory since many records were destroyed. For example, the surgeon general's office in Richmond was destroyed when the city was burned in 1865.⁶ While the South was working to recover from a disastrous defeat, there were many in the North compiling and preserving records. Even so, Northern records are not immune to errors. However, most historians agree that exactly 178,975 African Americans fought for the Union.⁷ Another 29,000 served in the navy (one quarter of the strength).⁸ This includes volunteers and those who were conscripted. The best estimate is that more than 200,000 African Americans enlisted or were conscripted to fight in the army for the Union.

Some understanding of the numbers of people involved is necessary in order to measure the impact of African Americans on the Civil War. With this in mind, I have attempted to summarize the numbers. The population of the United States in the 1860 Census was 31,364,367. Of this number, 3,953,760 were slaves and 498,070 were free African Americans.⁹ All but eighteen of the slaves were located in the slave states, which included the border states such as Kentucky.¹⁰ Total population of the Northern states was 18,737,425, including 225,224 free African Americans. Southern state population was 12,127,977, including 3,950,511 slaves and 250,787 free African Americans. One hundred eighty-two thousand free blacks were in the eleven Southern states that would join the Confederacy, nearly 60,000 in Virginia.¹¹ The remaining free African Americans were in the border states: Maryland, Kentucky, Missouri and Delaware. In terms of percentages, 14.1 percent of the population of the United States was African American. In the South 34.6 percent was African American while in the North the percentage was 1.2 percent.¹²

One of the factors determining the outcome of the war would be how free African Americans chose to serve. Would they be armed to fight for the South or flee north to join the Union?

The *Montgomery* (Alabama) *Advertiser* in 1861 predicted that 10 percent of the white population of the South would be needed to fight and said that this could be achieved because the slaves would stay on the plantations while whites unable to fight would be used to oversee their work. The *Advertiser* went on to say that in the North, every man enlisted would reduce the manufacturing and farming capability of the Union.

The conclusion was that the institution of slavery allowed the South to put a greater percentage of its population in the field to fight than the North.[13] But the fact was that the majority of men in the Confederate Army owned no slaves and their departure from their farms and industry hurt the South as much as the departure of working men in the North who went to war. More important, it was assumed that the location and occupation of African Americans was static when nothing was further from the truth. By the end of the war, 500,000 slaves had fled the South and many would join the Union Army. Added to that number were tens of thousands of laborers and body servants who left the plantations to serve their masters and the Confederacy. In the end, the Confederacy was no better off than the Union in diminished manpower resources to support the homefront.

When considering numbers, it would probably be better to label people non-white rather than African American, since there were thousands of Native Americans who were often counted as African Americans (for instance, the Cherokee who fought at the Battle of Pea Ridge). Furthermore, unsavory practices developed that made accurate counting more difficult. It was said that in some regions an African American soldier killed on patrol or picket duty would be immediately replaced by a new man who was told to answer to the dead man's name at pay call. An order was soon issued to prevent the drawing by collusion of the dead man's pay.[14] As a consequence, the total number that entered the Union Army may have been 20,000 to 40,000 more than the officially counted 178,795.

Many records written by African Americans have been incorporated into this book. Many in the North were literate, and the Union also pursued many programs to teach African Americans soldiers who had escaped from

U. S. Population in 1860
(From the U. S. 1860 Census)

	Population of the U. S.	Slaves	Free African Americans
North	18,737,425	18	225,224
South	12,127,977	3,950,511	250,787
Total	31,364,367	3,953,760	498,070

Total : 14.1% African American
North: 1.2% African American
South: 34.6% African American

U.S. Census of 1860 (courtesy Al Andreoni).

slavery how to read and write, as seen in Chapter 3. Eager students, they realized that the ability to read and write would help them in the future. Dozens of letters and diaries are quoted within. Spelling and grammatical errors have not been corrected and quotes are presented as they were written nearly one hundred and fifty years ago.

The Battle of Nashville brought together the valor of African American units faced with the hatred of the Confederates and the skepticism of the Union commanders. Still, the USCT won the decisive part of the battle. We are all somewhat confused by the array of units from Tennessee that fought there since many were Confederate while others fought for the Union. This was because while Tennessee was a Confederate state, many citizens, especially in eastern Tennessee, sided with the Union. Nearly all of the blacks who fought at Nashville were from Tennessee. I have tried to clarify statements from Tennessee soldiers by indicating whether they were from Union or Confederate units.

The Civil War was the first total war that involved not only the military but the civilian population. It was also the first time that technology was used to maximum advantage by both sides. A good example of this is the use of the telegraph instead of a courier (a man on a fast horse). We see this in exchanges that took place within hours by telegraph between Lincoln, Stanton, and Lorenzo Thomas after the Battle of Gettysburg in Chapter 4. It is difficult to identify battles won or lost through technology, but it was a major factor.

Introduction

Two men were instrumental in achieving the right for African Americans to fight: Frederick Douglass, the abolitionist, and Lorenzo Thomas, the adjutant general of the Union Army. This book focuses on Lorenzo Thomas, as much has already been written about Frederick Douglass.

The problem with Lorenzo Thomas is that some historians considered him to be a bureaucrat, an incompetent overage general disliked by many, as well as a drunk, both during and after the Civil War. As historian Chester G. Hearn stated: "A typical army bureaucrat who had seen little action during the war.... Thomas represented the older cadre of professional soldiers who understood military policy better than fighting."[1] Lincoln's secretary of war, Edwin Stanton, was more direct in his assessment of Thomas: "only fit for presiding over a crypt of Egyptian mummies like himself."[2] While some or all of these charges may be valid, they are unanswered because Thomas left behind no memoirs and no biographies have been written about him. In modern terms, he has been marginalized by history. This book is not a defense of Thomas and all of his faults, but instead presents his life and his impact on our nation's history.

Lincoln expressed the nation's enthusiasm for the recruitment of blacks to fight for the Union in a note to Andrew Johnson of Tennessee: "The bare sight of 50,000 armed and drilled black soldiers upon the banks of the Mississippi would end the rebellion at once."[3] On the same day that Lincoln sent this note, Lorenzo Thomas was sent west to recruit African Americans.

As the presidential election of 1860 approached, it was apparent to African Americans such as Frederick Douglass that none of the four political parties involved (Republican, Democratic, Constitution Union and Southern Democratic) favored the abolition of slavery. While it might be expected that the Republican Party, an anti-slavery party, would take a stand against the institution of slavery, the Republicans for the most part only opposed slavery in new territories.⁴ The two factions of the Democratic Party and the Constitution Party were pro-slavery. And so it was that when the war broke out, it was greeted with enthusiasm by the African Americans. As Frederick Douglass said in a speech in Boston on 3 December 1860, "I am for the dissolution of the Union ... and men can be found ... who would venture into these states [Confederacy] and raise the standard of liberty there."⁵

Secretary of War Edwin Stanton (Library of Congress).

General Winfield Scott, the army's general-in-chief, arrived in Washington on 12 December 1860 to meet with then Secretary of War Simon Cameron. His purpose was to argue for the manning of forts in the South. He also had a grand plan should war begin: blockade all southern ports and maintain control of the Mississippi River. Neither the secretary nor President Buchanan endorsed his views.⁶ Scott called his proposal the "Anaconda Plan" and, although rejected at that time, it would eventually be followed as the war progressed. It would also have a major impact on recruiting African Americans since it provided an exit for slaves from the South.

When the war started, patriotism swept the North and African Americans were ready to fight. Jacob Dobson wrote to the secretary of war, "Sir: I desire to inform you that I know of some three hundred of reliable colored citizens of this city [Washington], who desire to enter the service for the defense of the City."⁷ The problem was the reply that they received: this was a white man's war to restore the Union.⁸ Other African Americans took a view opposite that of Dobson: Why should they shed their blood for the North when the Union did not oppose, but rather perpetuated, slavery?⁹ Another African American from Troy, New York, simply stated, "We have nothing to gain, and everything to lose by entering the list of combatants."¹⁰

While the war would eventually become the means of abolishing slavery, it did not appear that way at the start. Abraham Lincoln and Jefferson Davis were performing a balancing act. Lincoln maintained that the war was to restore the Union.[11] He initially did not attack the institution of slavery, fearing that if he did so, the Southern states would not return to the Union and border states might also secede. Others grasped the problem. William P. Powell, an African American physician in New York City, wrote, "Will the government prosecute this war of subjugation, and bring the rebel states,— slavery and all,— back to their allegiance? Ah! sir, if that is the sole aim of the government of President Lincoln and the federal army, they will be surely and shamefully beaten. This war, disguise it as they may, is virtually nothing more nor less than perpetual slavery against universal freedom, and to this end the free states will have to come."[12]

General Winfield Scott — the longest serving general in the U.S. Army (Library of Congress).

Jefferson Davis, the president of the Confederacy, maintained that the Southern states had seceded to preserve their rights as states. He hoped to win foreign recognition, and admitting that the war was intended to preserve slavery would hardly win the recognition he desired. By the time of the Civil War, except for the United States, Brazil and Cuba, civilized nations had abolished slavery, (Great Britain abolished slavery by the Slavery Abolition Act of 1833).

Statistics would determine the outcome of the war and African Americans may have been the deciding factor. Quantifying the extent of African American manpower serving the North and South in the war is difficult but the best estimate of *laboring* manpower in the Union and Confederacy was 10 percent or more African American.[13] African American soldiers in the Union Army comprised about 10 percent of the force. (Chapter 3 provides details.) During the Civil War the Union organized African Americans into units called U.S. Colored Troops (USCT). A total of 170 regiments of USCT were formed.[14] The accomplishments of USCT can be seen in the chapters that follow. As the war continued and available white manpower diminished on both sides, the use of African Americans became crucial.

Throughout the Civil War, African Americans in the Union Army had to prove that they could fight effectively time after time. Eventually they were recognized as valuable soldiers who were needed to win the war. Details of several battles that show the valor and competence of the African American soldiers are found in Appendix F.

Over 200,000 enlisted and 7,122 officers served in African American regiments in the Civil War for the Union. Unfortunately, this officer strength included not more than one hundred African Americans excluding chaplains,[15] for reasons defined in Appendix B. African Americans fought in 449 engagements, including thirty-nine major battles, for the Union, and approximately 68,000 African Americans lost their lives while serving.[16] This represents a mortality rate that far exceeds that of the whites. The nation's highest award then and now is the Medal of Honor. Seventeen African American soldiers and four sailors received this award (see Appendix G).[17] To the total of African Americans who served in the army must be added 29,000 African Americans in the Union Navy,[18] and perhaps as many as 200,000 African Americans who were hired as laborers. The contribution to the Union victory was immense.

There are always problems with definitions. An example is free men versus freed men. During the Civil War, free men were those who were freed by their masters while freed men were those who escaped slavery and fled north to Union lines, where they became free. Today it makes little difference, but during the Civil War it affected the pay that Union soldiers received, as seen in Appendix B.[19] Nearly 200,000 African American soldiers served in the Union Army, or about 10 percent of the force. These numbers are only approximate estimates, and they likely leave out hundreds of thousands of laborers and support people who served in both the Confederate and Union armies and occasionally took up a rifle to fight.

African Americans and white troops had the splendid ability to sum up a problem with only a few words. "Avalanches" described the incredibly uncomfortable and sometimes fatal two-wheeled ambulances used during the Civil War. "Worm castles" referred to the hard bread that was eaten at night so the consumer did not have to look at the maggots. These perceptions are captured within.

The reader may be struck by the ingenuity displayed by the North and the South during the war. In most cases inventive ideas worked, such as seeking roots and plants to replace drugs when the Union blockade prevented delivery of medicine to Southern ports. Other solutions were a disaster, such as the Union's infamous "desiccated" (dried) potatoes (for more details, see Chapter 3). As in most wars, the various successes and failures formed an integral part of the soldiers' experiences.

Chapter 1

The River and the Rock[1]

Young Lorenzo

Lorenzo Thomas was born on 26 October 1804 in New Castle, Delaware. He was the son of Evan Thomas and Elizabeth Sherer. Lorenzo was the fifth of six children. Evan had emigrated from Wales and settled in New Castle after he met and married Elizabeth Sherer in Philadelphia on 7 January 1796. The family history of Lorenzo Thomas is provided in Appendix A. Most of the family spent their lives in New Castle and Lorenzo's parents were buried there in the Immanuel churchyard. New Castle is one of the oldest towns in the United States. It was founded in 1651 by the Dutch as Fort Casimir and by the Colonial period the name had been changed to New Castle. It was a transportation hub via land and water between Philadelphia and Baltimore since it was on the Delaware River.[2] Business had declined due to a depression in the colonial period but had picked up by the time Lorenzo was born. In 1804, the town contained 1,200 inhabitants and 160 houses.[3]

The Thomas family was, to some extent, a military family. One of Lorenzo's uncles had served on General Washington's staff during the American Revolution and both Lorenzo's father and his brother, Theodore, were in the militia organized during the War of 1812.[4] Lorenzo Thomas attended the New Castle Academy. His initial interest was in mercantile pursuits, but that would change. In May of 1819, Evan started promoting Lorenzo for an appointment to West Point, which was located north of New York City. At that time Evan held the office of Registrar for the Probate of Wills in New Castle.[5] He secured recommendations from a number of leading citizens of Delaware and wrote letters to the U.S. President James Monroe and John C. Calhoun, the secretary of war. Lorenzo was described as a youth with good morals who had received a good English education.[6] The Honorable Nicholas Van Dyke, U.S. senator from Delaware, acquired an appointment for him to the U.S. Military Academy at West Point.[7]

West Point had a long history before Lorenzo arrived. It was a Patriot stronghold during the American Revolution because of its location. It stood on high ground (the Rock) overlooking the Hudson (River) at a point where the Hudson makes a sharp turn. Sailing vessels needed to slow down in order to negotiate the turn and this afforded an opportunity for the Patriot shore batteries to concentrate fire on the British vessels that were trying to sail north from New York City to cut off New England and lay siege to such places as Albany and other Patriot strongholds. To add to the British chagrin, the Patriots stretched a chain across the Hudson that made passage more difficult, if not impossible. It was an engineering marvel and links of the chain may be seen at West Point today at the location known as Trophy Point. The British were unsuccessful in attempts to seize West Point by land attack, such as the Battle of Stony Point. General Benedict Arnold was placed in command of West Point and later in the war attempted to hand it over to the British. The plot was discovered and Arnold fled in disgrace to England, where he eventually died. His British contact, Major Andre, was captured and hanged. Late in the war, Washington established his headquarters at Newburgh, north of West Point. He was there when the war ended and many of the Continental soldiers were discharged in Newburgh. After the Revolutionary War, West Point remained an army garrison with the few soldiers who still remained in the army that would later become the United States Army.

After George Washington served two terms as president of the United States, he retired in 1796 and gave this farewell address to the nation:

26 September 1796

Friends and Citizens:

The period for a new election of a citizen to administer the executive government of the United States being not far distant, and the time actually arrived when your thoughts must be employed in designating the person who is to be clothed with that important trust, it appears to me proper, especially as it may conduce to a more distinct expression of the public voice, that I should now apprise you of the resolution I have formed, to decline being considered among the number of those out of whom a choice is to be made.... Hence, likewise, they will avoid the necessity of those overgrown military establishments which, under any form of government, are inauspicious to liberty, and which are to be regarded as particularly hostile to republican liberty. In this sense it is that your union ought to be considered as a main prop of your liberty, and that the love of the one ought to endear to you the preservation of the other.

1. The River and the Rock

Despite arguing against an overgrown military establishment in his farewell address, he took a different view shortly before he died in a letter to Alexander Hamilton, the acting commander of the nation's 10,000-man army:

Mount Vernon December 12, 1799

Sir,

I have duly received your letter of the 28th ultimo, enclosing a copy of what you had written to the Secretary of War, on the subject of a Military Academy.

The Establishment of an institution of this kind, upon a respectable and extensive basis, has ever been considered by me as an object of primary importance to this Country;—and while I was in the Chair of Government I omitted no proper opportunity of recommending it, in my public speeches, and otherwise, to the attention of the Legislature:—But I never undertook to go into detail of the organization of such an Academy;—leaving this task to others, whose pursuits in the paths of Science and attention to the Arrangements of such institutions,—had better qualified them for the execution of it.

For the same reason I must decline making any observations on the details of your plan;—and as it has already been submitted to the Secretary of War, through whom it would naturally be laid before Congress, it might be too late for alterations if any should be suggested.

I sincerely hope that the subject will meet with due attention, and that the reasons for its establishment, which you have so clearly pointed out in your letter to the Secretary, will prevail upon the Legislature to place it upon permanent and respectable footing.

With very great esteem & regard,
I am. Sir,
Your most obedt. Servt.
G. Washington

General Hamilton

President Thomas Jefferson proposed legislation to Congress in 1802 and on 16 March 1802, Congress authorized the president to organize a Corps of Engineers, which "shall be stationed at West Point ... and shall constitute a military academy."[8] The need for engineers to build fortifications and survey had always been a driving force that helped gain support for a military academy. Founded in 1802, the academy had its first graduates that same year since graduation relied upon examination rather than the four-year program that was introduced later. Two early graduates would have an effect on Lorenzo's education: Sylvanus Thayer (Class of 1808) and, to a lesser extent, Alden Partridge (Class of 1806).

Young Lorenzo was admitted to West Point on 1 September 1819 at the age of fourteen and joined the Class of 1823. There was a wide span of ages: the Class of 1823 had cadets from ages fourteen through twenty. The mean age was sixteen. Lorenzo arrived on the heels of a national scandal that required the intervention of the president of the United States, James Monroe, and many of the participants were still in place at West Point when Lorenzo arrived. It started with the superintendent of USMA, Alden Partridge.

The Cadet Mutiny

Alden Partridge was a puzzle. His conduct as superintendent of the USMA can be described as disgraceful, but his life after he was dismissed from the army demonstrated great talent and brilliance (see the Biographical Dictionary). "Old Pewter," as he was called, played favorites with the cadets whom he liked, allowing them to ignore regulations and graduate without taking an examination. He also hired friends and relatives, placing them on the academy payroll.[9] One friend grazed sheep on the drill field, and when mutton was served in the mess hall (dining room) the cadets threatened mutiny. Word of Partridge's indiscretions reached the chief engineer, Joseph G. Swift, and President Monroe, who directed that an investigation be conducted. Monroe concluded that Captain Partridge had to go and he was removed, court-martialed and dismissed (later changed to allow him to resign) from the army.

Monroe picked Major Sylvanus Thayer to replace Partridge. Thayer was a brilliant engineer and soldier who would show that he was also a great educator when he later reorganized West Point and its curriculum. Thayer was born in Braintree, Massachusetts, and became known as the "Father of West Point." He never married and spent a very long career in the U.S. Army. Thayer was faced with a major cleanup task when he arrived. Five faculty members had been arrested by Partridge for no valid reason and most of the cadets were on an extended summer vacation. Thayer freed the faculty and ordered the cadets back to West Point. To add to Thayer's problems, Partridge returned, parading the cadets and informing them that he had returned to take full command. However, he was arrested and not seen again at West Point, though his departure and later events spawned great media interest. Many of the cadets friendly with Partridge gave him a grand send-off as he boarded the steamship to New York City. When Captain John Bliss was brought in as a drill master, his tough discipline offended some of the cadets and they collected signatures on a petition to have Bliss dismissed. When they were warned that they were on the edge of mutiny, they persisted and Thayer dismissed the cadets, ordering the offenders off of the military reservation. The New York City tabloids provided their readers with details of the "Cadet Mutiny," which was by any standard a very mild (and boring) one.

Thayer next had to deal with the indifference with which Partridge had treated academics. Testing found that 20 percent of the cadet student body was incompetent and not able to pass the simplest of tests. Thayer sent half of them home and they would not return. The other half would start over with freshmen academics even though some had spent four or more years at West Point already.[10] The Partridge affair and the cadet mutiny covered in the press came very close to shutting down the academy, since it had many enemies, one of whom was U.S. Representative Davy Crockett of Tennessee. The objection of many was that the academy established a class of people that appeared to be above other professions such as doctors, lawyers and ministers.[11] This came close to the concerns expressed by President Washington in his farewell address, as seen earlier.

Lorenzo Thomas and most of the other members (some others had arrived a year earlier, awaiting the start of classes) of the West Point Class of 1823 arrived at the tail end of this giant shake-up and these cadets would benefit from the new academic standards that Thayer was putting into place. Lorenzo and his classmates would also benefit from the latest science textbooks acquired by Thayer and shipped to West Point from Europe. Thayer established a system of daily recitations in every class by the cadets (perhaps cursed by most cadets since then) and small sections divided according to ability.[12]

Cadet Thomas was described as tall and garrulous.[13] Academically, Lorenzo did quite well. In his first year, at age fifteen, he stood thirteenth of eighty-six in the class order of merit in 1820; sixteenth of sixty-three in 1821; eleventh of forty-three in 1822; and seventeenth of thirty-five at graduation in 1823. As each year moved past, some cadets failed and departed. The statistics in the 1820s were about the same as today: about one third of those who entered did not graduate.

Lorenzo's cadet career was not without difficulty. Near Christmas of 1822, liquor was discovered in his room and he was court-martialed, found guilty and dismissed from the army, but reinstated a few days later.[14] His defense was that it was near Christmas and people were allowed to bend the rules.[15]

Lorenzo's most memorable experience as a cadet must have been the cadet march from West Point to Massachusetts to meet with former president John Adams. The following account is from his obituary, published over half a century later:

> In the summer of 1821, the Corps of Cadets made an excursion under Major Worth, the Commandant. After encamping three days at Albany, it marched across to Springfield, where it remained three days. In another week it arrived in Boston. During its twelve days' stay in Boston it was entertained with the most distinguished kindness and hospitality, and visited all the places of note in the city and vicinity. On the 11th of August, "The Selectmen of the Town of Boston," presented the Corps with a stand of colors. On the 14th the Corps visited the town of Quincy, to pay honor to the venerable Ex-President John Adams, who received it with a complimentary address, and gave it an elegant breakfast, spread under an awning near his mansion. On its return the Corps marched by way of Dedham, Providence, and New London; took steamboat there for New York *via* New Haven, and reached West Point the 25th of August. The most hearty welcome was given it at every place through which it passed, the citizens sparing no pains to do it honor. The unexceptionable conduct and bearing of the cadets won for them everywhere a cordial respect and esteem. The subject of this memoir appears as "Private L. Thomas" on the roll of the Fourth Company of the Battalion, in the journal of this march.[16]

The West Point Class of 1823 graduated in June of that year. At graduation, Lieutenant Lorenzo Thomas was assigned to the Fourth U.S. Infantry Regiment. As a lieutenant fresh out of West Point, he engaged in combat against the Seminole Indians in Florida. He was decorated for gallantry and meritorious service during the Mexican War.[17] Beyond that, Thomas found his niche in the army very early in his career. He would spend nearly his entire career as an administrator. He was both a recruiter and a quartermaster, and logged over thirty years as an adjutant general at various levels, leading to his assignment as U.S. Army adjutant general in Washington during and after the Civil War.

CHAPTER 2

Life in the Fourth U.S. Infantry Regiment

The Fourth Regiment, where Lorenzo was assigned, was one of a very few regiments in the U.S. Army in the early nineteenth century. As such, it frequently was ordered to move to various locations to meet military challenges. The regimental history lists one to four moves a year. Most of these were in response to the Indian and Mexican campaigns.[1]

The Fourth Regiment of Infantry was organized by an act of Congress on 30 May 1796. After it was formed, it fought against Native Americans at the Battle of Tippecanoe and the British during the War of 1812. In May through August of that year, it served under General Hull, who surrendered his entire command to the British and was later convicted of cowardice. The Fourth's enlisted men and most of the officers were held prisoner in Canada and the regiment was subsequently disbanded.[2] In 1815 it was reorganized and fought against the British at the Siege of Plattsburg. It was then ordered south to subdue Native American tribes in Florida. By 1823, when Lorenzo Thomas joined the regiment, the headquarters and most companies were stationed in Alabama.[3] His service with the Fourth is found in Appendix E.[4]

The Seminole Wars (1818–1858)

The United States fought three wars against the Seminole Native Americans in Florida. Florida was a colony of Spain when the first war occurred. Historian John Mahon states:

> The turning point for the Seminoles came during the first two decades of the nineteenth century. Americans in the southern states coveted Spanish Florida. They felt that Florida belonged to the United States as a foot belongs to a leg.

Moreover, the Spanish government was responsible for the Indians but lacked the power to control them. Since the United States government could not, or did not, restrain its settlers along the Florida border, there were numerous clashes between American whites and the Indians living in Spanish territory. Some of these clashes sprang from cattle raids which occurred steadily on both sides. Others stemmed from slavery.[5]

Incidents continued to occur between the Seminoles, escaped slaves who had joined them, and white squatters, militia and army units. The more serious incidents occurred when the Spanish black garrison at Fort Negro killed a group of American sailors. This was followed by the ambush of a white supply boat with forty to fifty people onboard. Nearly all were killed.

For nearly twenty years the Fourth Regiment fought the Creek Indians in Georgia and the Seminoles in Florida. The regiment served under General Andrew Jackson. In March 1818, General Andrew Jackson invaded Florida to punish the Seminoles and clashes followed, with many Indian villages destroyed and much loss of life. Two citizens of Great Britain were captured and executed for providing weapons to the Seminoles. Britain protested the execution of two of its citizens and Spain protested Jackson's invasion at the time when John Quincy Adams, the U.S. secretary of state, was negotiating a treaty with Spain for the sale of Florida to the United States. After some delays, Adams told the Spanish that they should control their Indians or cede Florida to the United States. Since the Spanish had no military power to protect their interests, the United States took possession of Florida in 1821 while the members of the West Point Class of 1823 were enjoying their visit with John Adams in Boston. Throughout the First Seminole War, which ended in 1821 (the exact date is contested), the Fourth Infantry Regiment served in Florida at Pensacola and Barrancas. Yellow fever made its appearance and reduced the number of soldiers available to serve.[6] During the period of time that followed, the regiment built cantonments and raked roads to open the state.[7] Lorenzo Thomas described the work:

> Each company built its own double block of logs and a house of one story for the officers quarters. The troops also saved the boards for flooring, and rived the pine shingles for roofs. In truth, the troops did the entire work, the quartermaster department only furnishing the few tools to work with, such as nails and other hardware. Scarcely a nail was used to secure the shingles, they being hung on the rafters with wooden pegs. The spaces between the logs were chinked with moss and clay and afterward the whole was whitewashed. All completed with scarcely any expense to the government.[8]

Thomas was promoted and served as adjutant of the Fourth from 1 March 1828 to 15 February 1831.[9] By 1831, however, Thomas had contracted yellow fever and was sent north to recover his health. He was assigned to recruiting duty during the period 1831–1833.[10] During his recovery he married Elizabeth B. Colesberry in the Immanuel Church in New Castle on 4 December 1832.[11] There is no record that he knew her before he left for West Point at age fourteen. Lorenzo Thomas was baptized in that same church on 25 September 1836, soon after his father Evan Thomas died.[12] Thomas had several assignments after his recovery from yellow fever, including duty in the Adjutant General's Office in Washington, D.C., but returned to the Fourth in time to serve in the Second Seminole War (see Appendix E).

After the first Seminole War, a treaty was negotiated between the Seminoles and the United States, which provided that the Seminoles would move west. Some moved, but most did not and clashes continued between the Seminoles and the whites. On 28 December 1835, Major Francis L. Dade and 110 men of the Fourth Regiment and other units were ambushed while moving to reinforce Fort King. Nearly all were killed by the Seminoles under Chief Osceola.[13] This precipitated the Second Seminole War, which would drag on until 1841 and beyond, with most of the Seminoles removed to Indian Territory (Oklahoma). The war cost over fifteen hundred U.S. casualties, including the first Native American (Creek tribe) graduate of West Point (Class of 1822), Major David Moniac.[14]

The Fourth fought against the Seminoles throughout the war. Lorenzo Thomas was chief of staff of the army in Florida during the period 1839–1840. After the war, Thomas served in Washington, D.C., as assistant adjutant general and in other capacities until the start of the Mexican War. By this time he had risen to the rank of brevet major.

After the Second Seminole War, the Fourth enjoyed garrison duty for the first time in many years. In 1842, the regiment was ordered to Jefferson Barracks in Missouri, where it trained for two years.[15] As tension mounted between Mexico and the U.S., the Fourth was ordered to Corpus Christi, Texas. Ulysses Grant, a lieutenant in the Fourth and later president of the United States), wrote to his wife, Julia, "Our orders are for the Western borders of Texas but how far up the Rio Grand [sic] is hard to tell."[16]

The Mexican-American War

Following the defeat of the Texans at the Alamo in March 1836, Sam Houston rallied the Texan army to defeat the Mexican General Santa Anna at the Battle of San Jacinto on 21 April 1836. Santa Anna was captured and forced to sign a treaty that provided for the ceding of lands that are now Texas north of the Rio Grande. Following that, eight years of turbulence in Mexico and U.S. ambitions for more land led to another confrontation between the two nations. When the United States annexed Texas and it was admitted to the Union to become the 28th state in 1845, Mexico broke diplomatic relations with the United States. In January 1846, President Polk ordered General Zachary Taylor to Texas to a disputed strip of land between the Rio Grande and the Nueces Rivers.[17] By this time, Lorenzo Thomas, a brevet major, was assigned as assistant adjutant general to General William O. Butler, who reported to General Taylor.

The Mexican-American War of 1846–1848 was triggered by the murder of Colonel Truman Cross and a detachment of the Fourth U.S. Infantry Regiment by Mexican raiders. Colonel Cross was an assistant quartermaster general serving under General Taylor on the Mexican border. As tension over war was building, so were the armies of Mexico and the United States near the Rio Grande. Cross had gone riding alone on 10 April 1846 and disappeared. Taylor sent inquiries to the Mexican Army, which disclaimed any knowledge of Cross. Later, Lieutenant Theodoric Porter of the Fourth Regiment was killed, along with another member of his detachment, while searching for Cross on 19 April 1846. Lieutenant Ulysses Grant wrote to his wife, "Col. Cross has been killed by the Mexicans and Mr. Porter and one man killed while the rest escaped." Porter was a close friend of Grant. Searchers found Cross's body on 21 April 1846.[18] The situation escalated to war when the Mexicans sent significant forces (1,500–2,000) to attack the Americans on 25 April 1846.[19] Word went to Washington. President Polk sent a message to Congress that American blood had been shed on American soil and later he sent a declaration of war to Congress on 12 May 1846 and it was approved.[20] The United States was now at war with Mexico.

Zachary Taylor would command the U.S. troops and he was a most unlikely general. He was informal, wore no brass, and used a straw hat and civilian clothes. He was sixty-one at the start of the war and his troops called him "Old Zac" or "Rough and Ready." He spent a good amount of his time sitting outside his hut to enjoy the air. Samuel Chamberlain, who served in the war, tells this story:

> OLD ZACK was the hero of many a camp story, and the following is reliable.... When the 1st Virginia Volunteers (F.F.V.) under Colonel Hamtranck arrived they were as curious as any Yankees to see General Taylor. A certain Lieutenant who prided himself on belonging to one of the first families of the State went

up to Headquarters to obtain a glimpse of the General. Seeing an old man cleaning a sword in a bower, the officer went in and with that high-toned dignity which the descendents of Pocahontas and other Virginians are so famous for, addressed the bronze-faced old gentlemen who was hard [at] work in his shirt sleeves, "I say, old fell, can you tell me where I can see General Taylor?" The old "fell" without rising replied, "Wull, stranger, thar is the old hoss's tent," pointing to the Headquarters. "Lieutenant, if you please," said the F.F.V. "And so that is the humble abode of the great hero. Can I see him? And by the way, my old trump, whose sword is that you are cleaning?" "Wull Colonel," replied the old man, "I don't see there is any harm in telling you, seeing's you are an officer. This sword belongs to the General himself." "Ah! Then this is the victorious blade of the immortal hero! And I suppose then, my worthy man, that you work for the General?" The worthy man replied, "I reckon, and doggone hard, and little thanks and small pay I get too." The Lieutenant took off his sword and said, "My good man, I would like to have you clean my sword, and I shall come tomorrow to see the General and then I will give you a dollar." The Lieutenant was on hand the next day and seeing his old friend of the day before standing under an awning conversing with some officers, beckoned for him to come out and see him. The old gentleman came out, bringing the Lieutenant's sword. The Lieutenant was profuse in his thanks and giving the old man a poke in the ribs said, "Come, old fatty, show me General Taylor and the dollar is yours." The "old fatty" drew himself up and said, "Lieutenant! I am General Taylor," and turning slowly round, "and I will take that dollar!" The next day the General related the incident to Colonel Hamtranck and had the Lieutenant introduced in due form.[21]

After the declaration of war, Zachary Taylor and General John Wool were ordered to invade Mexico and instructed to occupy Mexico as far south as Monterrey. Monterrey, a key objective, lay on the thoroughfare from Mexico City to northern Mexico. Loss of Monterrey would be a serious blow to the Mexican government and a political advantage to the United States in any negotiations that might follow. A series of battles were thus fought, leading to the Battle of Monterrey.[22]

On 29 June 1846, Butler was appointed major general of volunteers and commanded the 1st Volunteer Division in the Army of Occupation. He served as second-in-command to Zachary Taylor during the Battle of Monterrey. Butler was described by Frank P. Blair (obviously a great admirer of Butler) in 1848:

In person, Gen. Butler is tall, straight, and handsomely formed; exceedingly active and alert. His mien is inviting — his manners graceful his gait and air military — his countenance frank and pleasing — the outline of his features of the aquiline cast, thin and pointed in expression the general contour of his head is Roman. The character of General Butler in private life is in fine keeping with that exhibited in his public career. In the domestic circle, care, kindness,

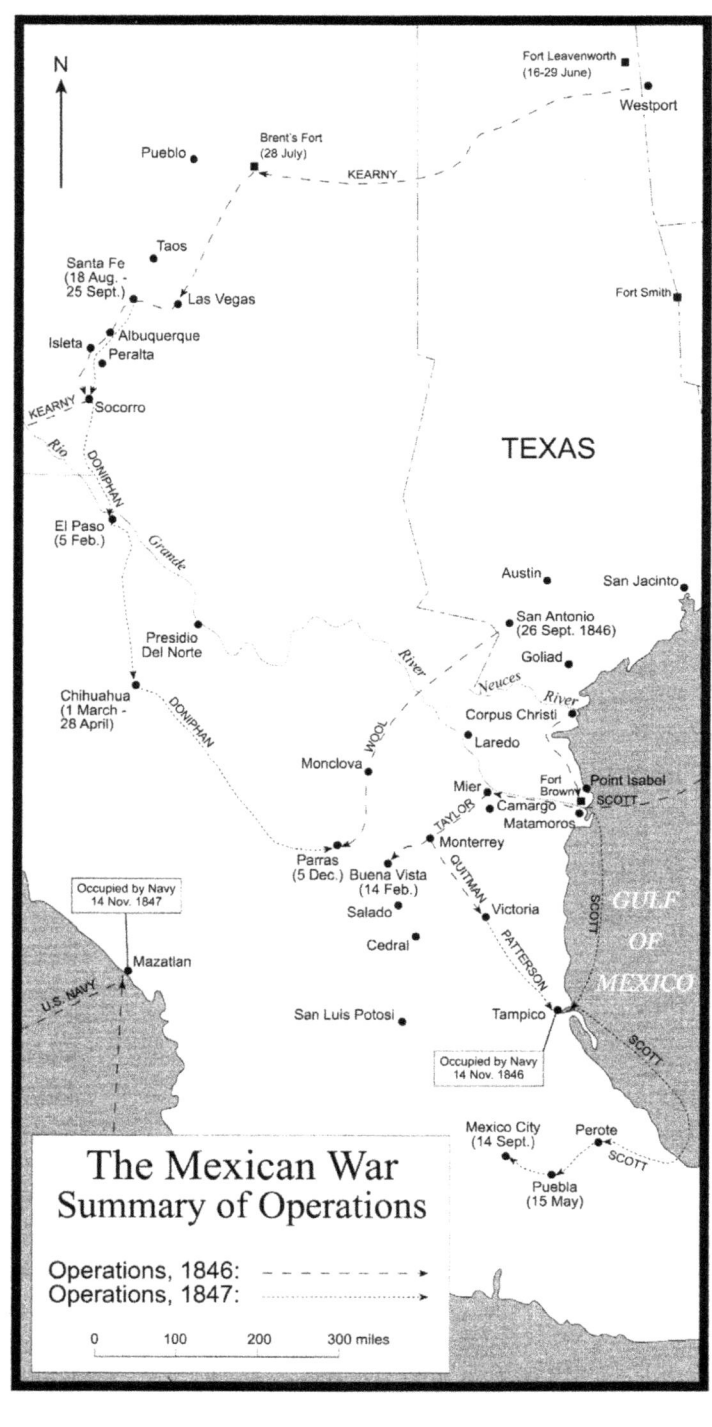

2. Life in the Fourth U.S. Infantry Regiment

assiduous activity in anticipating the wants of all around him readiness to forego his own gratifications to gratify others, have become habits growing out of his affections. His love makes perpetual sunshine at his home. Among his neighbors, liberality, affability, and active sympathy mark his social intercourse, and unbending integrity and justice all his dealings. His home is one of unpretending simplicity. It is too much the habit in Kentucky, with stern and fierce men, to carry their personal and political ends with a high hand. Gen. Butler, with all the masculine strength, courage, and reputation, to give success to attempts of this sort, never evinced the slightest disposition to indulge the power; whilst his well-known firmness always forbade such attempts on him. His life has been one of peace with all men, except the enemies of his country.[23]

The first day of the Battle of Monterrey on 21 September 1846 was a disaster for the American Army. Many U.S. casualties occurred because the army did not know how to fight in an urban environment. The Mexicans mowed down the U.S. troops from adobe huts that allowed them to fire down the streets and from rooftops.[24] Texan soldiers showed the U.S. regular troops how to fight: they had to move, using a "mouse hole" to cut through the adobe walls inside without exposing the troops to gunfire on the streets.[25] Use of rooftops also allowed the troops to move without exposure to direct fire.[26] The lessons learned at Monterrey in 1846 are still used today by the U.S. Army. It was during this battle that General Butler was wounded in the leg, and Lorenzo Thomas was later promoted and cited for gallant and meritorious service at Monterrey. Lorenzo recorded what he saw in the struggle for Monterrey:

> The army arrived at their camp in the vicinity of Monterrey about noon, September 19. That afternoon the General [Butler] endeavored by personal observation to get information of the enemy's position.... On entering the town, the General and his troops became at once hotly engaged at short musket range. He had to make his reconnaissance's under heavy fire. This he did unflinchingly, and by exposing his person — on one occasion passing through a large gateway into a yard, which was entirely open to the enemy. When he was wounded, at the intersection of the two streets, he was exposed to a crossfire of musketry and grape. In battle the General's bearing was truly that of a soldier; and those under him felt the influence of his presence. He had the entire confidence of his men.[27]

The American Army moved through Monterrey, eventually trapping the Mexican Army under General Ampudia in the city's central plaza. Negotiations followed that allowed Ampudia to evacuate in return for the

Opposite: Mexican War locations (from Felize Flannery Lewis, *Trailing Clouds Glory*, University of Alabama Press).

surrender of the city.²⁸ In his report, Butler praised his generals and added a "special thanks" to Lorenzo Thomas, who "remained in the field."²⁹

THE CASUALTIES

Casualties during this war were small compared to the U.S. Civil War, but are worth summarizing since many talented officers and enlisted soldiers were lost during this campaign. A total of 13,283 American deaths occurred in the Mexican-American War. Most of these were from disease. Additionally, over 9,000 deserted out of a total force of 111,000.³⁰ Deserting in enemy territory was a risky business. The United States did not seize and hold terrain. The strategy was to defeat the Mexican Army and continue the invasion. However, there were many reasons to desert. Camp life was miserable, wages were low, and treatment of the troops was not designed to encourage reenlistment. Many deserted to join a second unit and get another enlistment bonus (a bounty). Some say the troops deserted to join the gold rush to California but that is unlikely, since word of gold in California reached the troops only a short time before the war ended. Some deserted to join the Mexican Army. Most of these were Catholic immigrants who chafed under an army controlled by Protestants and objected to the treatment of Mexican Catholics by the American Army that they observed.³¹

SAINT PATRICK'S BATTALION

The Americans who joined the Mexican Army were organized into a unit that was most commonly known as Saint Patrick's Battalion (El Batallon de San Patricio). There were other names, such as the "Red Guards" because many were redheaded. Even in a small war, this was not an overwhelming force, although it increased to over two hundred by August 1846.³² The battalion's greatest contribution to the Mexican Army was their skill with artillery. The leader of the battalion was John Riley, a deserter from the 5th U.S. Infantry. There were also many deserters from the 4th U.S. Infantry and other units in the American Army. When the U.S. 4th Infantry and the other units of Butler's division assaulted Monterrey on 21 September 1846, the opposing force included Saint Patrick's Battalion. Lorenzo Thomas makes no references to Saint Patrick's Battalion in his report, but they were there and served well, killing many of their former comrades in the American Army.³³ They escaped when Monterrey was surrendered to the American Army.

The end came for Saint Patrick's Battalion at the Battle of Churubusco on 20 August 1847. It was one of the bloodiest battles of the war, and ended with a great American victory. Many of the American casualties were attributed to the Mexican guns served by the San Patricio Battalion.³⁴ Over one thousand Mexican prisoners were taken, including John Riley and members of his battalion. A special fate awaited them. Santa Anna remarked after the battle that if he had a few more men like them, he could have won the battle. The San Patricio casualties at Churubusco were devastating. Sixty percent were dead, wounded or captured. Only eighty-four escaped.³⁵ About eighty-five of the traitors were captured and tried. Those who deserted before the start of the war received reduced sentences. Sixty-eight were sentenced to be hanged while the others were branded with a "D" for "deserter" and flogged. General Winfield Scott, the commander, reviewed all cases. Scott confirmed the death sentences for fifty while the others got reduced sentences. John Riley was among those reprieved. These were given fifty lashes and branded with the "D."³⁶

END OF THE WAR

Following the Battle of Monterrey, several more battles were fought. The most important of these was the Battle of Buena Vista. Following the Battle of Monterrey, President Polk ordered General Taylor to join the expedition under General Scott, who would land at Vera Cruz and advance on Mexico City. Santa Anna planned to move quickly with a force of 20,000 to crush Taylor and then move south to attack Scott. In February 1847, the Fourth Infantry moved by sea to support General Scott's campaign against Mexico City. The regiment disembarked on February 9 and set up two miles to the rear of Vera Cruz.³⁷ From there the regiment continued on to the American victory at Chapultepec in Mexico City.³⁸

When Taylor heard of Santa Anna's advance, he decided to defend at a mountain pass near Buena Vista since Santa Anna outnumbered him by about four to one. Santa Anna attacked on 23 February 1847. The Mexicans broke through using cavalry, but Taylor strengthened his line by sending in his reserve, the 1st Mississippi Rifles under Colonel Jefferson Davis (later president of the Confederacy). This routed the breakthrough. Taylor ordered a counter-attack, which threw the Mexicans into confusion, and when night fell, 3,400 Mexicans lay dead on the field along with 650 Americans. Santa Anna received word of upheaval in Mexico City and abandoned the field later that night to return and restore order in Mexico City. This left Taylor in control of most of northern Mexico. In separate letters, Scott ordered Taylor and Butler to move to support his attack on Vera Cruz.

Scott landed at Vera Cruz on 9 March 1847, conducting the first U.S. major amphibious landing with a force of about 12,000 troops. The successful siege of Vera Cruz followed and Scott then marched on Mexico City. The march to Mexico City was not without incident. At Cerro Gordo, Santa Anna established a defensive position with 12,000 troops while Scott was down to 8,500 due to disease. Scott flanked the Mexican position, inflicting 1,000 Mexican casualties and taking 3,000 prisoners. Scott lost four hundred. In August 1847, Captain Kirby Smith, of Scott's 5th Infantry, remarked:

> What stupid people they are! They have lost six great battles; we have captured six hundred and eight cannon, nearly one hundred thousand stands of arms, made twenty thousand prisoners, have the greatest portion of their country and are fast advancing on their Capital which must be ours, — yet they refuse to treat [i.e., negotiate terms]![39]

Scott advanced on Mexico City on 7 August 1847. After a series of skirmishes, the Battle of Chapultepec Castle was fought on 18 September 1847, and with this victory, Scott occupied the city.

It was at Chapultepec that the last of the San Patricios were executed. Samuel Chamberlain described the execution[40]:

> The execution of the last number was attended with unusual and unwarranted acts of cruelty. The day selected was the one on which the Fortress of Chapultepec was to be stormed, and the gallows was erected on a rising piece of ground just outside of the charming little village of Mixcoac, in full view of the attack on the Castle. Colonel Harney, on account of the proficiency he had acquired as an executioner in hanging Seminoles in Florida, was selected to carry out the sentence. The man who "had ravished young Indian girls at night, and then strung them up to the limb of a live oak in the morning" was certainly well fitted to carry out the barbarous order: "To have the men placed under gallows with ropes around their necks, to remain until the American flag was displayed from the walls of Chapultepec, and then swing them off." A long beam supported by four uprights formed the gallows, from which dangled thirty lariats. As General Pillow's division moved forward to the assault, the Patricios were brought out with their arms and legs tied, seated on boards laid across wagons, and faced to the rear. When twenty-nine had been brought the Surgeon informed Harney that the other one was dying, having lost both legs at Contreras. Harney replied, "Bring the d — d s — n of a b — h out! My order is to hang thirty and by G — d I'll do it!" So the dying man was brought out and laid in a wagon and hauled to the gallows. When the order of execution was read to them, these reckless and desperate men, many of them wounded, made it the subject of mirth. One said, "If we won't be hung until yer dirty ould rag flies from the Castle, we will live to eat the goose that will fatten on the grass that grows on yer own grave, Colonel." Others cheered for "Old

Bravo," the Mexican commander in the fortress. While the fight raged in the dense grove at the foot of Chapultepec and the result seemed doubtful, they became more reserved, but when our troops appeared beyond the copse driving the Mexicans up the hill their levity returned. One said, "Colonel! Oh colonel dear! Will ye grant a favor to a dying man, one of the old Second, a Florida man, Colonel?" When Harney asked what he wanted, the Irishman replied, "Thanks, thanks, Colonel, I knew ye had a kind heart. Please take my dudeen out of me pocket, and light it by yer eligant hair, that's all, Colonel!" The red headed Colonel struck the jester a dastard blow on the mouth with his Sabre hilt, knocking some of his teeth out. As the poor wretch spit out blood he cried out, "Bad luck to ye! Ye have spoilt my smoking entirely! I shan't be able to hold a pipe in my mouth as long as I live." The battle raged for hours, with varying fortune, before Chapultepec was won. When Harney saw our flag flung to the breeze from the highest tower of the Castle, he gave the order for the wagons to start up, and thirty bodies hung whirling, swinging, kicking and rubbing against each other in a fearful Dance of Death. Just as their legless comrade died, one of the desperados cried out, "Oh, ye old brick top, is it kind ye are to make Murphy dance on nothing, now that he has lost his legs!" Such was the miserable end of the infamous Legion of San Patricio.[41]

Santa Anna's Last Campaign

Following the fall of Mexico City, Santa Anna made one last attempt to defeat the Americans in September 1847 by cutting them off from their supply base on the coast. This failed and Santa Anna was replaced by General Jose Joaquin de Herrera. Mexico now found itself outnumbered with much of its territory occupied. It had internal divisions and was unable to defend itself. Mexico sued for peace.

Aftermath

Ulysses Grant opposed the war, as did many others. He knew the army was there "really as a menace to Mexico in case she appeared to contemplate war," and he "was bitterly opposed to the measure." Grant continued to "regard the war, which resulted, as one of the most unjust ever waged by a stronger against a weaker nation. It was an instance of a republic following the bad example of European monarchies, in not considering justice in their desire to acquire additional territory."[42] In a comment that seems more appropriate to the 20th century than the 19th, he went on to say:

> It was very doubtful whether Congress would declare war; but if Mexico should attack our troops, the Executive could announce, "Whereas, war exists by the acts of, etc.," and prosecute the contest with vigor. Once initiated there were

but few public men who would have the courage to oppose it. Experience proves that the man who obstructs a war in which his nation is engaged, no matter whether right or wrong, occupies no enviable place in life or history. Better for him, individually, to advocate "war, pestilence, and famine," than to act as obstructionist to a war already begun.[43]

Lincoln, a member of Congress at that time, also opposed the war and took a view similar to Grant's. In what have been called his "Spot Resolutions," on 22 December 1847 he noted that President Polk had claimed that American blood had been shed on American soil. Lincoln countered that the House was "desirous to obtain a full knowledge of all the facts which go to establish whether the particular spot on which the blood of our citizens was so shed was or was not at that time our own soil."[44] These discussions accomplished very little. The war was fought and won by the United States and added an enormous amount of territory to the country. The Treaty of Guadalupe Hidalgo, signed on 2 February 1848, added the present-day states of California, Nevada, Utah, New Mexico, and most of Arizona and Colorado, as well as parts of Texas, Oklahoma, Kansas, and Wyoming.

With the end of the war, many of the members of the Fourth, including Ulysses Grant and Lorenzo Thomas, left the regiment and moved on to other things. The Fourth would continue to serve in the wars that followed, including the Civil War and the Indian wars. Lorenzo Thomas would spend the years after the Mexican War in Washington, first as General Scott's chief of staff and then as the adjutant general of the army, the post he held at the start of the Civil War (see Appendix E for additional details).

CHAPTER 3

President Lincoln's Recruiter

Lorenzo Thomas was adjutant general of the U.S. Army at the start of the Civil War.[1] He was flooded with paperwork, much from officers who were resigning from the U.S. Army in order to fight for the South:

May 1861
To: Colonel LORENZO THOMAS,
Adjutant-General U.S. Army, Washington, D.C.:

COLONEL: I have the honor to tender the resignation of my commission in the Army of the United States, and to request that it may be submitted to the President for his action; and I have also respectfully to ask that my successor may be appointed and ordered to relieve me as soon as practicable.

With great respect, your obedient servant,

A. S. JOHNSTON,

Colonel Second Cavalry, Brevet Brigadier-General.[2]

Albert Sidney Johnston commanded the Confederacy's western armies and was killed at the Battle of Shiloh.

Shortly after the start of the war, Secretary of War Simon Cameron was fired by President Lincoln for reasons outlined in Appendix B and he was replaced by Edwin Stanton, who took office on 15 January 1862.[3] Stanton was a holdover from President Buchanan's administration, in which he had served for a brief time as attorney general.[4] He was considered to be one of the best legal minds in the United States. Stanton had little experience with military matters and his sole qualification appears to be that he was acting as an advisor to Cameron when Lincoln felt compelled to fire the secretary of war. Lorenzo Thomas and Edwin Stanton took an instant dislike to each other. Thomas was a person focused on paperwork, protocols and regulations — in other words, an ideal person to act as adjutant general. Stanton, however, was determined to slash red tape and avoid military channels.[5]

31

Stanton, when he took office, was quoted as saying that he would pick up Thomas with a pair of tongs and drop him in the Potomac.[6] Afterwards, Stanton did his best to keep Lorenzo Thomas out of Washington. As an example, Thomas was assigned as the U.S. agent for the exchange of prisoners of war, as seen in the following letter to General Robert E. Lee:

> HEADQUARTERS ARMY OF THE POTOMAC,
> July 28, 1862.
> General R. E. LEE,
> Commanding Army of Northern Virginia.
> GENERAL: I have the honor to inform you that the Government has appointed Brigadier General Lorenzo Thomas as agent on the part of the United States for the exchange of prisoners. He will accompany the prisoners of war from Fort Delaware for whom transports have already been ordered and may be expected in the James River within a very few days. I will endeavor to give you as early notice as possible of the time when he will be at Aiken's that there may be no unnecessary delay in making the exchange at that place.
> I am, sir, very respectfully, your obedient servant,
> [GEO. B. McCLELLAN,]
> Major-General, Commanding[7]

Stanton would ultimately send Thomas west to recruit African Americans, but first other people would step up to the recruiting challenge, as seen in Appendix B. They would set the stage for Lorenzo Thomas' effort, which would follow later.

In the first year of the Civil War, Union African American regiments were organized by generals, governors and other individuals. Later it was decided that the War Department should take over and direct the organization of African American units on a large scale.[8] In March 1863, Stanton gave General Lorenzo Thomas twenty-four hours to move west and start recruiting African Americans on a massive scale. Stanton achieved two goals: he got Thomas out of Washington and at the same time he put this senior officer in charge of a major recruiting mission.[9] On the same day that Thomas moved West, Lincoln wrote to Andrew Johnson in Tennessee suggesting that "the bare sight of 50,000 armed and drilled black soldiers upon the banks of the Mississippi would end the rebellion at once."[10]

Stanton's order to Thomas was as follows:

> You will ascertain what military officers are willing to take command of colored troops; ascertain their qualifications for that purpose, and if troops can be raised and organized, you will, so far as can be done without prejudice to the service, relieve officers and privates from the service in which they are engaged, to receive commissions such as they may be qualified to exercise in the organ-

ization of brigades, regiments, and companies of colored troops. You are authorized in this connection to issue in the name of this Department letters of appointment for field and company officers, and to organize such troops for military service to the utmost extent to which they can be obtained in accordance with the rules and regulations of the service.[11]

Historian Michael T. Meier has described Lorenzo Thomas' trip west. Thomas would spend much of his subsequent time traveling back and forth from the West to Washington, D.C.:

> The order of March 25 was wide-ranging and gave Thomas a significant amount of leverage. The inspection tour was to take him first to Cairo, Illinois, to take note of the "military condition" while paying particular attention to the black refugees flooding the city. Stanton wanted to know how they were being treated by the army. The secretary gave Thomas authority to issue orders designed to provide "humane and proper treatment in respect to food, clothing, compensation for their service, and whatever is necessary to enable them to support themselves and to furnish useful service in any capacity to the Government." Thomas was to make similar observations at Columbus, Kentucky, at Memphis, Tennessee, and at the numerous posts on his way to General Ulysses S. Grant's headquarters at Milliken's Bend, Louisiana. At each stop, he was to explain the U.S. government's policy to the troops toward the "use of the colored population emancipated by the Presidents proclamation," especially their use as soldiers. In Thomas's mind, the most important section of his orders instructed him to work out a plan for organizing blacks into military units and finding officers willing to command them. He could reassign men from other regiments and promote enlisted men to officer rank if they qualified. Thomas could appoint officers for brigades, regiments, and companies and was to see to their supplies and uniforms. Through all of this, the adjutant general was to communicate frequently with the War Department, being candid as to the state of things.[12]

Thomas was to start recruiting new African American regiments along the Mississippi; this area was later expanded to include Maryland, Missouri and Tennessee.[13] He was not simply a senior recruiter, but a man charged with initiating a new Union policy, breaking down white opposition to African American soldiers and resolve issues with the new policy.[14] He did more: as adjutant general of the army, he was the channel that commanders followed to resolve problems and coordinate actions with the secretary of war and the president. He was also responsible for the welfare of the troops that he had recruited and their deployment, as seen in this telegram from General William Sherman to General Granger at Decatur.

> 3 August 1864, Near Atlanta, Georgia
> I want that brigade. Stephen D. Lee [Confederate General] is here from Mississippi with 3,500 cavalry, dismounted. Deserters say also that Forrest is here,

but, if so, only for consultation. Get General Lorenzo Thomas to give you some negro regiments to hold the railroad stations and bring forward any troops you can get. Consult General Rousseau.

W. T. SHERMAN,
Major-General, Commanding[15]

At the same time that he was recruiting, he continued his duties as adjutant general in the eastern battles. At the Battle of Gettysburg, Lorenzo Thomas was located nearby at Harrisburg. After Lee's defeat, Lincoln pressed General Meade, the Union commander, to move quickly to pursue Lee. It did not happen. Lincoln saw this report from Thomas to Stanton:

Harrisburg, PA, 8 July 1863

General Yates, with three regiments and a battery of artillery of twelve 4-pounders, is beyond Carlisle. He will be joined by two regiments, ready to move from this place. This force can make a junction with Pierce, and move down the Cumberland Valley on the enemy's rear. Four regiments are nearly ready at Reading. These will also be pushed forward. We have no definite information this morning of the enemy's movements or position.

L. THOMAS,
Adjutant-General[16]

Lincoln's response was prompt and addressed directly to Lorenzo Thomas:

8 July 1863

Your dispatch of this morning to the Secretary of War is before me. The forces you speak of will be of no imaginable service if they cannot go forward with a little more expedition. Lee is now passing the Potomac faster than the forces you mention are passing Carlisle. Forces now beyond Carlisle to be joined by regiments still at Harrisburg, and the united force again to join Pierce somewhere, and the whole to move down the Cumberland Valley, will, in my unprofessional opinion, be quite as likely to capture the "man in the moon" as any part of Lee's army.

A. LINCOLN[17]

Thomas replied to Stanton, not Lincoln:

Harrisburg, PA, 8 July 1863

Telegram of the President received. It is a slow business to organize militia and put them in march. I am afraid the President supposed the troops in advance were to delay until those behind came up, but not so, as the orders are to press forward. Pierce's infantry have been ordered to the Clear Spring country. The Forty-fifth Regiment, just arrived from Philadelphia, will go forward to Shippensburg without change of cars. Nothing of interest from the front.

L. THOMAS,
Adjutant-General[18]

In spite of the efforts of Lincoln and others, Lee escaped with his army.

Lincoln told Stanton, "Thomas was one of the best if not the best instruments for this service."[19] He had spent his career as an administrator and was best at turning chaos into order. He had also served in his early days as a recruiter for the Fourth U.S. Infantry (see Chapter 2). His assignment worked out perfectly: he managed to recruit and organize 41 percent of the African Americans who fought in the Civil War.[20]

Raising Troops in the West

Thomas did not set up a headquarters in the West and simply issue orders. He was a hands-on person and his letters show that he was constantly on the move to recruit African Americans and address issues described in this chapter. He visited centers where African Americans had been collected, urging them to enlist to fight for the Union. He was an effective speaker and had an orator's talent for motivating the troops.[21] In April 1863, he wrote Stanton "They eagerly seek to enter military organization."[22] He also spoke to white troops and, after addressing 7,000 at Helena, Arkansas, on 6 April, he wrote to Stanton that the policy of arming the blacks was "most enthusiastically received ... and infused new spirit into the troops."[23]

Lorenzo Thomas moved back and forth between the Deep South and Washington. Exhaustion and sickness nearly cost him his life in the hot June weather.[24] He recovered and returned to recruiting duty, but while he was convalescing (June–August 1863), recruiting slowed down in his absence.[25]

> Adjutant General Thomas was brought home on Sunday, in easy stages from the hospital in Louisville, saved literally from the jaws of death. The North will be interested to hear that Gen. Thomas has organized 20 negro regiments in Lower Mississippi, has put under cultivation 60 abandoned Louisiana, Mississippi, and Arkansas plantations, and, better than all, has totally changed in all the armies of the West and South the pro-slavery feeling. The services rendered by this veteran officer to the government, in organizing and pushing forward the enrollment of the contrabands of the Southwest, ought never to be forgotten.
> — Washington *Daily Morning Chronicle*, June 23, 1863

Thomas' persuasiveness was effective. By issuing orders to commanders along the Mississippi and talking to the troops, white and African

The African American Civil War Memorial in Washington, D.C. (photograph by the author).

American, the regiments were quickly formed. Thomas made it clear to all: "I come from Washington clothed with the fullest power in this matter ... I can act as if the President of the United States were himself present. I am directed to refer nothing to Washington, but to act promptly. What I have to do, to do at once ... to strike down the unworthy and elevate the deserving."[26]

The approach to recruiting was simple. First, he explained to white regiments the new government policy. Next, he asked each division commander to organize two black regiments and he enticed cooperation by offering promotions in the new regiments that were formed to whites who presented themselves to division examining boards. To General John M. Schofield, commanding at St. Louis, he said, "Collect as many black men, women, and children as possible ... you can organize the men into regiments, and I will commission the officers."[27] Division commanders or district commanders in turn passed down to their brigade commanders the order to organize regiments of African Americans. Brigade commanders found convenient ways to get this done. One method was to select officers to do the recruit-

Frederick Douglass, who urged Lincoln to enlist African Americans to fight (Library of Congress).

John C. Frémont, who played a key role in the conquest of California before the Civil War (Library of Congress).

Contraband — the escaped slaves (Library of Congress).

ing. If successful, the officer would be discharged from his unit and commissioned to a higher rank in the regiment that he had recruited.[28] Another method was to send out groups of white soldiers to recruit blacks. The recruiters would nail up posters and gather African Americans, telling them that they should fight to strike a blow against slavery.[29] Horace Greeley, an abolitionist, complained:

> There are few, if any, instances of a White sergeant or corporal whose dignity or whose nose revolted at the proximity of Blacks as private soldiers, if he might secure a lieutenancy by deeming them not unsavory, or not quite intolerably so; while there is no case on record where a soldier deemed fit for a captaincy in a colored regiment rejected it and clung to the ranks, in deference to his invincible antipathy to "niggers."[30]

The methods used to recruit were sometimes heavy-handed. Robert Cowden, who would become the commander of the Fifty-ninth Regiment USCT, described recruiting:

> The plan for "persuading" recruits while it could hardly be called the shot-gun policy was equally as convincing, and never failed to get the "recruit." ... The cavalry of the division was continually employed as scouts and skirmishers, and almost daily brought into camp hundreds of animals and negroes as spoils. The former were used in replenishing the army and increasing its effectiveness

for the summer campaign, and the latter were turned over to Colonel Bouton, whose recruiting agents accompanied all these excursions.... In this way, in the space of six weeks, the entire command was made up, without the expense of a single dollar to the Government, and on the 27th of June, 1863, was mustered into the United States military service.[31]

The incentives were enormous, as Thomas stated: "I am authorized to give commissions, from the highest to the lowest, and I desire those persons who are earnest in the work to take hold of it."[32] Thomas' authority to promote and appoint was impressive. In round numbers he could appoint thirty-five officers and dozens of noncommissioned officers for each African American regiment.[33] As William O. Stoddard, Lincoln's secretary, noted, "It was astonishing how large a number of second lieutenants of volunteers were willing to sacrifice themselves for the good of the service as majors and colonels."[34] The officers were nearly all white, but the noncom ranks were available to African Americans. This created a talent drain on white regiments in the West. Experienced officers from white regiments departed to join the African American regiments and get a promotion, but it also created vacancies in the white regiments that required promotions to back-fill vacancies. No doubt Thomas had this all figured out and it

The Integrated U.S. Navy (Library of Congress).

worked. By the end of 1863, Thomas had recruited twenty new regiments and a year later the number was up to fifty.³⁵

After Thomas moved west, General Order No. 143, issued on 22 May 1863, centralized control by the Bureau of Colored Troops under the adjutant general (Lorenzo Thomas). It may have been one of the most important general orders of the Civil War, since it established rules for the enlistment of African Americans on a grand scale. (General Order No. 143 is provided in its entirety in Appendix E.) A summary of the order follows: All of the African American regiments would be numbered consecutively and named "_____ Regiment of U.S. Colored Troops (USCT)." These were combat units:—infantry, cavalry and artillery. There were a few exceptions to the conversion to USCT in Massachusetts and Connecticut. General Hunter's original regiment (see Appendix B) was designated as the 33rd Regiment USCT.³⁶ Three screening boards were set up in Washington, Cincinnati, and St. Louis to examine those who wanted to volunteer as officers in the new regiments.³⁷ The movement to arm African Americans was now under the control of Washington.³⁸

General David Hunter — one of the first to recruit African Americans (Library of Congress).

The first task for Lorenzo Thomas was to consolidate and reorganize units formed by recruiters (identified in Appendix B). At the same time, he moved to recruit more. He faced many obstacles. The main problem remained that of finding locations where an abundance of African Americans lived who would volunteer or could be conscripted, if necessary.³⁹ This led to the raid at Jacksonville, Florida, in March 1863, in order to seize and hold the town. As Confederate General Joseph Finegan wrote, "That the entire negro population of East Florida will be lost and the country ruined there can be no doubt, unless the means of holding the St. John River are immediately provided."⁴⁰ Two African American regiments held Jacksonville and accomplished further forays up the St. John River, collecting supplies and more African Americans. The problem was that they were being worn down by constant Confederate probes, with the result that two white regiments were sent to reinforce Jacksonville. This was the first time that white and African American regiments fought together and it worked well.⁴¹

Lorenzo Thomas reported to Stanton in April, "The negroes themselves are beginning fully to comprehend the purposes of the government in regard to them, are well satisfied, and eagerly seek to enter military organizations."⁴² However, the *National Intelligencer* of 22 April reposted, "The negroes don't manifest much enthusiasm, and some have to be impressed."⁴³

For an African American, enlisting from a slave state presented challenges. In some cases, slave owners would move their slaves further south in order to escape Yankee recruiting. The slave had to first find his way to Union lines and then find a recruiting place. John Young, a slave, recalled his flight: "I run off from home in Drew County [Arkansas]. Five or six of us run off to Pine Bluff [Arkansas]. We heard that if we could get with the Yankees we'd be freed, so we run off to Pine Bluff and got with some Yankee soldiers ... then went to Little Rock and I joined."⁴⁴ The African Americans were organized into their own regiments and were not integrated into white units⁴⁵ although some groups of African Americans did join white regiments. Desegregation in the U.S. Armed Forces did not occur until 1948.

Lorenzo Thomas' recruiting efforts continued on a broad scale. In August, he contacted General John Schofield:

Jefferson Davis after the Civil War (Library of Congress).

> CINCINNATI, OHIO, August 5, 1863.
> Major General JOHN M. SCHOFIELD,
> Commanding, &., Saint Louis, Mo.:
>
> GENERAL: I am on my way to General Grant's army to organize additional regiments of volunteers of African descent, and understanding that you design making an expedition shortly into Arkansas, I request that you will in the course of your operations collect as many blacks — men, women, and children — as possible. The able-bodied men you can organize into regiments, and I will commission such officers for them as you may designate. You will, of course, be careful to give me only such officers whose hearts are in the work.
>
> I have the honor to be, very respectfully, your obedient servant,
>
> L.THOMAS,
> Adjutant-General.[46]

In his third annual message to Congress, President Lincoln stated, "Of those who were slaves at the beginning of the rebellion full 100,000 are now in the United States military service."[47] This was double trouble for the Confederacy. Not only had it lost slave manpower, but it had also added to the bayonets of the North. By the end of the war, the total number of African Americans comprised about 12 percent of the Union Army's strength.[48]

The Role of African Americans — Laborers or Soldiers?

Throughout the war Thomas would be involved in the challenge of to how to employ African Americans. The following letter from General William T. Sherman to Lorenzo Thomas defines the problem.

> 21 June 1864
> To: General Lorenzo Thomas
>
> It has repeatedly come to my knowledge, on the Mississippi, and recently Colonel Beckwith, my chief commissary, reported officially that his negro cattle drivers and gangs for unloading cars were stampeded and broken up by recruiting officers who actually used their authority to carry them off by a species of force. I had to stop it at once. I am receiving no negroes now, because their owners have driven them to Southwest Georgia. I believe that negroes better serve the Army as teamsters, pioneers, and servants, and have no objection to the surplus, if any, being enlisted as soldiers, but I must have labor and a large quantity of it. I confess I would prefer 300 negroes armed with spades and axes than 1,000 as soldiers. Still I repeat I have no objection to the enlistment of negroes if my working parties are not interfered with, and if they are inter-

fered with I must put a summary stop to it. For God's sake let the negro question develop itself slowly and naturally, and not by premature cultivation make it a weak element in our policy. I think I understand the negro as well as anybody, and profess as much conviction in the fact of his certain freedom as you or any one, but he, like all other of the guns homo, must pass through a probationary state before he is qualified for utter and complete freedom. As soldiers it is still an open question, which I am perfectly willing should be fairly and honestly tested. Negroes are as scarce in North Georgia as in Ohio. All are at and below Macon and Columbus, Ga.

W. T. SHERMAN,
Major-General, Commanding.[49]

This would continue to be a problem in both the North and the South: Would African Americans work as laborers or be allowed to fight? Lorenzo Thomas reported to Stanton:

> More troops would have been put into the army but for the pressing demands of the several departments on the Mississippi, and for laborers with the troops operating in the field. The number of blacks used in this way, excluding cooks and servants must be very large. Most of the labor is done by this class of men, and the forts on the Mississippi river have been mainly thrown up by them.... Where white and black troops come together in the same command the later [sic] have to do the work. At first this was always the case, and in vain did I endeavor to correct it, contending that if they were to be made soldiers, time

General James H. Lane — the jayhawker who recruited African Americans (Library of Congress).

would have to be afforded for drill and discipline, and that they should have only their fair share of fatigue duty. The prejudice in the army against their employment as troops was very great; but now, since the blacks have fully shown their fighting qualities and manliness it has greatly changed.[50]

The Duties

Although brought into the Union Army to fight, the blacks did more than their fair share of work on labor details. In spite of a general order prohibiting the practice, the abuses continued.

African Americans in the South were an excellent source of military intelligence to the North. Since they worked as laborers on fortifications and many other jobs, they could relate Confederate strengths and positions. Allan Pinkerton, the chief of the Union's intelligence network during the first two years of the war, would interview African Americans coming in to Union lines and he extracted a great deal of information during these interviews. Beyond that, he also hired African Americans as spies and they were well suited for this task, since they were not suspected by the Confederates and could cross lines and disappear into Confederate labor groups. Pinkerton recalled one African American spy, John Scobell, whom he recruited: "The manner in which his duties were performed, was always a source of satisfaction to me and apparently of gratification for himself. From the commencement of the war, I had found the negroes of invaluable assistance, and I never hesitated to employ them when after investigation, *I found them to be intelligent and trustworthy* [italics by the author]."[51]

Many were employed in food preparation. In 1862, four African American cooks per company were authorized.[52] Teamsters were hired by the Quartermaster's Department in large numbers because of their experience on the plantations.[53] Hospital workers, railroad workers and ambulance drivers were recruited in large numbers.[54] The greatest number were employed in construction tasks, such as digging defenses.[55]

Over 200,000 free African Americans served as laborers, teamsters, cooks, carpenters, scouts, and so on for the Union forces.[56] They loaded and unloaded ships and performed a variety of other tasks outside of the duties of a soldier. This work would continue while other African Americans later enlisted to fight. These non-military duties were not without danger. On 12 March 1863, a party of soldiers with twelve African Americans left Elizabeth City, North Carolina, to collect wood. A group of forty guerrillas attacked, killing one African American and wounding two others.[57]

Dock workers (Library of Congress).

African Americans were called on to work in the ambulance corps and infirmary corps, and years later both Union and Confederate African American veterans would relate the duties that they bravely performed. African Americans inevitably got the worst assigned duties, such as burial details, digging latrines and other heavy labor work.

After the USCT regiments were formed, African Americans were doing dirty jobs when they should have been drilling and practicing with their rifles. The result was that heavy labor details hurt readiness and the health of the command, which drove up the number of people who died. Part of the problem was a holdover of the earlier policy to use African Americans only as laborers and garrison troops in order to free up white units to fight.[58] When General W. T. Sherman prepared to march on Atlanta, he set the African American regiments to work building fortifications at Chattanooga. He kept them busy on that because he did not trust their fighting ability.[59] As a consequence, the march on Atlanta was, for the most part, an all-white affair and Sherman continued to focus on the use of African Americans as laborers.

What it came down to was how the department and divisional commanders to which the African American regiments were assigned chose to employ the regiments. In some cases they fought shoulder to shoulder with white regiments. Elsewhere they did endless work building fortifications and other manual labor.[60] In part, the use of African American soldiers as laborers was caused by the notion that they were more acclimated than whites to working in the heat. Surveys at that time seemed to support this since it was believed that "the Black will do a greater amount of work than the white soldier, because he labors more consistent."[61]

Brigadier General Daniel Ullmann complained to Senator Henry Wilson that Negro troops in Louisiana were confined to work as "diggers and drudges." So much time was required for fatigue work, he added, that there was little opportunity for drill. "Months have passed at times without the possibility of any drill at all. At Chattanooga members of the Fourteenth Colored Infantry worked from six to seven hours every day on fortifications and on returning to camp had to prepare for dress parade which was held daily, except Sunday."[62]

The abuses went on. Colonel James C. Beecher of the 35th USCT found using black soldiers to do menial tasks, such as picking up the garbage of white soldiers, inexcusable, and stated:

> It is a draw-back that they are regarded as, and called " — d Niggers" by so-called "gentlemen" in uniform of U.S. Officers, but when they are set to menial work doing for white regiments what those Regiments are entitled to do for themselves, it simply throws them back where they were before and reduces them to the position of slaves again.[63]

General Daniel Ullmann, who accepted Lincoln's offer to command African American troops (Library of Congress).

The prejudice was also apparent at the highest levels of the army. General Meade relieved a division of black troops "to use these troops in the construction of Warren's redoubts, as they work so much better than the white troops, and save the latter for fighting."[64] The War Department finally issued a directive dated 14 June 1864 that required white units to do their fair share of the labor:

The incorporation into the Army of the United States of colored troops, renders it necessary that they should be brought as speedily as possible to the highest state of discipline. Accordingly the practice which has hitherto prevailed, no doubt from necessity, of requiring these troops to perform most of the labor of fortifications, and the labor and fatigue duties of permanent stations and camps, will cease, and they will only be required to take their fair share of fatigue duty with white troops. This is necessary to prepare them for the higher duties of conflict with the enemy.[65]

Something was needed to break this mold if the African Americans were to serve as soldiers. Victories by the African American regiments gradually brought the army around to the point of view that they should serve as soldiers fighting side by side with the white regiments. The victory of the 2nd Kansas Colored over Quantrill's raiders at Baxter Springs in October 1863 was one of many battles that earned the African Americans the right to fight.[66] (See Appendix F for a summary of these battles.)

African American regiments usually got the least desirable duties when they signed up to fight. Occupation duty and guarding supply trains and prisoners were standard duties assigned to African American units. Confederate prisoners complained, to no avail, that they wanted white guards, stating that the African Americans would shoot to kill for any minor prisoner infraction. The black response was, "The bottom rail is now on the top."[67] The African American regiments were also assigned to hunt down guerrillas. These duties could be intensely boring but also at times could become very dangerous. When Southern guerrillas were cornered by African Americans, they could expect a stiff fight and instant justice if they were captured. Lieutenant Anson Hemingway of the 70th USCT wrote home, "There has been a party of guerillas prowling about here, stealing horses and mules.... A scouting party of African Americans was sent out ... and came upon the party of whom they were in pursuit. There were seventeen prisoners captured and shot by the colored soldiers."[68] The executions were in accordance with the rules of war established by the Lieber Code.[69]

In some cases, the African American soldiers were required to perform menial labor for the whites. At Morris Island, South Carolina, the following General Order 77 was issued on 17 September 1863: "It has come to the knowledge of the Brig. Gen. Commanding that detachments of colored troops, detailed for fatigue duty, have been employed in one instance at least, to prepare camps and perform menial duty for the white troops. Such use of these details is unauthorized and improper, and is here after expressly prohibited."[70]

Picket (guard) duty was never-ending for the African Americans, but it was not without some entertainment. Thomas Morgan of the 14th USCT wrote, "Colored soldiers acted as pickets, and no citizen was allowed to pass our lines, either to enter the village or out, without a proper permit. Thus many proud southern slaveholders found themselves marched through streets guarded by those who three months earlier had been slaves. These negroes often laughed over these changed relationships as they sat around their camp fires, or chatted together while off duty, but it was rare that any southerner had reason to complain of any unkind or uncivil treatment from a colored soldier."[71]

The Pay

White privates received $13 a month, plus $3.50 for clothing, and sergeants got $21. African American privates received $10 a month, $3 of which was in clothing. For higher ranks, the difference was even greater. It took two years to rectify this situation. A part of the problem was an interpretation of the Militia Act of 1862 that held that African Americans should be paid as laborers and not as soldiers.[72] African American soldiers were thus getting the same pay as laborers.[73] White soldiers could also expect a bounty (a bonus for enlisting) but African Americans received very little or none.[74] Congress authorized a $100 bounty in July 1861 for white men enlisting for three years. With the passage of the Enrollment Act (3 March 1863), three-year white enlistees received $300 and five-year recruits got $400, but these sums were divided up and paid in monthly install-

General Benjamin Butler — the first to recruit African Americans (Library of Congress).

ments with the soldiers' regular compensation. African American soldiers could make considerably more money by enlisting as a paid substitute soldier than by enlisting without a bounty. Frederick Douglass protested the inequality of pay to Lincoln and recalled Lincoln's reply:

> The employment of colored troops at all was a great gain to the colored people — that the measure could not have been successfully adopted at the beginning of the war, that the wisdom of making colored men soldiers was still doubted — that their enlistment was a serious offense to popular prejudice ... that the fact that they were not to receive the same pay as white soldiers seemed a necessary concession to smooth the way to their employment at all as soldiers, but that ultimately they would receive the same.[75]

There were efforts to rectify the inequality. In August of 1864, General Butler established a bounty of $100 to be paid to the African American recruits.[76] Furthermore, the bounty laws of 1865 and 1873 finally established equality. This had a profound effect on the soldiers' lives. One observer who returned to South Carolina and Florida in the late 1870s noted, "I rarely met an ex-soldier [African American] who did not own his house and ground, the enclosures varying from five to two hundred acres." This helped make up for the inequalities of the war when the problems of pay and bounties caused near-mutinies among the troops and hardship for the families of African Americans, some of whom ended up in the poorhouse. Captain Charles P. Bowditch of the Fifty-fifth Regiment recalled that an anonymous letter promised that half the regiment would stack arms and do no duty if pay was not received.[77]

The Army Appropriation Bill of 1864, passed on 15 June 1864, helped fix the

Robert Gould Shaw, who commanded the 54th Massachusetts (Library of Congress).

inequality of pay but problems of back pay and inequality in bounties still presented a morale problem for the African Americans.[78] The devil was in the details of this act. The bill was retroactive only to 1 January 1864. It applied to persons of color who were free on the 19th day of April 1861, and who had enlisted between December 1862 and 16 June 1864. Fortunately, it was relatively easy for a soldier to apply for and receive back pay dating to 19 April 1861. But this left many out; those who were freed after 19 April 1861 would not get the back pay. As veteran Joseph T. Wilson put it, "In other words, if one half of a company escaped from slavery on 18 April 1861, they are to be paid thirteen dollars per month and allowed three and one half dollars per month for clothing. If the other half delayed two days, they receive seven dollars a month and are allowed three dollars per month for precisely the same articles of clothing."[79]

It was not until March 1865 that Congress granted equal pay to all black soldiers who would receive the same pay as whites from the date that they were mustered into service. There were two unintended consequences of unequal pay. First, the families of the black soldiers suffered the most from the low pay. Second, it demonstrated to the blacks that white prejudice was prevalent in the North as in the South.[80]

General Nathan Banks — former governor of Massachusetts (Library of Congress).

The Physical Examinations

Each recruit was required to receive a physical examination, but few actually did. Of those examined, many African Americans were found unfit for service due to abuse by slaveholders and the rigors of life as a slave. In the North, those who enlisted and were later found unfit for service could volunteer for the Invalid Corps (later renamed Veteran Reserve Corps). This offered service and they would be given light duty, such as guarding facilities. Many unfit soldiers who had been wounded joined. As with whites, African American conscripts reported for the physical exam claiming a variety of illnesses, real and imagined. Some limped into the medical facility on crutches recently cut from a nearby forest. A volunteer doctor recalled, "The stubbornness with which they persist in shamming disease [both blacks and whites], in order to escape soldiering is truly wonderful."[81] Most who enlisted when a regiment was being formed were committed to three years of service while those enlisting in the field had a one-year obligation.[82]

General Edward A. Wild organized two African American regiments (Library of Congress).

Many African Americans who escaped slavery were in poor health. They had traveled long distances and endured hardships in order to reach Union lines. An extreme example is found in the 65th USCT regiment — thirty men died after they arrived and before they could be mustered.[83] A common practice at the time was to photograph African Americans when they reached Union lines and after they had been equipped. Scars on their backs from floggings provided ample evidence of their treatment in the South. This was done in part for Union propaganda purposes but it was also very revealing about the condition of the recruits when they arrived. All recruits were supposed to undergo a surgeon's examination so that individuals unfit for service could be weeded out (perhaps saving their lives, since they would be more likely to die from disease than a healthy person).

52   President Lincoln's Recruiter

Unfortunately, only about 11 percent of the African American recruits were examined when they enlisted.[84] Of those examined, one out of four was rejected. Whites fared little better than blacks and one survey found that one out of three whites was rejected.[85] There was an aspect of malingering in all of this. A conscripted white would be more likely to fake illness than an African American who might have traveled hundreds of miles to enlist.

Union Surgeon General Barnes was faced with old problems. Inadequate physical exams of recruits led to an influx of old people, many with degenerative diseases. These had burdened Grant's army in 1862 when a U.S. Sanitary Commission (USSC) report found a large number of patients with degenerative diseases occupying beds in the Department of the Gulf.[86] The list of disabilities was impressive: imbecility, insanity, epilepsy, paralysis, atrophied limbs, tuberculosis, secondary syphilis and many other disabling diseases.[87] Many of these unfit people were pursuing bounties and others were being paid as substitutes in the subscription system in place at that time. They attempted to hide their disabilities and local politicians would persuade the examiners to be lenient.[88] At the other end of the spectrum were the very young people who had felt compelled to answer the call in defense of the nation. Young people, age thirteen or younger, were enlisting. Undoubtedly, many who enlisted reported an age much older than they really were. It was generally agreed at that time that soldiers under the age of twenty (29 percent of the soldiers were twenty or younger) were a liability to the army.[89] Since they had not developed any immunity to common camp diseases, they were often the first to sicken and die and they could not withstand the rigors of service in the very hostile environment of war. Many of these deaths could have been avoided if decent recruit-

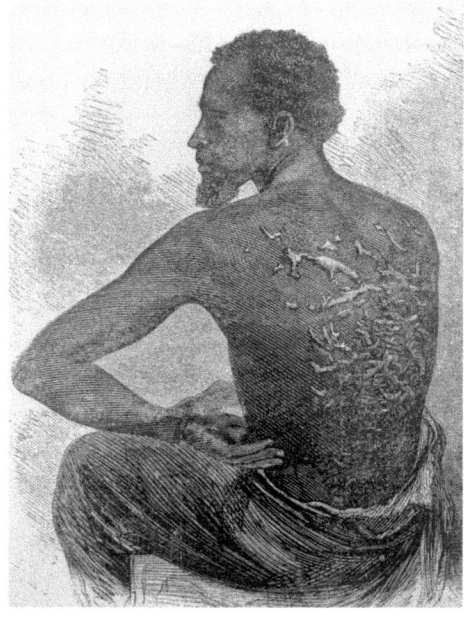

The African American recruit (Library of Congress).

ing standards and an adequate system of examining recruits had been in place.

Some say that the differences in the biology of the races had an effect on their susceptibility to diseases, but it is difficult to find any evidence to support this. Built-in immunity is another suggested cause for differences in mortality between the races, but this argument frequently falls apart. As an example, because of their environment, many African Americans in the Deep South had built up immunity to malaria.[90] Whites in the same environment would also have built up immunity to the disease. Nevertheless, malaria mortality rates for African Americans were actually higher than for whites.[91] Many of the African Americans came from areas not known for malaria, such as Kentucky, so these enjoyed no built-in immunity.[92] Surgeons, however, were convinced that African Americans were immune to malaria, so when an African American appeared at sick call with symptoms of malaria, the surgeon would ascribe the symptoms to some other disease; this misdiagnosis could be fatal. The conclusion would be that the high death rate among African Americans was caused by other factors such as poor diet or lack of the medical care (and quinine) that the whites enjoyed.

Yellow fever is another case to consider. It is a product of environment, so much so that the Confederacy was convinced that yellow fever would become the "scourge of the Yankees" as they moved south.[93] The built-in immunity of the African Americans appears to have been a factor considered by Union commanders when they sent African American troops into areas with a high incidence of yellow fever. While the yellow fever mortality among whites was higher than among African Americans, the disease resulted in very few deaths in the Civil War (23 African Americans and 409 whites) and was not significant to the health of the Union Army.[94]

The Diet of the Soldiers

The Union Army's diet was also a cause of casualties: "Beans killed more soldiers than bullets."[95] Twelve ounces of salt pork or one pound four ounces of salt beef and one pound two ounces of flour was the basic daily diet. To that was added one vegetable, navy beans, peas or 1.6 ounces of rice. This was a skimpy diet and scurvy often resulted.[96] Food quality was also a problem and beef was frequently bad in spite of efforts to pickle it and prevent decay.[97] The troops called it "salt horse" and sometimes it was a mystery meat of unknown origin. As one soldier described, "It was black as a shoe; on the inside often yellow with putrefaction."⁹⁸ The troops called the hard bread "worm castles."⁹⁹ They preferred eating the bread at night so that they did not have to look at the maggots. Fortunately, this bad diet was supplemented by food sent by relief organizations. Funds were made available to purchase additional items, especially vegetables if the unit was in a location where such items were available. More often than not, the troops used their own pay to buy more rations. Foraging (stealing food from the locals) also added to the diet.

Cooking was a disaster. The problem was that the troops preferred to cook their own rations rather than use the unit cook. As a result, filthy

A cook at work (Library of Congress).

disease-ridden utensils and pans were used to cook up the beans and other food. People frequently got sick from the practice. Pressure increased to force the troops to use the unit cook, and enough cooks were hired to provide one cook per company, usually an African American. Surgeons and line officers were made jointly responsible for supervision and instruction.[100] This reduced illness, but many soldiers continued to cook on their own: old habits die slowly.

Science entered the scene to find a way to increase the quantity of potatoes available to the troops. "Desiccated potatoes" (dried potatoes) were introduced to fix the problem of potatoes rotting in shipment. Desiccated potatoes came in large, disgusting slabs that, when boiled, resembled, as one soldier put it, "a dirty brook with all the dead leaves floating around promiscuously."[101] They were strongly loaded with pepper to make them "antiseptic." The result was indigestible by any creature and surgeons were surprised to find that scurvy reappeared even though soldiers who were hungry enough would eat anything, even this product. What was not known until many years later was that the act of drying the potatoes removed the vitamin C that prevented scurvy.

Other grand experiments followed. The "Horsford ration" (invented

Union mess hall (Library of Congress).

by a Harvard professor of that name) provided the bread and meat rations to give a Union soldier everything he needed. The meat was "sausage," consisting of such items as heart, liver, tongue and kidney, and "varnished" with gelatin. The bread was coarsely ground wheat with salt and sugar added. The idea was that this would save the government $10,000,000 per year.[102] A test was tried in Texas in 1864. The bread arrived loaded with vermin, the meat was spoiled and the troops (many of whom were African Americans) got sick.[103] There is no record to indicate that Professor Horsford ever tried his own product. He is remembered for his reformulation of baking powder which was more successful than his Civil War experiments.

The African American Casualties

Death entered the ranks of African American regiments from very unlikely sources. A Union officer, Robert Cowden, described the first summer with the African American recruits:

> During the months of July and August, the condition of the health of the regiment was very discouraging,— more than forty dying in July, and nearly as many in August. The principal cause, doubtless, was that meal, from which the corn-bread to which they were accustomed was made, could not be obtained, and they were obliged to live on wheat-bread. Their superstitions may also have increased mortalities, for so frightened were they that, going to the regimental hospital was considered equivalent to death. As soon as cornmeal was obtained and the hot weather was past, health was restored. Meantime panic had seized upon many and they had absented themselves from camp for a time, but most of them returned, and after slight punishment were restored to duty.[104]

The death rate among African Americans was considerably higher than that of their white counterparts during the war. Slaves were often in poor health when entering the army, more so than their white colleagues, because of poor diet and mistreatment

Historian Margaret Humphreys states that of the nearly 200,000 African Americans who served for the Union, 33,000 died: 29,000 from disease and only four thousand from battle wounds.[105] On the other hand, Joseph T. Wilson states that the total deaths from all causes were 68,178, and he provides a state-by-state breakdown of the deaths[106] that is close to estimates of other authors. Statistics from the war are often confusing. In the case described above, Humphreys was counting Union casualties while Wilson was counting all on both sides. According to Humphreys, whites sustained a 4.5 percent death rate from battle wounds while the African Americans fared much better and lost only 1.8 percent.[107] This is easily explained: African Americans were assigned garrison duty in order to free up white regiments to fight battles. However, garrison duty was a death sentence in many respects. Disease was rampant in the camps for such reasons as poor sanitation. The mortality rate in the Union camps for African Americans was 25 percent.[108] While far fewer African Americans died in combat or as a result of wounds, death by disease was much more common than among the whites. From all causes, battle and disease, in the Union Army 13.5 percent of white soldiers died during the Civil War, but the African American death toll was 18.5 percent.[109] The difference may have been much higher depending upon which historian's numbers one wishes to trust. The 65th Regiment USCT had no combat deaths but lost nearly half of its strength due to disease.[110] After the war, the 65th was scrutinized because it had no combat deaths, but had the highest mortality

Collecting the bones after the Battle of Cold Harbor (Library of Congress).

rate of any Union regiment in the war.[111] Some ascribe this high death rate to the locations of the camps to which they were assigned, Benton Barracks in St. Louis and the Mississippi camps in Louisiana.[112]

Other diseases were examined by the USSC to determine if susceptibility had anything to do with race, but the results were inconclusive. The higher death rates of African Americans were not a result of racial deficiencies but rather of other factors, such as medical care. African Americans in the Civil War received second-class medical care.[113] Part of the problem was the surge to recruit African American regiments in 1863–1864. While white regiments were already in place with medical staff, the African Americans were new. As mentioned above, the much-studied 65th Regiment USCT had the highest death rate of all 2,000 Union regiments, due entirely to medical problems. All of the benefits of the sick, such as better food, clothing and shelter, were not available to the men of the 65th and other African American regiments.[114]

Regiments were authorized a surgeon and two assistant surgeons, but few of the African American regiments had their full complement, and those that did had surgeons and assistant surgeons assigned late in the war. Some regiments had none. (See *Official Army Register of the Volunteer Force of the United States Army for the Years 1861, 1862, 1863, 1864; Volume 8* for a listing of surgeons and assistant surgeons assigned to African American regiments.[115]) The point is that in the surge to create new African American regiments, medical doctors were offered an opportunity for promotion and good pay, but there were not enough qualified people to assign to this duty. As a consequence, unqualified people were assigned. For example, the 1st Regiment USCT had a physician appointed who did not want to go South when the regiment was assigned there. He was replaced by a surgeon who disliked the duty, did nothing and was fired. Then a private stepped forward, claiming that he had medical experience (he had none). It appears that his motivation was the ample supply of medicinal alcohol, which he greatly enjoyed. Finally, a competent surgeon stepped forward, but inspectors found that he also had a liking for medicinal whiskey and on the day of the inspection found him with a black eye and bruised nose from his previous night's activities.[116]

The army did its best to find qualified surgeons for the African American regiments, with uneven results. Calls to medical colleges were put out to enroll medical students. While some colleges had excellent curricula, others were merely diploma factories that inflicted more medical incompetence on the troops. The soldiers' opinion of these students' work: "They poison the soldiers."[117] General Lorenzo Thomas, who was given the task of forming the new African American regiments by Secretary of War Stanton, refused to appoint anyone without a medical degree.[118] It was a hopeless situation; in the end, the troops paid the price for the Union Army's inability to find qualified surgeons.

Even cultural differences and language played a role in the high mortality rates. If a white surgeon did not understand his African American patient, it would be difficult to diagnose and treat the disease.[119] The consequence of all of these problems with the white surgeons was the creation of a gulf between the soldiers and their surgeons.[120] This caused the soldiers to avoid treatment, which further drove up the death rate.

As the war progressed, Union forces were ordered east and south from Benton Barracks to fight a number of campaigns for which neither the whites nor African Americans were acclimated. They entered into one of the most unhealthy regions of the United States. There was a buildup of African American regiments in Louisiana and the plan was to replace whites, who were thought to be more susceptible to diseases such as malaria and yellow fever. It was thought that African Americans, with their acquired immunity, were better suited to defending forts in this area.[121] While this approach reduced African American battle casualties, death from disease increased because of inadequate food and lack of decent shelter and the heavy labor that had to be performed in building fortifications. The high water table in the region served as an excellent breeding ground for mosquitoes and the water was frequently contaminated with fecal matter.[122] While the official policy was that whites and African Americans would divide the labor, in fact the division was less than equal, with the African Americans doing the vast major-

General Edmund Kirby Smith (Library of Congress).

ity of the work. Three of the African American regiments in Louisiana lost four men in combat and 1,374 to disease. James E. Yeatman of the Western Sanitary Commission visited Youngs Point, Louisiana, in late 1863. The camp housed about 2,100 people. "There appears to be more squalid misery and destitution here than any other place that I have visited. The sickness and deaths were most frightful. During the summer from thirty to fifty died in a day and some days as many as seventy-five."[123]

As the war ended, 25,000 African American troops were ordered to Texas.[124] First, they were to defeat Confederate General Kirby Smith. Even after Lee and Johnston had surrendered and Jefferson Davis had been captured, Smith refused to give up the fight. The second goal was for Union forces to secure the border with Mexico, which was in a state of upheaval due to warfare between Benito Juarez and the French emperor Maximilan. The last target was to deal with recalcitrant Texans who wanted to continue the war. However, this last point was not valid. By the summer of 1865, even Texans were war weary and wanted no further part in fighting.

Scurvy now became the major killer of African American troops. Scurvy continued unabated because of poor planning in setting up a

Benito Juarez — the Mexican leader (Library of Congress).

Maximilian — the emperor of Mexico (Library of Congress).

General Sterling Price — "Old Pap" (Library of Congress).

system to supply the troops, but more important, white Union officers were diverting supplies and funding to their own purposes. Surgeon Charles Radmore, in charge of Brownsville Hospital, ordered "certain quantities of Brandy, Whiskey, Claret Wine, Champaign, Hostetters Bitters and Malt Liquors for the Gov't Service, almost none of which ever found its way to the sick in Hospital or elsewhere."[125] The result of this sad affair in Texas was that about 2,500 African Americans perished from scurvy in the summer and fall of 1865. In a severe case of underreporting, the Union Army listed 128 African American soldiers who had died.[126] The USSC commission had done much during the war to supplement the diets of Union soldiers, but by late 1865 it was shutting down, so the soldiers' "safety net" was not available when it was needed the most in Texas.

Throughout the war there appeared to be trends that caused more deaths among African Americans than should have occurred. First, at all levels of the army, the accepted cause of high death rates was the racist view that African Americans were an inferior race that could not survive. As a result, when the high death rates occurred, they were accepted as yet more proof of inferiority without looking further. Second, the African American regiments were supported by incompetent surgeons and some white officers who were determined to profit from the war at the expense of the troops. Third, as with whites, many volunteers were enlisted in the army without adequate physicals or no examinations at all. As a result, people with diseases and disabilities were accepted into the Union Army and it was their death sentence. Fourth, African American regiments were singled out as the bottom of the supply chain, receiving rations and all other supplies after white regiments had been served. Finally, the Union Army moved troops without regard to their background or acquired immunity (except for the Louisiana assignments of African Americans). No one suggests that the army leaders had the time to consider this, but preventive measures and adequate equipment would have helped. As an example, the 10th Minnesota Regiment was moved from Minnesota south to Benton Barracks at the same time that the influx of African American regiments took place. The Minnesota troops had winter clothing and knew how to survive in cold weather. They may also have had built-in immunities to counter some of the diseases at Benton Barracks. The African Americans were brought in from the southern climates where they had been raised. Whether or not they had cold-weather clothing is not known. What is known is that while hundreds of African Americans were dying at Benton Barracks from pneumonia and dysentery, a total of five Minnesotans lost their lives. However, another factor has to be entered into this equation. Throughout the war African Americans generally had living quarters far less satisfactory than those of the white troops. Ira Russell described the quarters assigned to the African Americans as follows: "One hundred men were crowded into rooms originally meant for fifty, necessarily rendering the air very impure; and this evil was rendered greater by faulty construction of the barracks and imperfect ventilation."[127] The result was a perfect breeding ground for tuberculosis, pneumonia and other diseases. While this was going on, members of white regiments were writing home about winter sports, guard duty and a winter fair.

Historian and physician Margaret Humphreys has summarized it best: "Had they [African Americans] received even the minimal care meted out to white troops, the same (though still inadequate) diet, the same amount of fatigue duty, the same uniforms, the same tents, and had they been led by experienced, caring officers, much of the disease that mowed them down could have been prevented."[128]

The Families

General Hunter's approach toward recruiting in the Carolinas was heavy-handed. Under Sherman, African American "contrabands" had been put back on their masters' former plantations. Hunter, however, had them conscripted from their plantations to be armed and equipped as the 1st Carolina Colored Regiment: "Wives and children embraced the husband and father thus taken away, [to serve in the Union Army] they knew not where, and whom, as they said, they should never see again."[129] Army recruiters soon discovered that a willingness to enlist rested on the army's commitment to the dependents of recruits. General Butler, recognizing this, pledged family protection and support to his recruits in December

1863. Other military officials, including Adjutant General Lorenzo Thomas in the Mississippi Valley, soon followed suit, with positive results.[130]

As Lorenzo Thomas moved west to recruit, he found that many of the recruits had recently been slaves or came directly from the farms. Loyal slave owners received compensation when their men signed on; slaves owned by men with known Confederate sympathies were just taken as contraband of war. Some plantation owners, loyal or not, resisted the impressment of their slaves into the Union Army, and reprisals were threatened on the families of men who volunteered. The women who remained would have to do the men's full work in the fields, or the women would be sold "down river." Slave women were also subject to physical reprisal, such as rape or brutal beatings, if their men left. It was not until March of 1865 that Congress acted to liberate the families of black soldiers whose owners were not in rebellion.[131]

As recruiting expanded, the army found that it could find little work for the families, which meant that the army had to feed and care for the women and the children. Some recommended that the families be relocated

Lorenzo Thomas addressing the USCT (Library of Congress).

to free states, but Lorenzo Thomas resisted: "the prejudice of the people of those states are against such a measure." The army concluded that the families should be kept in the vicinity of the soldiers on abandoned plantations, which the Confederates viewed as important targets (because the families of Union soldiers were located there). Federal manpower would thus be needed to protect the families.[132]

Thomas knew that successful recruiting depended upon having adequate provisions to care for the families of the soldiers. Even General William T. Sherman lectured Lorenzo Thomas on this subject: "If negroes are taken as soldiers by undue influence or force and compelled to leave their women in the uncertainty of their new condition, they cannot be relied on." Sherman believed that if the government enabled them to "put their families in some safe place and then earn money as soldiers or laborers, the transition will be more easy and the effect more permanent."[133] Sherman wrote to Thomas in April 1864:

HDQRS. MILITARY DIVISION OF THE MISSISSIPPI,
Nashville, Tenn., April 12, 1864.
General LORENZO THOMAS,
Adjutant-General U.S. Army, Vicksburg, Miss.:
DEAR GENERAL: Yours of march 30, from Natchez, is received, and I take pleasure in answering. I confess I fear to enunciate any plan that can reconcile all objections, but am willing to say that I will use all my official power and influence to carry out yours or that of the War Department. My objections to the plantation scheme are purely military. The Mississippi is a long, weak line, easily approached from the rear. Plantations of, say, three whites and fifty blacks to a mile of river can be broken at any point by a guerrilla band of 100 with perfect impunity. You and I know the temper of the whites in the South.

I heard a young lady in Canton, educated at Philadelphia, who was a communicant of a Christian church, thank her God that her negroes, who had attempted to escape into our lines at Big Black, had been overtaken by Ross' Texas brigade and killed. *She thanked God, and did so in religious sincerity* [italics by author]. Now, a stranger to the sentiment of the South would consider this unnatural, but it is not only natural but universal. All the people of the South, old and young, rich and poor, educated and ignorant, unite in this, that they will kill as vipers the whites who attempt to free slaves, and also the "ungrateful slaves" who attempt to change their character from slave to free.

Therefore, in making this change, which I regard as a decree of nature, we have to combat not only with organized resistance of the Confederate forces, but the entire people of the South. Now, I would prefer much to colonize the negroes on lands clearly forfeited to us by treason, and for the Government to buy or extinguish the claims other and loyal people in the districts chosen. I look upon the lands bordering the Mississippi, Steele's Bayou, Deer Creek,

Sunflower, Bogue Phalia, Yazoo, &c., in that rich alluvial region lying between Memphis and Vicksburg, of which Haines' Bluff, Yazoo City, and Grenada are the key points, as the very country in which we might collect the negroes, will find more good land already cleared than in any district I know of, and it would enable the negro at once to be useful. If, however, the Government prefer the "lessee" system, then I shall favor the occupation by a black brigade of Harrisonburg, and cover as well as may be the Mississippi country lying between the Washita and Yazoo. General Slocum will soon come down, and we believe he will co-operate with you [with] his whole heart. Of course the possession of Vicksburg is a sine qua non. We don't want the task of taking it again; but if he can spare troops he will be instructed, in connection with Natchez, to hold Harrisonburg, with one or more gun-boats up the Washita and Tensas.

Steele is ordered to hold the line of Red River, but I must have Smith's command, which I loaned for but thirty days, and I have reason to know that banks must swing over against Mobile, so Steele will have only his Arkansas command, and that may be sufficient; of this we cannot judge until we know what is already done. If Shreveport be taken before these orders reach Steele, he may hold that point; otherwise, all he should attempt would be Alexandria, in connection with the gun-boats.

We have sure enough a big job on hand, and the only way is to go on trusting to consequences following naturally grand results. Lee and Johnson must be whipped, and it should not be deferred an hour beyond the first possible practicable moment.

I necessarily write in some haste, but you will catch the drift of my argument.

With respect, your friend and servant,

W. T. SHERMAN,
Major-General, Commanding.[134]

Thomas had written to Stanton on 1 April 1863 regarding the condition of the colored population and urged that they "be employed with our armies as laborers and teamsters, and those who can be induced to do so, or conscripted if necessary, be mustered as soldiers." Regiments of Negroes, Thomas believed, would give protection to the free colored people working abandoned plantations along the Mississippi. "They could garrison positions," he concluded, "and thus additional [white] regiments could be sent to the front."[135] However, a year later, Sherman remained focused on the safety of black families and the use of African Americans as laborers:

HEADQUARTERS MILITARY DIVISION OF THE MISSISSIPPI,
Near Kensaw Mountain, June 26, 1864.

General LORENZO THOMAS,
Louisville, Ky.:

I was gratified at the receipt of your dispatch from Chattanooga. I would have answered sooner if our telegraph had not been broken so often of late. As I wrote you, I know all the people have left North Georgia for the regions of the Flint and Applachicola with their negroes.

The regiments of blacks now in Chattanooga and Tennessee will absorb all the recruits we can get, but if you raise new regiments they could be well employed about Clarksville, Bowling Green, and on the Tennessee River, say at the terminus of the Northwestern Railroad. My preference is to make this radical change with natural slowness. If negroes are taken as soldiers by undue influence or force and compelled to leave their women in the uncertainty of their new condition, they cannot be relied on; but if they can put their families in some safe place and then earn money as soldiers or laborers, the transition will be more easy and the effect more permanent.

What my order contemplated was the eagerness of recruiting captains and lieutenants to make up their quota in order to be commissioned.

They would use a species of force or undue influence and break up our gangs of laborers as necessary as soldiers. We find gangs of negro laborers well organized on the Mississippi at Nashville and along the railroads most useful, and I have used them with great success as pioneer companies attached to divisions, and I think it would be well if a law would sanction such an organization—say of 100 to each division of 4,000 men.

The first step in the liberation of the negro from bondage will be to get him and family to a place of safety, then to afford him the means of providing for his family, for their instincts are very strong, then gradually use a proportion—greater and greater each year—as sailors and soldiers. There will be no great difficulty in our absorbing the four million of slaves in this great industrious country of ours, and being lost to their masters the cause of war is gone, for this great money interest then ceases to be an element in our politics and civil economy. If you divert too large a proportion of the able-bodied into the ranks, you will leave too large a class of black paupers on our hands; the great mass of our soldiery must be of the white race, and the black troops should for some years be used with caution and with due regard to the prejudice of the races. As was to be expected, in some instances they have done well, in others badly, but on the whole the experiment is worthy a fair trial, and all I ask is that it be not forced beyond the laws of natural development.

In Maryland, Missouri, and Kentucky it may be wisely used to secure their freedom with the consent of owners.

W. T. SHERMAN,
Major-General, Commanding[136]

Thomas wrote to Stanton:

NASHVILLE, TENN., June 25, 1864.
Honorable E. M. STANTON,
Secretary of War:

I repaired to Chattanooga and opened communication with General Sherman. He reports that he is receiving no negroes, as they are scarce in Northern Georgia, having been driven to Macon and Columbus. The general prefers them armed with spades and axes to soldiers at the present time, but does not object to the enlistment of any surplus negroes coming within his lines. I may have to fill the two incomplete regiments at Chattanooga with recruits from Kentucky. They made an excellent appearance. I shall have to investigate the acts of Lieutenant-Colonel Brown, a Tennessee officer commanding at Gallatin, Tenn., reported as driving the negro refugees beyond his line, and returning fugitive slaves to rebel masters in Simpson County, KY. His Tennessee cavalry are reported as treating them harshly and cruelly, kicking and abusing them. The heavy artillery regiment at Paducah numbers, 1,019. I will send infantry officers there as soon as I can get them. There are near 1,000 blacks at the camp at Louisville and 1,000 at Camp Nelson. As soon as the officers arrive I will organize two regiments and distribute them for recruiting purposes. The same system will be carried out in Tennessee. The negroes, seeing armed parties of their own people passing through the country, will readily join them, being satisfied of protection. I leave for Louisville the 26th instant.

L. THOMAS,
Adjutant-General.[137]

Thomas devised a plan to make use of the African Americans without making them wards of the government. He appointed a commission of three people to supervise the leasing of plantations and the assignment of African Americans to work the fields. The wages were very low. Men received seven dollars a month, women were given five dollars and children between twelve and fifteen received half these rates (children below twelve were not permitted to work in the fields). The families would be provided food and clothing, but the cost of clothing was deducted from their wages, which left very little. Thomas was criticized for his plan, but it was probably the best that he could have devised at that time.[138]

John Eaton had been assigned to supervise contraband activities in Mississippi, Tennessee, and Arkansas. The problem was that he was a civilian without any authority to enforce his orders. Lorenzo Thomas stepped in and commissioned him a colonel of an African American regiment. A month later he added another regiment to Eaton's command. These actions not only established Eaton's authority but also provided him with the forces needed to defend the camps and plantations that were frequently targeted by Confederate raids. Unfortunately, more problems followed. The Treasury Department became involved and tried to revoke the leases established by Eaton and Thomas, replacing them with their own versions. Plantation owners realized that the Treasury leases were impractical and wanted no part of them, but conflict continued. Finally, the plantation owners decided to return the African Americans to military control for support. Thomas wrote Stanton of his intentions:

> I consider the Negroes under my control ... furnishing of course labor under the calls of the Treasury agent; but Mr. Mellen [Treasury Department] assumes that they are entirely under him, and he desires to issue orders accordingly. The military authorities must have command of the Negroes or there will be an endless confusion. I will keep this control unless ordered to the contrary.[139]

Thomas followed up with a telegraph to Stanton that was seen by Lincoln, who immediately replied directly to Lorenzo Thomas by telegraph:

> I wish you would go to the Mississippi River at once and take hold of and be master in the contraband and leasing business.... Mr. Mellen's system doubtless is well intended, but from what I hear, I fear that if persisted in it would fall dead within its own entangling details. Go there and be the judge.[140]

Thomas met with Mellen and the result was that the military would assume control of all estates, except for abandoned plantations. The Treasury Department would be allowed to continue writing leases for these.[141]

The Officers

Secretary of War Stanton gave Lorenzo Thomas the authority he needed to appoint officers to the USCT regiments. This amounted to thousands of men since each regiment needed thirty-five officers.[142] Thomas wrote to the commanders in the field:

> You will ascertain what military officers are willing to take command of colored troops; ascertain their qualifications for *that* purpose, and if troops can be raised and organized, you will, so far as can be done without prejudice to the service, relieve officers and privates from the service in which they are engaged, to receive commissions such as they may be qualified to exercise in the organization of brigades, regiments, and companies of colored troops. You are authorized in this connection to issue in the name of this Department letters of appointment for field and company officers, and to organize such troops for military service to the utmost extent to which they can be obtained in accordance with the rules and regulations of the service.[143]

In a letter to General Frederick Steele on 15 April 1863, Lorenzo Thomas explained how officers should be selected.

> It is the wish of the War Department that each Division Commander interest himself in the officering and recruiting of two regiments; the officers to be selected by a Board of Officers appointed by the Division Commander to determine on the fitness of the applicants, and to assign them to positions, without regard to present rank, merit alone being the test." White soldiers were to be appointed to fill all the commissioned ranks of each regiment, the positions

of first sergeant, and the noncommissioned grades. Those recommended by the boards for appointment were to be mustered out of their old regiments and mustered into their new colored organizations "as fast as companies, battalions, and regiments are organized."[144]

Private George W. Baird, for example, was qualified for and appointed to the rank of colonel in the 32nd U.S. Colored Troops. While this large a jump in rank was not a common promotion, other white privates and sergeants were also promoted to higher ranks. Thirty-three percent of lieutenants had been privates.[145] Baird later won the Medal of Honor and was promoted to flag officer rank.

The illiteracy of the African Americans who enlisted demanded a better educated and versatile white officer corps that could improve the new soldiers and educate them beyond drill and rifle practice. Officers in white regiments frequently volunteered for service with the USCT since promotion went with the reassignment. In this way, the USCT received a flow of experienced white officers who knew how to fight and train. Additionally, a candidate officer training academy, the Free Military School, was established in Philadelphia for new candidate officers who would be assigned to USCT. It was similar to the Officer Candidate School in the U.S. Army today. At the conclusion of training, a board examination was administered to the white officers; this arrangement was very successful.[146] A few African Americans also served as officers in the USCT.[147]

In spite of Jefferson Davis' threat that white officers of African American regiments would be executed if captured by the Confederate Army, the surge of applications to serve in African American regiments increased. The Confederates apparently never realized that their murders of prisoners of war had created a crusade in the North and molded a fighting force that would fight to the death. By 26 December 1863, 1,051 applications had been received and 560 were approved.[148]

The search for qualified officers eventually led to the establishment of boards at the division level in the field or post level in the northern cities to review applicants and select those who would be officers in the African American regiments.[149] Boards usually selected white applicants, although, as mentioned above, a few African Americans served as officers during the Civil War.[150] About one hundred African Americans served as officers and most of these appointments stemmed from Benjamin Butler's decision to create black regiments in Louisiana early in the war. Lorenzo Thomas wrote to General John A. McClernand explaining the boards:

> In the Divisions, the plan has been to institute a board of one officer from each Brigade to examine the several applicants and make a roster for the Regiment

and this being approved is sufficient. I desire none but those well qualified and whose heart is in the work.[151]

In August 1863, General John Beatty of Ohio reported the results of the examining boards:

> The time was, when we thought it would be impossible to obtain good officers for colored regiments. Now we feel assured that they will have as good if not better officers than the white regiments. From sergeants applying for commissions, we are able to select splendid men — strong, healthy, well informed, and of considerable military experience. In fact, we occasionally find a noncommissioned officer who is better qualified to command a regiment than nine-tenths of the colonels.[152]

As George R. Sherman, an officer in the 7th USCT, pointed out, "These slaves came to us ignorant of anything outside of their plantation. They were kept that way on the plantation since an ignorant African American was less likely to hold disruptive ideas."[153] Daniel Ullmann outlined the task ahead for officers of the African American regiments in his General Order, Number 7, dated 10 June 1863:

> [They] were selected for qualities which ... eminently qualify them for this duty, namely: accurate knowledge of drill, long experience in the field, patience, diligence, and patriotism the constant exercise of all these qualities necessary. You are brought into contact with a race, who, having lived in abnormal condition all of the days of their lives, are now suddenly elevated into being soldiers of the United States fighting against their oppressors, as well for their own liberties as for the integrity of the republic. They are to be molded by you into drilled and disciplined troops. You cannot display too much wisdom in your conduct, both as regards yourselves and them. Let the law of kindness be your guide.[154]

The requirement that all officers of African American regiments be white hampered recruitment. Robert Purvis, a disgusted African American in Philadelphia, wrote, "It argues a sad misrepresentation of the character, aspirations and self-respect of colored men, to suppose that they would submit to the degrading limitations which the government imposes in regard to the officering of said regiments [whites only]. From that position and error, the government must recede, or else ... failure to secure the right kind of men will result."[155] During the Battle of Gettysburg, the problem became more apparent.

HEADQUARTERS Department of the Susquehanna, Harrisburg, Pa., July 2, 1863.

Brigadier General LORENZO THOMAS,
Adjutant-General, U.S. Army, Washington, D.C.

GENERAL: The colored company recruited in this city for six months' service refused by unanimous vote to be mustered in with white officers. Is it not the understanding that they should have white officers? It would certainly make them far more efficient.

I am, general, very respectfully, yours,

D. N. COUCH,
Major-General, Commanding.[156]

Lorenzo Thomas followed up with this note to Stanton:

HARRISBURG, PA., July 4, 1863. (Received 2.30 P.M.)

Honorable E. M. STANTON:

No additional information. There are two companies of blacks here, who desire to enter the service with their own officers. I do not know whether you have authorized the muster of any black officers. I have been opposed to it, and I find General Couch also objects. Please let me know your decision, to cover this and similar cases in the free States.

L. THOMAS,
Adjutant-General[157]

Lincoln and Stanton would not budge. From their point of view, the public needed to digest the enlistment of African American privates who would be armed before they had to swallow the concept of African American officers.[158]

The Search for Competent Physicians

The USCT were formed over two years after the start of the war, which meant that most available physicians had already been assigned to white regiments.[159] A problem faced by both the North and the South was the qualifications of the physicians. At the start of the war, army physicians had to choose sides. Of the 122 physicians in the army, 24 joined the Confederacy and 98 remained with the Union. Very few on either side had experience in treating mass casualties. Only those physicians serving on the frontier had ever seen a gunshot wound, and if so, it was a novelty. Those who had served in the Mexican War were senior citizens by 1861 and likely to do more harm than good. New physicians joining either army were generally young and inexperienced, with poor qualifications. In the North the best surgeons were placed as surgeons of volunteers. Others settled for the less stressful jobs, such as examining recruits. Examining boards for surgeons turned this around. The boards got rid of incompetent surgeons and others resigned rather than face a board. Medical degrees at that time were in many cases meaningless, presented by "diploma mills." Even the Harvard medical school was backward: it had no stethoscope (invented in France in 1816) until 1868 and no microscope until 1869. States had no licensing systems. But thanks to the examining boards, by spring of 1864, incompetent surgeons had nearly disappeared from Union ranks.[160]

Finding an African American with a medical degree during the Civil War was difficult, but there were a few out there. These faced the problem of racism on the part of those empowered to make appointments and many were rejected, but it was a numbers game. Even if every African American physician who applied had been enlisted, it would not have made a dent in the requirement for surgeons in African American regiments. The story of African American Dr. Alexander Augusta is a relevant case. Dr. Augusta was assigned to the 7th Regiment USCT and had seniority over white surgeons who followed him. They created a cause célèbre, complaining all the way up the chain of command to Lincoln that they could not be subordinate to an African American. There is no record of Lincoln's reply, but Augusta was later reassigned to a recruitment center in Baltimore.[161] As a brevet lieutenant colonel, Augusta became the highest-ranking African American to serve in the war.[162]

In spite of efforts at all levels to find physicians for the USCT, the endeavor for the most part failed because of timing. In a desperate attempt to provide physicians for USCT, the army turned to the use of hospital stewards. Hospital stewards performed a variety of tasks, serving as pharmacists, hospital administrators and clerks. N. P. Banks, commanding in the Department of the Gulf, objected to the use of hospital stewards as surgeons: "Hospital Stewards of low order of qualification were appointed to the office of Assistant Surgeon and Surgeon. Well-grounded objections were made from every quarter against the inhumanity of subjecting the colored soldiers to medical treatment and surgical operations from such men."[163] Lorenzo Thomas also registered strong objections to the use of hospital stewards as physicians. He told Colonel E. D. Townsend in December 1863, "The rule laid down by me, and which I have adhered to, was that I would not give an appointment to a Hospital Steward, or any person, who was not a graduate of a Medical College. I place the Negro Troops on a perfect equality, in this aspect, with the white troops." In February 1864 he reiterated his position: "No Surgeons or Assistant Surgeons will be appointed in Regiments of African Descent unless it is certified that they are graduates of medicine."[164]

Lorenzo Thomas mounted his own effort to obtain physicians for the USCT. He sent a medical officer to New England to persuade physicians to appear before the medical board for commissions in the USCT. He also arranged an early graduation program with selected medical schools for those who agreed to enter the USCT immediately after successful completion of the college's oral examination and written thesis. In Tennessee, Colonel Mussey appointed anyone who "can procure a diploma from some recognized medical school." Next, contract surgeons were sought and asked to sign a one-year agreement to work for the military, as were medical cadets employed by the War and Navy Departments. Both of these groups were attractive because they had an understanding of military structure and experience with the types of injuries and illnesses they were likely to encounter in the USCT.[165]

During the war, the buildup of surgeons was impressive. A survey in 1916 identified a total of 3,237 Confederate surgeons who had served in the army and 107 in the navy.[166] The North had over 13,000.

The Equipment

Lack of adequate clothing was a problem for both sides during the war. One of Stonewall Jackson's troops had a vivid recollection of the march from Romney to Winchester, Virginia, and back in January 1862:

> As the men "marched along," he wrote, "icicles hung from their clothing, guns, and knapsacks; many were badly frost bitten, and I have heard of many freezing to death along the road side. My feet peeled off like a peeled onion on a march, and I have not recovered from its effects to this day.... The soldiers in the whole army got rebellious — almost mutinous — and would curse and abuse Stonewall Jackson; in fact, they called him 'Fool Tom Jackson.'" This same Confederate chronicler also related that eleven members of the Fourteenth Georgia and Third Arkansas regiments froze to death while on guard duty near Hampshire Crossing during the same campaign. "Some were sitting down," he recalled, "and some were lying down; but each and everyone was as cold and as hard frozen as the icicles that hung from their hands and faces and clothing — dead! They had died at their post of duty. Two of them, a little in advance of the others, were standing with their guns in their hands, as cold and as hard frozen as a monument of marble — standing sentinel with loaded guns in their frozen hands!"[167]

Many similar stories were related by soldiers in the North. After a long campaign in Missouri pursuing Confederate General Sterling Price, T. J. Hunt of the 10th Minnesota Volunteers described the end of a 1,000-mile march, much of which was accomplished by soldiers marching barefoot in the snow.

When near Jefferson City, we forded the Osage River, thirty rods wide (snow having covered the ground in the morning) during a severe rain, lest it should rise so we could not cross at all. With the wet and cold, our sufferings were intense, as we could not start fires with green wood which was all that could be gotten. On Nov. 3rd we faced a northeast snowstorm, the whole day. Minnesota never had so severe a one so early. At first it melted freely, then freezing, it lay more than four inches deep before night, which it ceased snowing but froze hard. We spent [the] night in open fields with little fuel and no shelter from wind. I got some sleep lying on a brush heap from which I had shaken the snow. Others sat or lay on their rubber blankets, but were obliged to get up and stir briskly and keep our little fires going, taking turns in warming one side at a time, as our scanty fires were made against stumps while wood was cut from other stumps to feed them. Axes were too few but were in constant use. Three houses nearby sheltered a few sick, probably saving a few lives. I thought many would die that terrible night, but I believe none did. The next day, the snow melted and the second day, it nearly disappeared. Mud took its place, and we moved on. In a few days we reached St. Louis, a muddy, ragged worn army.[168]

Thomas Jefferson Hunt of the Tenth Minnesota Volunteers in his old age (Minnesota Historical Society).

The USCT suffered more from bad equipment than the white regiments. It appeared that the Ordnance Department was using the USCT as a dumping ground for unserviceable equipment. Bayonets that were poorly constructed or did not fit the soldiers' rifled muskets

The firing line (Library of Congress).

were a frequent source of complaints. In December 1863, General Ullmann complained that he sent his African American regiment into battle with "arms almost entirely unserviceable." Lorenzo Thomas, after an inspection of the eight companies of a colored regiment stationed on Ship Island, Mississippi, wrote Stanton on 7 April 1864: "This Regiment, like most of this class of soldiers, have the old flintlock muskets, altered to percussion, which have been in use for a long time. The muskets of this Regiment were condemned once, and have been condemned by an Inspector a second time."[169]

Uniforms were always a problem throughout the war. Fortunately, the USCT were organized in 1863, when the army supply system had caught up with demand. Additionally, their late arrival worked in their favor in that some of the African American regiments were equipped with lightweight uniforms that were the envy of white regiments who still suffered from heavy uniforms weighing up to six pounds.[170] However, the uniforms were only a small amount of the weight that a soldier had to carry. The cartridge box alone weighed over four pounds and to that was added the weight of the rifle, canteen and all the other items that a soldier needed to sustain himself in battle. The result was that many soldiers developed hernias, bad backs and other physical problems. There is nothing new about this and it has been an issue in wars before and since. The major problem is that in a campaign, replacement items are generally not immediately available. As an example, the 10th Minnesota Volunteers arrived at Benton Barracks, Missouri, after a long campaign defeating General Price. Some were without uniforms (except for undergarments) in December of 1864.[171] Fortunately, they were quickly rearmed and re-equipped for the Battle of Nashville. One historian has suggested that western units fared better because they were composed of "outdoor men" who could survive hardship, but there is no statistical evidence to support this.[172] On the contrary, western units suffered a higher percentage of losses due to battle and disease (most historians agree with this assessment).[173] They suffered because they were at the end of the supply chain.[174]

White regiments occasionally received bad rations, but for African American regiments, bad rations such as wormy meat and bug-infested bread were the order of the day. Both whites, and African Americans were supposed to receive the same rations.[175] The problem was the quality. The commissariats steered the bad rations to the African Americans. They were the newest units and were less likely to complain because of inexperience. African American regiments learned fast, and by the time they were being organized into brigades they had ample rank and experience to refuse the bad rations, as did the white regiments.[176]

Education and Training

Trying to track individual black soldiers after the war was a nightmare. Many enlisted under an alias (to avoid retribution against their kin back home) while others had no surname. A soldier might enlist as "George" or "Jim," and that was it. To make matters worse, most were illiterate because it was against the law in the South to educate slaves. One recruiter asked the soldier his name. "Dick," was the reply. When told he needed a second name, the reply was "Don't want none — one name enough for me." After some persuasion, most would select a second name. Since many did not want the name of their slave holder, they selected names like Grant, Sherman, Lincoln, Butler, and so forth.[177]

Education became a priority. In March 1864, Lorenzo Thomas issued General Order No. 9, which required that at least one school be established in each police district along the Mississippi River. These schools were for the education of African American children. There were problems with compliance and uniformity of the schools, so Thomas placed the schools under the supervision of Colonel John Eaton, who was required to appoint superintendents who would manage the activities of schools within their districts. The schools were later expanded to include Tennessee, Arkansas, and Kentucky.[178]

Training was difficult due to illiteracy, and also because few of the new soldiers knew how to handle a firearm. Once trained with weaponry, it became clear to all that trained African Americans were too dangerous to keep as slaves and they would never be slaves again.[179] The African Americans worked hard at training and were highly motivated. For slaves, the opportunity for freedom was important. For Northern free African Americans, the motivation was to gain acceptance and equality through their service.[180] Training meant drill, and a great deal of it. The regiments were divided into lettered companies of one hundred men each. Many African Americans were promoted to corporal and sergeant based upon literacy, appearance and leadership skills, but literacy was not a prerequisite, especially for those who enlisted from the South.

Enlisted slaves quickly learned to read and write since they saw this as important to their future.[181] Education was important for their performance in their regiment as well. By August 1865, more than 200,000 free African Americans had received instruction in reading and writing.[182] As the Annual Cyclopedia stated, "When deprived of their commanders [they] would not in general fight independently as well as those who have had more education."[183] Frances Beecher, the wife of Colonel James Beecher (commander of the Thirty-fifth Infantry), recalled, "My mornings were spent in teaching the men of our regiment to read and write, and it became my pleasing duty and habit whenever our moving tents were pitched there to set up school ... the result was when the men came to be mustered out, each one of them could proudly sign his name to pay-roll in a good legible hand. When enlisted, all but two or three of them were obliged to put a mark to their names."[184] James T. Wilson of the Fifty-fourth Regiment recalled that every company had someone to instruct reading if nothing more.[185]

Lack of education had an impact on promotions and assignments to officer and non-commissioned officer ranks. Lorenzo Thomas would only assign whites to officer positions. Some non-commissioned officer positions, such as first sergeant, also went to whites because the jobs required handling of extensive paperwork and a high degree of literacy. This arrangement provided that the white sergeants would be promoted to officer ranks as vacancies occurred and blacks would replace the white sergeants as literacy improved. Thomas' plan did not work out very well. White sergeants had joined to obtain promotion to officer ranks and when vacancies did not occur they became disgruntled. The blacks were blocked from promotion by whites in sergeant positions, but when a black was promoted, the white sergeants became unhappy. The morale of the unit thus declined.[186]

In Enemy Hands

Jefferson Davis' Christmas Eve Proclamation of 1862 stated that "all negro slaves captured in arms [will] be at once delivered over to the executive authorities of the respective States to which they belong to be dealt with according to the laws of the said States."[187] This could be a death sentence because they would be found guilty of insurrection. Free blacks would not necessarily be executed, but could be sold into slavery. A more common practice was to return slaves to their masters, sell them or put them to work on Confederate fortifications. African American soldiers were well aware of the dangers of being captured as a Union soldier. Corporal Gooding wrote, "There is not a man in the regiment who does not appre-

General Patrick R. Cleburne — the "Stonewall of the West" (Library of Congress).

ciate the difficulties, the dangers and maybe the ignoble death that awaits him, if captured by the foe."[188]

Thousands of African American Union troops and their white officers were murdered by the Confederate Army. The prevailing view of Confederate generals such as Forrest and Pickett and many other Confederate troops was that African American Union soldiers were insurgent armed murderers who wanted to kill all Southern whites. Armed African Americans should therefore be executed immediately when captured or returned to slavery. Obviously, it was easier for a Confederate soldier to just shoot prisoners than to try to figure out how to return them. The Confederate policy also maintained that Union white officers were promoting an African American uprising and should be put to death or otherwise punished at the discretion of a military tribunal.[189] However, publicly promoting murder or carrying it out does not make good copy in the press. There followed public statements and Confederate policies that fell short of advocating murder but still encouraged it, and this led to countless murders by the Confederates.

General Nathaniel Bedford Forrest — "The Wizard of the Saddle" (Library of Congress).

In many cases, the murders of African Americans and their white officers were conducted secretly and exact numbers are not known. Frequently, however, Union troops would respond to the Confederate executions by doing the same thing to Confederate prisoners. A typical reaction to the Confederate murders follows. This incident occurred near Baxter Springs in what is now Oklahoma:

> While encamped there, on the 18th of May [1863], a foraging party, consisting of twenty-five men from the Phalanx [African American] regiment and twenty men of the 2nd Kansas Battery, Major R. G. Ward commanding, was sent into Jasper County, MO. This party was surprised and attacked by a force of three hundred Confederates commanded by Major Livingston, and defeated, with

a loss of sixteen killed and five prisoners, three of whom belonged to the 2nd Kansas Battery and two of the black regiment. The men of the 2nd Kansas Battery were afterwards exchanged under a flag of truce for a like number of prisoners captured by the negro regiment. Livingston refused to exchange the black prisoners in his possession, and gave as his excuse that he should hold them subject to the orders of the Confederate War Department. Shortly after this Colonel Williams received information that one of the prisoners held by Livingston had been murdered by the enemy. He immediately sent a flag of truce to Livingston demanding the body of the person who had committed the barbarous act. Receiving an evasive and unsatisfactory reply, Colonel Williams determined to convince the Major that this was a game at which two could play, and directed that one of the prisoners in his possession be shot, and within thirty minutes the order was executed. He immediately informed Major Livingston of his action, sending the information by the same party that brought the dispatch to him. Suffice it to say that this ended the barbarous practice of murdering prisoners of war, so far as Livingston's command was concerned.[190]

It was obvious to those on both sides that the South could not afford to lose soldiers as a result of Union retaliation. As the number of white executed Confederate prisoners started to mount, it occurred to some in the Confederacy that it might be a good idea to establish a policy that made sense and had teeth to prevent the execution of Confederate soldiers by the North in retaliation for Confederate murders. Unfortunately, that was not the course chosen by Davis. Initially Jefferson Davis and the Confederate government followed a very clever policy designed to avoid suborning murder but at the same time left it up to the states and the army to continue murder without the blessing of the government. The official policy was vague and permissive. On 1 May 1862, the Confederate Congress authorized Jefferson Davis to direct that white officers of African American regiments be executed and armed African Americans be turned over to the state where captured.[191] Confederate General Order Number 60, of 21 August 1862, established that Union officers who recruited African Americans were to be treated as "outlaws," not prisoners of war. The punishment was that these should be held for execution as felons at such time as the president should order.[192] Jefferson Davis received a blunt response from Union General David Hunter, who was recruiting African Americans at that time:

> Mr. Davis, we have been acquainted intimately in the past. We have campaigned together, and our social relations have been such as to make each understand the other thoroughly. That you mean, if it be ever in your power, to execute the full rigor of your threats, I am well assured; and you will believe my assertion, that I thank you for having raised in connection with me and

my acts, this sharp and decisive issue. I shall proudly accept, if such be the chance of war, the martyrdom you menace; and hereby give you notice that unless your General Order against me and my officers be formally revoked, within thirty days from the date of the transmission of this letter, sent under a flag of truce, I shall take your action in the matter as finale; and will reciprocate it by hanging every rebel officer who now is, or may hereafter be taken, prisoner by the troops of the command to which I am about returning.[193]

With Lincoln's Emancipation Proclamation on 1 January 1863, which freed the slaves in all states at war with the Union, came the realization in the South that a large pool of African American labor was being encouraged to fight for the North and their freedom. Jefferson Davis responded by stating that all white officers of African American regiments should be handed over to the state where captured for action by that state; African Americans were to be returned to slavery.[194] There were a few officers in the Confederate Army who had qualms with this. General Beauregard, commanding at Charleston, had men of the 54th Massachusetts captured at Fort Wagner. He objected to treating them like slaves and he queried the governor of South Carolina, proposing that he turn over his prisoners to the governor.[195] Instead, these troops were imprisoned until the end of the war.

Grant and other Union generals adopted a very pragmatic policy: for every African American murdered by the Confederate Army, a white Confederate prisoner would be executed.[196] As the scale of the murders increased and rumors of 54th Massachusetts soldiers who had been murdered began to circulate, Frederick Douglass protested to Lincoln. He would stop recruiting for the Union unless Lincoln took action against the Confederacy. Lincoln responded by quoting General Order 100, the Lieber Code, which established a code of conduct for those engaged in war. Lincoln's General Order No. 233, passed on 31 July 1863, provided that "for every soldier of the United States killed in violation of the laws of war a rebel soldier shall be executed and for every one enslaved by the enemy or sold into slavery by the enemy a rebel soldier shall be placed at hard labor on the public works."[197] This only drove the Confederate murders of prisoners underground. Henry Freeman of the 12th Regiment USCT reported three cases of murder by the Confederate Army: "Lieutenant W. L. Clark, captured on a train, was made to kneel down and shot in cold blood, because he belonged to this colored regiment. Three other officers captured after the battle of Nashville, were led off, under pretense of being sent to General Forrest's headquarters and in a secluded ravine, without warning, were shot down like so many dogs. Two were killed instantly; a third ... left for dead, subsequently recovered to tell the story."[198] The total number murdered by the Confederates during the war and left in unmarked graves will never be known.[199]

Among the outcomes of the Emancipation Proclamation was the destruction of any hope of foreign recognition of the Confederacy. The barbaric treatment of prisoners by the South also ended any such hopes. Rather than discouraging recruitment of African American soldiers, the Confederate policy may have turned the war into a crusade for the African Americans. More important, the African Americans would fight more stubbornly than before to defeat the Confederacy.[200] As one African American soldier put it, "Dere's no flags ob truce for us."[201]

Prisoner exchanges were common during the Civil War, but the South initially refused to exchange African American prisoners. The Confederate exchange agent, Robert Ould, stated, "We would die in the last ditch rather than return an ex-slave to the Union Army."[202] This stopped all prisoner exchanges. But, as the manpower squeeze increased in the Confederacy, the South reconsidered and notified General Benjamin Butler, the Union exchange agent, that it would consider free negroes as eligible for exchange. Grant intervened. He knew that the South needed the exchanged manpower far more than the Union and he instructed Benjamin Butler to refuse exchanges.[203] As a result, prisoners of war on both sides continued to rot in their camps.

Historian Michael T. Meier summarized Lorenzo Thomas' final report on the Civil War, dated 3 October 1865:

> Thomas reflected on his experiences in the Mississippi Valley. Stanton was reminded that the instructions to Thomas were given on short notice and that the issue of recruiting and arming blacks "was new to me;" "I entered upon the duty by no means certain at what I might be able to effect." Thomas, ever confident, concluded that "most of my military service was performed in the Slave States, and I was perfectly familiar with plantation life. I felt that I knew the peculiarities of the whole race." Thomas was without a command when he went to the Mississippi Valley and had to depend on others much of the time. Furthermore, there was much chaos, and the previous raising of black regiments had been done without regard to regulations. Thomas ended this practice and ordered that all black regiments raised would conform to regulations of ten companies of one hundred men each.[204]

CHAPTER 4

The Impeachment of President Andrew Johnson

While Lorenzo Thomas was still the adjutant general of the U.S. Army, the impeachment of Andrew Johnson took place in 1868. It occurred when the print media was coming of age and had learned how to handle daily coverage and immediate reporting. It involved not only President Andrew Johnson but also two future presidents of the United States, a future prime minister of France (Georges Clemenceau) and an assortment of other people who would later achieve national notoriety, including a German revolutionary (Carl Schurz) who would become a national reformer in the United States. It also included Lorenzo Thomas. This chapter tells their story.

When President Lincoln, a moderate Republican, was assassinated by John Wilkes Booth on 15 April 1865, the Civil War had just ended. He was succeeded by his vice president, Andrew Johnson of Tennessee. At the time that he assumed the office of president, Johnson appeared to be a Radical Republican because he was known to hate the wealthy Southerners who had seceded from the Union. Johnson was a self-made man who had struggled in poverty in Tennessee before he achieved success. Southerners could no longer expect the reconciliation that Lincoln had promised after the war, or so it appeared when Johnson took office. Such things as readmission to the Union and pardons of those who had fought for the South were not on Johnson's agenda. To the Radical Republicans in Congress, it appeared that Johnson was their man: they wanted harsher treatment of the South. According to these men, the states that had seceded should be treated as conquered territories and dealt with in any manner desired by the Union.[1] As Senator Ben Wade, a leading Radical, observed, "Lincoln had too much of the milk of human kindness."[2] Over time, however, Johnson's opinion changed and he became aligned with Lincoln's policy of reconciliation, which infuriated the Radical Republicans in Congress led by Charles Sumner in the U.S. Senate and Thaddeus Stevens in the House. These men would continue to press for revenge in legislation, much of which was vetoed by Johnson. The Radicals were demanding civil rights for the African Americans and harsh treatment for the South while Johnson wanted more lenient treatment for the South and states' rights. He also opposed African American civil rights. People in the North were infuriated by the state governments in the South, supported by Johnson, that were repressing African Americans. Carl Schurz was sent south to examine conditions in mid–1865. He reported:

President Andrew Johnson (Library of Congress).

I saw in various hospitals negroes, women as well as men, whose ears had been cut off or whose bodies were slashed with knives or bruised with whips, or bludgeons, or punctured with shot wounds. Dead negroes were found in considerable number in the country roads or on the fields, shot to death, or strung on the limbs of trees. In many districts the colored people were in a panic of fright, and the whites in an almost insane state of irritation against them.[3]

Johnson continued to infuriate the Radicals in Congress with his vetoes, demonstrating his lack of the compromise skills that Lincoln had always used with great success. Instead of compromise, he specialized in confrontation. When he vetoed the Freedmen's Bureau legislation (which would have provided relief to former slaves and reunited families), he stated, with a blind eye to what Schurz had reported, "The freedman is not so exposed as may first be imagined. He possesses a perfect right to change his place of abode."[4] The Republican press responded, "[Johnson's approach] ties up children so that they shall not bite the rabid dog, and turns loose the rabid dog so that he can protect the children."[5] Lincoln would have been pleased with Johnson's attempt to reconcile with the

South but would have been horrified at the fact that Johnson ignored the plight of African Americans in the post-war South. Perhaps Johnson's greatest blunder was his veto of the Civil Rights Act of 1866, which provided that African Americans would have the same rights as white citizens.[6] This alone ensured that he would not be nominated for reelection by his party and would sink into oblivion (see Biographical Dictionary).

Many viewed Johnson as a drunkard, confrontational in his actions, and frequently unable to control his temper, as evidenced by the diary entry of Confederate soldier Private Copley of the 49th Tennessee Regiment that was written after the Battle of Nashville in December 1864:

> We arrived ... before noon ... hungry and tired. Many of the prisoners were barefooted and could have been easily tracked by the marks of blood behind them. We were ragged, dirty and blood-bespattered.... We were paraded on the capitol grounds. We were kept on public exhibition for five or six hours, and near five thousand people came out to view us. Amongst the number was the noted Andrew Johnson, afterwards President of the United States, who greeted this little handful of half-starved, unarmed and defenseless men with a volume of abuse and vituperation; of course, he could afford to do this and be in no danger while we were enclosed by a wall of ... bayonets.... A majority of the citizens who came to look at us were ladies. They were not allowed to approach nearer than the bayonet's point of the double chain-guard of Federal troops who were between us and them, nor permitted to exchange any words with us. But we saw their looks of tenderness and affection.... We were ... ordered away ... to the enclosure of the outer dismal walls of the State penitentiary.[7]

Unfortunately, Johnson was the standard-bearer of Lincoln's policy of forgiveness for those states that had seceded from the Union. Presidents do not pick their vice presidents for talent or brains, but rather in order to secure more votes. Lincoln himself described Johnson as a "queer fellow" who initially declined to participate in his own inauguration in March 1865.

As the new president, Johnson had many problems, not the least of which was his secretary of war, Edwin Stanton. Stanton was a Radical Republican and a holdover from Lincoln's administration who became a disloyal obstructionist in the Johnson administration.[8] After Lincoln's death, he had taken control of the State Department (Secretary Seward had been injured when Lincoln was assassinated).[9] With so much power in the hands of Stanton, people were left to ponder who was in charge of the government: Johnson, the moderate, or Stanton, the Radical.

The first major blow to Johnson was his three-week "Swing around the Circle" of 1866, which was designed to secure the election or reelection to Congress of people friendly to his views. His speaking tour around the country turned into a debacle. He lost his temper (he was drinking, again) and engaged in shrieking contests with hecklers, demonstrating that he was unsuited to be president. Johnson's problem was that when he was confronted, he lost control. His opponents realized this and staged confrontations.[10] Johnson played into their hands. A deadly mix of alcohol and lack of self-control, fueled by an unsympathetic press, made Johnson the laughingstock of the nation. At his last stop in Indianapolis, he was driven from the stage by a hostile crowd.[11] Ulysses S. Grant later remarked, "I have never been so tired of anything before as I have been with the political stump speeches of Mr. Johnson. I look upon them as a national disgrace."[12] Grant, who was obviously no fan of Johnson, later remarked to Senator John Henderson of Missouri that Johnson should be removed from office "if for nothing else than because he is such an infernal liar." Henderson replied, "On such terms, it would be nearly impossible to find the right sort of man to serve as President."[13]

It was estimated that Johnson's tour cost the Democratic Party a million votes.[14] The result was that his candidates lost votes and Congress emerged from the mid-term elections as significantly favorable to the Radical Republicans, who now had more than a two-thirds majority in both houses.[15] The recently elected Southern legislators who could have helped Johnson were excluded by both the Senate and the House and were not seated. To make sure that they left town, Congress refused to pay their living expenses.[16] The final tally after the November 1866 election was that the Radicals won 173 of the 226 House seats as well as all but 9 of the 52 Senate seats.[17]

Johnson needed to replace Stanton. Since the Radical Republicans now had a veto-proof Congress thanks to Johnson's "Swing around the Circle," they contrived to prevent Stanton's departure by enacting the Tenure of Office Act, which denied the president's authority to replace a member of his cabinet — in this case, Stanton — without congressional approval. This was a departure from the Constitution, which required congressional consent to the appointment of a member of the president's cabinet, but made no mention of replacing a member. Congress was already planning to replace Johnson and included the stipulation that a president would be guilty of high crimes and misdemeanors should he replace a cabinet member without congressional approval. A new war was forming, but rather than North versus South, it was now the president versus Congress.[18]

There was a stipulation in the act that allowed the president to suspend a cabinet member with an interim appointment while Congress was not in session, subject to the approval of Congress when it returned.[19] Therefore, Johnson ordered Stanton out and named Ulysses S. Grant, the hero of the Civil War, as secretary of war. Not even Stanton would dare to oppose Grant, Johnson believed, and he awaited the return of Congress. But Grant was no fool. He realized that Congress would reinstate Stanton, and when this happened, he would be in violation of the law if he did not relinquish the office. He would be running for the presidency himself soon and did not need a conviction on his record. When Congress returned, they disapproved the appointment and Grant stepped down, despite the objections of Johnson. Stanton then resumed his job as secretary of war. Johnson could not name another secretary of war *ad interim* because Congress was now in session.

By December it appeared that the Radical Republicans were out of ammunition. The press summarized:

> If the great culprit [Johnson] had robbed a till; if he fired a barn; if he had forged a check; he would have been indicted, prosecuted, condemned, sentenced, and punished. But the evidence shows that he only oppressed the Negro; that he only conspired with the rebel; that he only betrayed the Union party; that he only attempted to overthrow the Republic — of course he goes unwhipped by justice.[20]

There was mounting fear that Johnson might do something desperate, such as simply replacing Congress through force of arms. Carl Schurz described Johnson "as a mad dog that bites all around him like an anger-crazed boar."[21] In August, Grant, the general-in-chief, sent a letter to General Sheridan then commanding troops in the South:

> I much fear that we are fast approaching the point where he [Johnson] will want to declare [Congress] itself illegal, unconstitutional, and revolutionary. Commanders in the Southern states will have to take great care to see, if a crisis does come, that no armed headway can be made against the Union.[22]

Benjamin Franklin described impeachment as a way to preserve peace in times of crisis.[23] Article Two of the United States Constitution gives the power of impeachment to the House of Representatives and the Senate has the power to try impeachments:

> The President, Vice President, and all civil Officers of the United States shall be removed from Office on Impeachment for, and Conviction of, Treason, Bribery, or other High Crimes and Misdemeanors. The House of Representatives has the sole power of impeaching, while the United States Senate has the sole power to try all impeachments. The removal of impeached officials is automatic upon conviction in the Senate.

Congress, of course, would define "high crimes and misdemeanors." As seen above, impeachment is a two-step process. The House of Representatives, by simple majority, passes the articles of impeachment and the Senate tries the case. A two-thirds majority in the Senate is required to convict and, if so convicted, the defendant is removed from office. It takes conviction on one article of impeachment, even if there is more than one. Two presidents have been impeached in the history of the United States. Bill Clinton's impeachment in the late 20th century is well known to citizens today, but the first was President Andrew Johnson's impeachment in 1868.

The members of the House were trying to determine on what basis they could get rid of Johnson through impeachment. Theories such as "[he] had up-ended the Constitution in order to hand over power to ex-rebels"[24] did not play well anywhere. There were others that made less sense. The question was this: If you do not like a president or his policies, can you impeach him? James Wilson in the House remarked, "Political unfitness and incapacity must be tried at the ballot box, not in the high court of impeachment."[25] If a later president made unpopular decisions, would he also be impeached? Another congressman put it this way: "Johnson was impeached for one series of misdemeanors [violation of the Tenure of Office Act] and tried for another [his policies]."[26]

The Sequence of Events

Thaddeus Stevens, in reviewing correspondence between Grant and Johnson, smelled blood: Johnson had continued to press Grant to remain as secretary after the Senate had ordered the reinstatement of Stanton.[27] Could this be a violation of the Tenure of Office Act, and if so, could they impeach based upon that? It did not work. Stevens got voted down and he declared that the Republican Party was full of cowards.[28] Impeachment was not dead, however, and would soon return. There were arguments in favor of Johnson's right to remove Stanton in spite of the act, but these did not receive much discussion.[29] Johnson tried to get General Sherman to accept the position. Sherman refused. In a letter to his wife he had stated, "Washington is as corrupt as Hell ... I will avoid it as a pest house."[30] Others were also offered the cabinet position of secretary of war, which they likewise refused.

On 18 February 1868, Johnson turned to Lorenzo Thomas. At first Thomas refused, as the others had done, but then indicated that if he were restored to his rank of major general (this was a pension issue and Thomas was long overdue to retire), he would accept. Also, replacing his old enemy (Stanton) was a bonus for Thomas. On that basis, Johnson replaced Stanton with Lorenzo Thomas as *ad interim* secretary. Orders were written to that effect and Johnson sent notification to Congress.

The congressional reaction was violent. The Tenure of Office Act allowed the president to name a cabinet member while Congress was not in session pending congressional approval when Congress returned. This occurred in the case of Grant. In the case of Thomas, however, Congress was in session and naming Thomas was a violation of the act. Stanton swore out an affidavit charging Thomas with a violation of the Tenure of Office Act. Stevens was delighted: he now had an impeachable offense against Johnson. Candles burned long in the House of Representatives that night.

It will never be known for certain if Lorenzo Thomas was a bumbling fool or a clever fox, since he left no memoirs. But based upon his many years of experience in Washington, D.C., and his subsequent actions, the latter seems to be the case. General Thomas never wrote of his motivations after the impeachment hearings, but his actions and testimony during the hearings indicate a very deliberate effort to get Johnson acquitted, and it worked. Also, eulogies after his death and comments by colleagues were strangely silent about this period of Thomas' career. Perhaps they thought that this excursion into politics was not relevant to his military career.

While Congress was working late into the night on impeachment and Stanton was barricading himself in his office, Lorenzo Thomas was attending a masquerade ball at Marini's Hall. Johnson would later remark, "Jesus Christ, a man of his age at a fancy ball!"[31] Much was made of Thomas' behavior at the ball before he attempted to take office.[32] On the way to the ball he made clear to his acquaintances that he would evict Stanton by force if required. He made similar statements when he stopped at the Willard Hotel for refreshments along the way. A notice found in many such establishments stated, "Members of Congress will go to the table first, and then gentlemen. Rowdies and blackguards must not mix with the Congressmen as it is hard to tell one from the other."[33] As one newspaper reported, "Lorenzo Thomas imbibed in true Johnsonian spirit."[34] At the ball that night, he pranced around while dancing and drinking, stating that he would rudely eject Stanton as secretary of war in the morning. As this was happening, word went to Stanton and key members of Congress that the morrow might bring interesting events. While dancing the night away, Thomas was served with a notice at the ball indicating he would be arrested if he moved to replace Stanton. While this temporarily dampened his spirits, after he refreshed his drink, Thomas moved forward with his plan to evict Stanton.

While awaiting his breakfast the next morning on 22 February 1868 at 8:00 A.M., a hung-over Lorenzo Thomas answered a knock at his front door and found an assistant U.S. Marshal and constable with a warrant for his arrest issued by Judge Carrter for violating the Tenure of Office Act. In the company of the marshal and constable, Thomas made stops at the White House to chat with Johnson and to visit with the attorney general. Judge Carrter set bail at $5,000, which was posted by two merchants on Thomas' behalf.[35] Grounds now existed to challenge the Tenure of Office Act using a writ of habeas corpus that could be carried to the Supreme Court. It is surprising that Stanton, a brilliant attorney, would have Thomas arrested because it gave Johnson the legal grounds to challenge the Tenure of Office Act, especially since, the Supreme Court membership could be expected to rule against the legality of the act.[36] When Stanton realized what he had done, he immediately ordered his lawyer to drop the prosecution. This ended the possibility of review of the Tenure of Office Act by the Supreme Court at that time, but in 1878 it was repealed.

After posting bail, Lorenzo Thomas moved to the War Department to confront Stanton. Thomas entered Stanton's office and found him with several Radical Republicans who took notes on the following discussion:

> THOMAS: I am Secretary of War *ad interim*, and am ordered by the President of the United States to take charge of this office.
> STANTON: I order you to repair to your room, and exercise your office as adjutant-general.
> THOMAS: I am Secretary of War *ad interim,* and I shall not obey your orders; but I shall obey the order of the President to take charge of this office.
> STANTON: As Secretary of War, I order you to repair to your office as adjutant-general.
> THOMAS: I shall not do so.
> STANTON: Then you may stand there, if you please; but you will attempt to act as Secretary of War at your peril.
> THOMAS: I *shall* act as Secretary of War.[37]

With that Thomas left and crossed the hall to the office of General Schriver to collect the secretary of war's mail. Stanton followed. Lorenzo Thomas recalled what followed:

> I said, "The next time you have me arrested, please do not do it before I get something to eat." I said I had nothing to eat or drink all day. He put his hand

around my neck, as he sometimes does, and ran his hand through my hair, and turned around to General Schriver and said, "Schriver, you have got a bottle here; bring it out." When Schriver's bottle turned out to be empty, a messenger fetched another. Pouring drinks, Stanton said, "Now this, at least, is neutral ground."³⁸

The *New York Herald* reported, "No two cooing doves ever met on milder terms."³⁹ People were starting to realize that this whole thing was a political charade and not worth another civil war between branches of the government. Thomas reported back to Johnson, who insisted that Thomas take over as secretary of war while Stanton was barricading himself in his office. It had become a comic opera. The *New York Herald* in jest reported:

> During the evening the President was arrested nineteen times. Grant was put in arrest five times, dismissed [from] the army eight times, relieved from duty three times, ordered to Alaska once, sent on a tour of inspection once, a court martial convened for his trial four times, and assassinated twice. Stanton committed suicide once, was arrested six times, had an indefinite number of quo warrantos, man-damuses and other awful things served upon him. Nine different files of marines were marching to eject him from the War Office, and

Stanton prepares to fire on Lorenzo Thomas and Andrew Johnson (*Harper's Weekly*).

the President, in a fit of rage, had gone over personally and unceremoniously pitched him out of the window of the War Office. As for [Lorenzo] Thomas, it was impossible to keep track of the number of times he had been seen drunk.[40]

The serious side to all of this was that violence and bloodshed could erupt at any time and there were few cool heads in Congress or the White House that could be counted upon to avoid a major disaster. Things became rather martial. Missouri promised 100,000 soldiers who would march to support the beleaguered president while the *New York Herald* reported that "if violence is used to eject Mr. Stanton[,] 100,000 men are ready to come to Washington and put him back."[41] Grant and the military could be relied upon to maintain order, but there is usually a high price paid in blood when soldiers are used to do a policeman's job, as they are not trained to be policemen.

On 22 February, Stevens was delighted to push through the House impeachment articles based upon the action of Johnson in dismissing Stanton and appointing Thomas. By now, Stevens was a dying man and his voice could hardly be heard. The *Cincinnati Commercial* reported, "He seems to breath[e] with difficulty. His voice has that dreadful low, grating sound that we hear from deathbeds."[42] The House voted in favor of the impeachment, charging Johnson with high crimes and misdemeanors, and the impeachment resolution passed to the Senate. It was a case of overkill — there were eleven separate articles, some of which overlapped. It would only take conviction on one to convict. The strongest article was number eleven, which was broad and offered the greatest likelihood of conviction. (The Articles of Impeachment are found in Appendix C; Lorenzo Thomas is frequently mentioned in these articles and very often as a co-conspirator). According to the Constitution, the Senate would need to vote on the Articles of Impeachment, requiring a two-thirds majority to convict. Since Johnson had no vice president, the next in line for president was Congressman Benjamin F. Wade of Ohio, president pro tempore of the Senate: a Radical Republican. The thought of Wade as president was frightening to many. He favored increased tariffs and, as the *Chicago Tribune* noted, "The gathering of evil birds about Wade leads [one] to think that a worse calamity might befall the Republican Party than the acquittal of Johnson."[43]

Meanwhile, Stanton's wife nearly accomplished what Johnson and Thomas had been trying to do. If Stanton vacated his office, Thomas could move in, since the office would have been abandoned, and Congress would have no case for impeachment. When Stanton sent a sergeant to his home

4. The Impeachment of President Andrew Johnson

to collect food and bedding for him while beseiged in his office, his wife refused, saying that her husband should resign and come home. The sergeant returned with the message and that night the two attempted to boil Irish stew in Stanton's office fireplace. It burned and stank up the office, and Stanton and his loyal sergeant went to bed without their supper. The next day, Stanton sent his sergeant to his home to get food and other necessities. Stanton's wife refused to provide anything and sent word to Stanton to resign and come home.[44] He refused. Stanton would pay a high price for this, later.

Politics in the Finest American Tradition

Extreme measures to obtain votes for conviction or acquittal were practiced by both sides. These ranged from political pressure to death threats (such as rumors that some senators would be poisoned in the Senate). Of course, bribery on a grand scale was the order of the day. The Radicals were at a disadvantage since they did not control government tax collection, funding, or patronage jobs, but they did their best to bribe Democrats and those who might favor acquittal.

The Whiskey Ring was a group of distillers, distributors and politicians who connived to defraud the government of taxes owed on liquor. Under Andrew Johnson this network of grafters was comfortable because all bribes were in place and the taxes were siphoned off and never arrived at the Treasury. If Johnson were convicted, the new president, Ben Wade, would take office, new civil servants would be appointed, and the bribery schemes would need to start over. The process would cost the grafters millions of dollars until all new bribes were in place. On this basis, plans moved forward to bribe senators to vote for acquittal. The success of the Whiskey Ring is not known, but the fact is that seven Radical Senators voted for acquittal. It was not until 1875 that members of the Whiskey Ring were indicted.

Everyone suspected bribery but no proof could be found to indict. However, Representative Ben Butler, a Radical Republican, was convinced that he could make a case. He had in his sights Cornelius Wendell, a notorious Washington figure who for years had operated slush funds that were used to bribe congressmen for legislation favorable to the Democrats. Johnson had appointed Wendell director of public printing, a highly lucrative position. Over a six-year period, he took in $3.8 million, half of which went into his pocket ($25 million in current dollars), a very respectable income for a civil servant.[45] Wendell knew all of the details of the bribery schemes to acquit Johnson. Butler amassed $100,000, an enormous amount of money in those days. He initiated a plot to bribe Wendell, the briber, to reveal details of the bribery schemes. What Butler did not know was that $100,000 was a pitiful amount compared to the illegal millions that Wendell was pocketing. Unsurprisingly, Wendell did not buy into the Butler plot to bribe the briber to tell the Senate of the bribery schemes.[46]

The extent of bribery on both sides has never been determined. It is said that while the Senate was voting, Johnson had a list of bribed senators in his coat pocket that he kept checking to make sure that they voted as bribed. If Senator Edmund Ross of Kansas had not voted to acquit, there were other senators on Johnson's list who had been paid to vote for acquittal.

THE PARTICIPANTS

On 30 March 1868, the Senate trial started. It was a circus atmosphere. Representative Ben Butler from Massachusetts would act as lead prosecutor. Butler was a former colleague of Thomas from their recruiting days in the Mississippi Valley. Attorney General Henry Stanberry was lead counsel for the defense, but became ill during the trial and was replaced by William Evarts, a New York lawyer. Chief Justice Salmon Chase would preside over the trial. Neither Andrew Johnson nor Edwin Stanton would testify.

THE TRIAL

The Radical Republicans had an overwhelming majority in the Senate. Johnson only had twelve votes to acquit and would need to convince seven Radical Republicans in order to win acquittal. As the hearings in the Senate got underway, it appeared at times that the Radicals were trying to derail their own case. They suggested that Stanton be called from his barricaded office to testify, but if he did that, Lorenzo Thomas could take control of the War Department in Stanton's absence and Johnson could claim that Stanton had abandoned his post and the Tenure of Office Act did not apply. Cooler heads prevailed and Stanton was not called. The proceedings nevertheless degenerated into many irrelevant excursions. Days of discussion followed on obscure legal points of the Tenure of Office Act and what Johnson had or had not done. These were discussions that only attorneys could understand. Some questioned exactly what Thomas said at the ball the night before he attempted to evict Stanton. It was a debacle, but it kept the public entertained and the proceedings may have prevented outright bloodshed over the issue.

The time came for Lorenzo Thomas to testify. Throughout his testimony, Thomas tried to establish that most of the actions that violated the Tenure of Office Act were taken of his own volition and not on Johnson's orders, and the entire purpose of the effort was to test the act in the courts. Over two days of testimony, it was established that Thomas, not Johnson, had decided to forcibly evict Stanton from the War Department. Furthermore, Thomas confirmed that in his discussion with Johnson, the purpose of replacing Stanton with Thomas was to challenge the act's legality in the courts:

The impeachment admission ticket (Library of Congress).

> QUESTION: "State when you next went to the War Department that day?"
> THOMAS ANSWER: "I immediately went to the President's Office after making bail, and stated the facts to him [Johnson]. He made the same answer — 'Very well, I wanted to get it into the courts.'"[47]

On 11 April 1868, Thomas testified, "The next correction [to his 10 April testimony] I want to make is this: I said the President told me to take possession of the office [this could mean forcible entry]; he expressed it 'take charge' of the office." Question: "Are you certain that was the expression?" Answer: "I am positive."[48]

Johnson himself would later confirm this to a reporter. He implied that Thomas' appetite for liquor was the cause of many problems and described him as "a queer old gentleman." Johnson also stated that he was not responsible for Thomas' actions or statements that "were independent of my orders."[49]

Later, General Sherman was called to testify. Before Thomas, Sherman had been asked to take over as secretary of war, but he had declined.

Johnson's defense team was trying to establish that Johnson was only attempting to challenge the Tenure of Office Act before the courts, not simply to violate the act. Question to Sherman: "Was anything said at the conversation by the President, as to any purpose of getting the question of Mr. Stanton's right to office before the courts?" There followed time-consuming legal arguments before Sherman could answer. The Senate adjourned and the proceedings reopened on 13 April 1868. After the question was restated to Sherman, he replied, "The President told me that the relations between himself and Mr. Stanton and other members of the Cabinet were such that he could not execute the duties of the office which he filled as President of the United States without making nominations, *ad interim* for the office of Secretary of War, and that he had the right under the law, and that his purpose was to have the office administered in the interests of the army and of the country, and he offered me the office in that view; he did not state to me then that the purpose was to bring it into the courts directly."[50]

Two questions carried a great deal of weight as the senators prepared to vote: Was the president attempting to raise a court case over the Tenure of Office Act, and was he trying to remove Stanton by force?[51] In his testimony, Lorenzo Thomas may have turned a number of Radicals toward acquittal. By mid–April the Radicals thought that impeachment might fail.[52] The press, as always, was having a grand time entertaining its readers, as can be seen in this piece written by Georges Clemenceau[53]:

> The president either did or did not violate the Tenure of Office Bill. Mr. Curtis [defense team] makes out that (1) he did not violate it, and (2) he set out to violate it, but that in doing so he acted with the best intentions in the world. I leave to someone more clever than I the task of finding some connection between these two propositions.[54]

There were all sorts of last-minute efforts by the Radicals to pressure wavering senators to vote for conviction, and on 16 May it was put to a vote. The voting in the Senate had little to do with the Tenure of Office Act; it was a power struggle between two branches of government, the executive and the legislative. When Radical Republican senators lined up to vote for conviction on Article XI, seven of their number voted to acquit. With only six voting to acquit, the measure would still pass, but the seventh vote for acquittal, that of Edmund G. Ross of Kansas, killed the measure. (A listing of the Senate votes is provided in Appendix D.) Much discussion subsequently occurred about voting on the other ten articles that offered less chance for success than Article XI, but the Senate could not muster enough votes to do this. Apparently everyone in the country had had enough. With that, Johnson's administration was saved. Stanton resigned and would die the following year. One newspaper wrote, "Andrew Johnson is innocent because Benjamin Wade is guilty of being his successor."[55] The new secretary of war was a former Civil War general, John M. Schofield, a Medal of Honor winner, who had fought well at Nashville. Johnson was not nominated by his party for the presidency later that year and the 1868 election was won by Ulysses S. Grant. Thaddeus Stevens died a few weeks after the hearings. As

Georges Clemenceau as prime minister of France (Library of Congress).

one historian put it, "He wasted the last few days of his life promoting hatred, a cause that he had promoted all of his life." Some thought that the nation was saved from a government dominated by a Congress that would control the executive branch of government — something not envisioned by the founding fathers.

Several years later, Edmund Ross summarized the reason why he voted to acquit:

> In a large sense, the independence of the executive office as a coordinate branch of the government was on trial.... If ... the President must step down ... a disgraced man and a political outcast ... upon insufficient proofs and from partisan considerations, the office of President would be degraded, cease to be a coordinate branch of the government, and ever after subordinated to the legislative will. It would practically have revolutionized our splendid political fabric into a partisan Congressional autocracy.... This government had never faced so insidious a danger ... control by the worst element of American politics.... If Andrew Johnson were acquitted by a nonpartisan vote ... America would pass the danger point of partisan rule and that intolerance which so often characterizes the sway of great majorities and makes them dangerous.[56]

In spite of his high-minded ideals, he was thought to have been bribed to acquit, but there is no evidence to prove this.[57]

James Dixon, a moderate Republican, summarized his reasons for voting to acquit a few months after the trial in a letter to Senator Fessenden:

> Whether Andrew Johnson should be removed from office, justly or unjustly, was comparatively of little consequence — but whether our government should be Mexicanized, and an example set which would surely, in the end, utterly overthrow our institutions, was a matter of vast consequence. To you and Mr. Grimes it is mainly due that impeachment has not become an ordinary means of changing the policy of the government by a violent removal of the Executive.[58]

Legends Revisited

During the 1950s, then-senator John F. Kennedy published a book titled *Profiles in Courage*. The joke in Congress at that time was that JFK should have shown less of his profile in claiming that he was the author and more courage in admitting that the book had been written by others, mostly by Ted Sorensen, his assistant.[59] Kennedy's only credit to Sorensen was that his criticisms helped improve the book.[60] More important, Kennedy's book promoted legends about the Johnson impeachment that were not true. The favorite was that the seven Radical Republican senators who voted to acquit were ostracized and never elected again. In actual fact death, switching to other parties and other reasons affected the futures of the seven. In the case of Edmund Ross, he was not reelected because, in

Edmund Ross, the senator from Kansas (Library of Congress).

the finest traditions of American politics, his home state electors were bribed to nominate someone else: a fitting end to a sad chapter in history.[61]

Michael Les Benedict, in his excellent book on the impeachment, gave an accounting of each of the seven Radicals and proved that none received significant retribution for their votes. As for Ross, Benedict simply stated that Ross switched parties and had a long, successful career as a Democrat.[62]

A myth that continues to this day is that the vote to acquit Johnson saved the republic from a White House dominated by Congress, essentially merging two branches of government into one.[63] Both Kennedy and Woodrow Wilson subscribed to this belief, but there is no evidence to support this. Had Johnson been convicted, the first bill in Congress, if it had a majority in the new president's party, would have been to repeal the Tenure of Office Act, which in fact occurred. A better example is found in the War Powers Resolution of 1973, which was an effort to limit Nixon's power to deploy U.S. forces overseas. The presidential answer after Nixon was to ignore the act or state that it did not apply. Both options worked for the executive branch.

A final legend should be addressed. Lorenzo Thomas was considered by the press, Congress and colleagues to be a befuddled old drunk who triggered the impeachment of Johnson. Was this a carefully designed plot between Johnson and Thomas to test the legality of the Tenure of Office Act by getting Thomas arrested and using the writ of habeas corpus to push the act to the Supreme Court? If so, the plot miscarried when Stanton withdrew the charges against Thomas, as seen above. Thomas' testimony, although awkward, drove home the points needed to achieve acquittal and he deserves more credit than he has previously been given for winning Johnson's acquittal. After the trial, Lorenzo Thomas returned to his job as adjutant general and retired the following year. He did very little after his retirement and his activities have not been recorded. He died in Washington, D.C., the city he knew best, on 2 March 1875. He was buried in Oak Hill Cemetery in Georgetown.[64]

Thomas had many detractors who considered him a meddler during the Civil War but the biographer of Massachusetts Governor John Andrew, Henry Greenleaf Pearson, understood Thomas better than most: "He did his business with dispatch if not thoroughness, moving rapidly from point to point; by the end of the year he could report twenty thousand negroes under arms as a result of his initiative."[65] Historian Dudley Taylor Cornish also states:

What many of the adjutant general's contemporaries misunderstood was what Lorenzo Thomas had been sent to do. He was, after all, no mere recruiting agent. Rather was his task that of initiating Union policy on a grand scale, of breaking down white opposition to the use of Negro soldiers, of educating Union troops in the valley [Mississippi] on this one subject, of starting the work of organization and then moving on to begin it anew at the next Union position while other officers took up the actual details of recruiting and organizing and carried them forward to completion. These things Thomas did and did well.[66]

Historian Michael T. Meier summarized the career of Lorenzo Thomas as follows:

The energy and capacity for work that Thomas brought to the effort impressed even his critics, and his efforts on behalf of freed people — a discussion of which is not within the scope of this essay — reflected an understanding and concern for their plight. Thomas's final report provides a glimpse of the complexities of the issues he confronted. In spite of the resistance, prejudice, and skepticism, Thomas estimated that 2,872 officers and 77,720 enlisted men entered into the service of the U.S. Colored Troops in the Mississippi Valley. As a career officer, Thomas undertook assignments as ordered. With black recruitment, though, he brought energy and commitment to the cause. Thomas continued in his role as adjutant general until 1868, when the events of that year proved his undoing following his embroilment in the impeachment crisis of President Andrew Johnson. Johnson told him that, after Stanton was fired, he was going to appoint him interim secretary of war.... The episode ended pathetically, and Thomas became a laughingstock to many. He retired in 1868, living out his life in Washington, D.C., and dying of debility and congestion of the lungs on March 2, 1875, at the age of seventy-one.[67]

His obituary summed up his life:

One who knew him long and intimately, now bears testimony which hundreds will corroborate: That no man ever went further to oblige a friend or to return a favor received; and but few men in this world have ever done less to resent an injury or pursue an enemy. In everything but this last trait — resentment — this man was well characterized by his family motto, *"Jamais arriere"* [Never Behind].[68]

Biographical Dictionary

This section provides a history of the lives of the key participants in this book.

John Quincy Adams ("Old Man Eloquent") the sixth president of the United States, was born in Braintree, Massachusetts, on 11 July 1867. John Quincy Adams was the U.S. secretary of state negotiating a treaty with Spain for the sale of Florida to the United States when the U.S. Army was campaigning to suppress the Seminoles. He was also the son of John Adams, the second president of the United States. He served as secretary of state (1817–1825) under James Monroe. He was then elected president of the United States and served from 1825 to 1829. He returned to Congress and served in the House of Representatives until his death on 23 February 1848. He was buried in Quincy, Massachusetts.[1]

John Andrew the governor of Massachusetts who recruited African Americans for the Civil War, served as governor between 1861 and 1866. He was born in Windham, Massachusetts, on 31 May 1818. He returned to his law practice after the war and died in Boston on 30 October 1867.

Alexander T. Augusta the physician who was the most senior African American officer of the war, taught at Howard University after the war. At his death in 1890, he was the first African American officer to be buried at Arlington National Cemetery in a plot separate from the white officers.

George W. Baird the army private promoted to colonel of the 32nd USCT, was born in Milford, Connecticut, on 13 December 1839. He remained in the army after the war. He served in the Indian Wars and it was during these conflicts that he won the Medal of Honor. He was adjutant to General Nelson Miles and eventually became deputy paymaster general of the army in 1899. He was promoted to general in 1903, shortly before he retired. Baird died in Asheville, North Carolina, on 26 November 1906 and was buried in Milford, Connecticut.

Nathan Banks (the "*Bobbin Boy*") from Massachusetts, was so named because he had gone to work at an early age in a cotton mill superintended by his father. He was born in Waltham, Massachusetts, on 30 January 1816. He was elected to the Massachusetts legislature and was later elected governor of the state. Lincoln appointed him a general in the Union Army in 1861. Banks improved the living conditions of the African Americans and included one provision supported by all: a school board was set up to educate African Americans. A series of military failures by Banks followed his appointment as general but he contributed greatly to recruiting, morale, money and propaganda for the Union cause. After the war, he was elected to the House of Representatives, where he served successive terms. He retired and died in Waltham on 1 September 1894, and was buried in Grove Hill Cemetery.[2]

Nick Biddle the first casualty of the Civil War was the African American soldier wounded by a Confederate mob attack on Union soldiers in Baltimore on 18 April 1861. The soldiers were marching to the train that would take them to Washington, D.C. Before the attack, one of Biddle's fellow soldiers joked with him and asked if he was afraid that the mob would capture him and sell him into slavery in Georgia. Biddle was not amused and replied that he was going to Washington trusting in the Lord and that he did not fear the devil himself or a bunch of thugs in Baltimore. As he marched through Baltimore, Private Biddle of the Washington Artillery was singled out by the mob because he was an African American. The mob shouted, "Nigger in Uniform." A rain of bricks showered down on the Pennsylvania unit and Biddle took a hit in the head, but he and his comrades made it to the railroad station and then to Washington. When they arrived in Washington, Lincoln greeted the Pennsylvanians and allegedly shook hands with Biddle. Biddle

Nick Biddle — the first casualty of the Civil War (**Library of Congress**).

survived the war but died in poverty in 1876. His white comrades made sure that he was properly honored and buried.

Benjamin Butler   the first to recruit African Americans, was born on 5 November 1818 in Deerfield, New Hampshire, and was well known as a Massachusetts politician who gained flag rank during the Civil War. He did great service for blacks, as seen in this book, but he is best remembered for his general order that stated that any females in New Orleans who disrespected Union soldiers would be treated as prostitutes. From that he got the nickname "Beast Butler." He was fired by Grant in January 1865 after his defeat at Fort Fisher. After the war he served in Congress as a Radical Republican and participated in the impeachment of President Andrew Johnson. He wrote the initial draft of the Civil Rights Act of 1871, which later passed after a less sweeping bill was written, and this was signed into law by President Grant. Butler died in Washington, D.C., on 11 January 1893 and was buried in the family plot in Lowell, Massachusetts.[3]

William O. Butler   who served as second-in-command to Zachary Taylor during the Battle of Monterrey (in which he was wounded), was born in Jessamine County, Kentucky, on 19 April 1791. He served in the War of 1812, in which he was captured by Indians and sent to Canada, where he was released on parole. After the war he served as a congressman. He returned to the army in 1846 at which time he was appointed a major general of volunteers. After the war he ran for vice president on the Lewis Cass ticket, but they were defeated by Zachary Taylor. He retired to his home in Carrollton, Kentucky, where he died on 6 August 1880. His remains were buried in the Butler family cemetery.

Edward Canby   was the Union general at the Battle of Spanish Fort, and remained in the army after the war. Canby was born in Piatt's Landing, Kentucky, on 9 November 1817. Canby graduated from the U.S. Military Academy with the Class of 1839; he was second to last in his class of thirty-one.[4] Following the Civil War, he served in the Modoc Indian War in California and became a member of the Peace Commission assigned to negotiate with the Modoc leader, Captain Jack, to end the war. On 11 April 1873, Canby met with Captain Jack at Laval Flats, California, but in an act of treachery, Captain Jack and his followers murdered Canby and several other members of the Peace Commission. Captain Jack and others were later apprehended and hanged. The other Modocs were imprisoned.

Samuel Chamberlain   a soldier, painter and author of *My Confession,* was born in Center Harbor, New Hampshire, on 27 November 1829. He joined the Illinois Second Volunteer Regiment and fought in several battles during the Mexican-American War. In 1849, he deserted from the army and returned home. He volunteered during the Civil War and achieved the rank of honorary brevet brigadier general. After the war he served as a warden of state prisons in Massachusetts and Connecticut. Chamberlain died in Worcester, Massachusetts, on 10 November 1908. At the time of his death, the Boston newspapers noted that he had fourteen horses shot in battle, was wounded seven times and had participated in more than 100 battles.[5]

Patrick Ronayne Cleburne ("Stonewall of the West") who was killed at the Battle of Franklin, was born on 16 (or 17) March 1828 in County Cork, Ireland. He enlisted in the British Army after he failed to gain entry to Trinity College in Dublin in 1846. He emigrated to the United States three years later. By 1860 he was a naturalized citizen and a practicing lawyer. He sided with the South and quickly rose through the ranks to the position of general. Robert E. Lee called him "a meteor shining from a clouded sky." Cleburne was killed at the Battle of Franklin, Tennessee, on 30 November 1864.

Georges Clemenceau ("The Tiger") covered Johnson's impeachment trial as a young reporter and later became the prime minister of France during World War I. Clemenceau was born in France on 28 September 1841. He was a man of many talents. He graduated as a doctor in 1865 and also founded several literary magazines. As a political activist in France, he was jailed and released, and eventually left for the United States in 1865. After the Johnson impeachment trial, Clemenceau continued to work as a reporter in New York City. He also practiced medicine, wrote for a Paris newspaper and taught French in Stamford, Connecticut, where he met his future wife. He later returned to Paris, where he was elected to the Chamber of Deputies in 1876. His political and writing career continued for forty years. After World War I broke out he was appointed prime minister in 1917 (for a second time). He continued as prime minister after the war and was defeated in his attempt for election to the French presidency in 1920. He then retired from political life and died on 24 November 1929.

Jefferson Davis the president of the Confederacy, was born on 3 June 1808 in Christian County, Kentucky. Davis graduated from the U.S. Military Academy in 1828 and served in the Mexican War. He was wounded at Buena Vista and later served as a senator from Mississippi and secretary of war in the Pierce administration. Davis served as the president of the Confederacy throughout the war; in the last days of the Confederacy he fled south, intending to maintain a government in exile (in Cuba). Davis and other members of his government stopped at Danville, Virginia, which has since been called the last capital of the Confederacy. Davis was captured in Georgia and imprisoned for two years on a charge of treason. The case was dropped in 1869. He was the first president of Texas A&M. In his final days he wrote extensively and completed *A Short History of the Confederate States of America*. Davis died on 6 December 1889 in New Orleans, Louisiana. He is buried in Hollywood Cemetery, Richmond, Virginia.[6]

Frederick Douglass was born into slavery around February 1818 in Talbot County, Maryland. After he escaped from slavery he became an orator, writer and statesman. He was a leader of the abolitionist movement and a champion for civil rights and women's suffrage. By the start of the Civil War he was perhaps the most famous African American in the United States and used his influence to recruit blacks for the Union Army. After the war he continued his work to achieve civil rights for African Americans and supported Grant's run for the presidency. In 1872, Douglass was the first African American to be nominated as vice president of the United States on the Equal Rights Party ticket but was not elected. Douglass died in Washington, D.C., on 20 February 1895. He was buried in Mount Hope Cemetery, Rochester, New York.

John Eaton the man assigned to supervise contraband activities in Mississippi, Tennessee, and Arkansas, was born in Sutton, New Hampshire, on 5 December 1829. He was appointed by General Grant to be the superintendent of Negro affairs for the Department of Tennessee and supervised the establishment of seventy-four schools for African Americans. He advanced to the rank of brevet brigadier general and after the war he was appointed as the U.S. commissioner of education in 1870. He was president of Marietta College and later he served as president of Sheldon Jackson College in Sitka, Alaska. Eaton died in Washington, D.C. on 9 February 1906.

Nathan Bedford Forrest ("The Wizard of the Saddle") who fought with Hood at Nashville, was born on 13 July 1821 at Chapel Hill, Tennessee. He was a Memphis merchant who became a general and is remembered as one of the greatest cavalry leaders of the South. After the war, both Jefferson Davis and Robert E. Lee agreed that the South had not fully utilized Forrest's talents. He was also accused of being a war criminal who was never prosecuted for the murder of African American Union soldiers after their surrender at Fort Pillow. This episode has been disputed by historians ever since. After the war he served as the first Grand Wizard of the Ku Klux Klan. Forrest died in Memphis, Tennessee, on 29 October 1877. He was buried in Forrest Park in Memphis.

John Charles Frémont one of the first to free African Americans in the West, was born in Savannah, Georgia, on 21 January 1813. He was the son of a French emigré dancing master and a Virginia housewife. He was described as precocious, handsome, and daring. He led expeditions in the West and played a key role in the conquest of California before the Civil War. He was selected as the presidential candidate for the Republican Party in 1856, but lost to James Buchanan. Lincoln appointed him general at the start of the war, but he failed at all of his military assignments and resigned in 1864. After the war, he served as territorial governor of Arizona and died in New York City on 13 July 1890. He was buried in Rockland Cemetery, Piedmont-on-Hudson, New York.[7]

William Lloyd Garrison the abolitionist journalist who promoted slave insurrections in the South, was born in Newburyport, Massachusetts, on 10 December 1805. He started his writing career at age fourteen working for the *Newburyport Herald*. In 1831 he founded *The Liberator,* an antislavery newspaper, perhaps the most famous of the Civil War. He set the tone for the paper in his first issue:

> I am aware that many object to the severity of my language; but is there not cause for severity? I will be as harsh as truth, and as uncompromising as justice. On this subject, I do not wish to think, or to speak, or write, with moderation. No! No! Tell a man whose house is on fire to give a moderate alarm; tell him to moderately rescue his wife from the hands of the ravisher; tell the mother to gradually extricate her babe from the fire into which it has fallen;—but urge me not to use moderation in a cause like the present. I am in earnest—I will not equivocate—I will not excuse—I will not retreat a single inch—AND I WILL BE HEARD. The apathy of the people is enough to make every statue leap from its pedestal, and to hasten the resurrection of the dead.

After the war, Garrison ended *The Liberator* but continued to support the reform issues of African American and women's rights. He died on 24 May 1879 and was buried in Boston.

Ulysses S. Grant ("Sam") was born on 27 April 1822 in Point Pleasant, Ohio. He was appointed to the U.S. Military Academy and graduated in the Class of 1843 with a class standing of twenty-one out of thirty-nine. He served with distinction during the Civil War, leading the Union Army by the end of the war. He served as the 18th president of the United States from 1869 to 1877. Grant was an honest man victimized by others during his presidency. After his presidency, he lived in poverty, but with the help of Mark Twain, he published his memoirs, which were immensely successful. He died of throat cancer in Mount McGregor, New York, on 23 July 1885. His book about his reminiscences served to provide for his wife after he died. His remains are in a mausoleum on Riverside Drive in New York City.[8]

Horace Greeley the abolitionist newspaper editor, was born in Amherst, New Hampshire, on 3 February 1811. He founded the Liberal Republican Party and the *New York Tribune*. He used the *Tribune* to support his opposition to slavery as well as the Republican Party and other causes. He ran in the 1872 presidential election but lost by a landslide. He died while the votes were being counted on 29 November 1872.

John Bell Hood ("Sam Woodenhead") who lost at the Battle of Nashville, was born in Owingsville, Kentucky, on 1 June (or 29 June) 1831. He graduated from the U.S. Military Academy with the Class of 1853. His class standing was forty-four out of fifty-two. Hood did well as a brigade and division commander but failed when he was promoted to larger independent commands.

General John Bell Hood, who lost at Nashville (Library of Congress).

The decisive defeats that he suffered at Atlanta and in the Franklin-Nashville campaigns destroyed his reputation. His attack at Franklin was called "Pickett's Charge of the West." After the war he retired to New Orleans, where he worked as a cotton broker and in the insurance industry. Hood died on 30 August 1879 in the yellow fever epidemic in New Orleans, along with his wife and oldest son. He was buried in Metairies Cemetery in New Orleans, and his ten orphans were farmed out to other families in Louisiana, Mississippi, Georgia, Kentucky and New York — a very sad ending for a hero. If his children ever had a family reunion, it must have been a very grand affair with much to discuss. His son, Duncan Norbert Hood, graduated from West Point in the Class of 1896. Apparently he inherited some of his father's leadership ability, for he was a colonel of U.S. Volunteers during the Spanish-American War in 1898.[9]

> *My feet are torn and bloody,*
> *My heart is full of woe,*
> *I'm going back to Georgia*
> *To find my uncle Joe [Johnston].*
> *You may talk about your Beauregard,*
> *You may sing of Bobby Lee,*
> *But the gallant Hood of Texas*
> *Played hell in Tennessee.*[10]
> *Anon*

Thomas Jefferson Hunt of B Company, Tenth Minnesota Regiment, was born in Vermont in 1831. His reminiscences were extensive and comprehensive, providing the reader with information not found elsewhere. Hunt's reminiscences were never published, but were transcribed onto a typed copy that is maintained at the Minnesota Historical Society. His description of one of the last major battles of the Civil War (the Battle of Spanish Fort) provides an unparalleled level of detail.[11] He was the last surviving officer of the Tenth.

During his career after the war he served in the Minnesota legislature and was elected a probate judge. His jaw wound sustained at the Battle of Nashville handicapped him for the rest of his life. He was a prohibitionist and author of the first dry laws. He died at age ninety-three in Minnesota in 1924.

David Hunter one of the first to recruit African Americans for the army, was born in Washington on 21 July 1802. He was the grandson of a signer of the Declaration of Independence, Richard Stockton. Hunter graduated from the U.S. Military Academy in 1822 (a year ahead of Lorenzo Thomas). Lincoln appointed him general in 1861. Hunter abolished slavery in the Department of the South in 1862, an action that was repudiated by Lincoln. He retired in 1866 and died on 2 February 1886. He was buried at Princeton, New Jersey.[12]

Andrew Jackson ("Old Hickory") was born in Waxhaw, South Carolina, on 15 March 1767. During the American Revolution he joined the militia and was taken prisoner by the British. After the war he moved to Tennessee and was elected to the U.S. House of Representatives, and later to the Senate. In the War of 1812, he was elected major general of Tennessee Volunteers. He is perhaps most famous for his defeat of the British at the Battle of New Orleans. Following the war, Jackson invaded Florida in a campaign against the Seminoles and captured Pensacola. He was elected president in 1829 and served two terms. He promoted and signed the Indian Removal Act of 1830, which caused the Cherokees and other tribes to be moved west to what is now Oklahoma. After his presidency he retired to the Hermitage, his home near Nashville, Tennessee, where he died on 8 June 1845, and was buried at the Hermitage.[13]

Benito Juarez the leader of Mexico in the fight against the French, was born on 21 March 1806 in San Pablo Guelatao, Oaxaca, Mexico. He was a lawyer and politician who served five terms as president of Mexico. His greatest challenge was to overthrow the empire of France established in Mexico, which ended when Juarez executed the French emperor Maximilian in 1867. The Confederate soldiers who had left the United States after the Civil War to fight for Maximilian departed Mexico before they would share Maximilian's fate. Juarez was reelected for two terms as president of Mexico (1867 and 1871) after the U.S. Civil War. Perhaps his greatest quote, which appears on monuments in Mexico, was this: "Among individuals as among nations, respect for the rights of others is peace." Juarez died in Mexico City on 18 July 1872 while reading a newspaper in his office.

James H. Lane recruited one of the first African American regiments to fight in the war. He was born on 22 June 1814 at Lawrenceburg, Indiana. Lane was a Kansas politician and Union general during the Civil War. He was accused of atrocities inflicted on Confederate sympathizers, but these allegations did not hamper his career. His 1st Regiment Kansas Volunteers (Colored) was successful in fighting Southern guerrillas and sympathizers. In their first action, thirty members of the 1st Regiment defeated 130 mounted Confederate guerrillas. After the war he served in the U.S. Senate but eventually became depressed. Lane shot himself on 1 July 1866 and died on 11 July 1866 in Leavenworth, Kansas.

Robert E. Lee the commander of Confederate forces, was born on 19 January 1807 in Stratford Hall, Virginia. His father served in the Revolutionary War as General Henry "Light Horse Harry" Lee III. Unfortunately, Light Horse Harry lost the family fortune, which put him into debtors' prison and left the family destitute. Robert Lee later received an appointment to the U.S. Military Academy and graduated second in the Class of 1829. After many military assignments, including superintendent of the U.S. Military Academy, Lee joined the Confederate Army and led it for most of the war. After the war, he accepted the position of president of Washington College in Lexington, Virginia. By all accounts, he was well liked by the student body and his prestige ensured the continued flow of funds to the college. Lee died at the college (now known as Washington and Lee University), on 12 October 1870. He was buried in Lee Chapel on the university campus.[14]

Maximilian the emperor of Mexico, was installed by Napoleon III of France in 1864 since the French believed that the United States, distracted by the Civil War, would not react to this violation of the Monroe Doctrine. In spite of the French effort to lure ex–Confederates, such as Sterling Price, into Mexico to join their cause, it was doomed. Many citizens of Mexico joined Maximilian in his war against Benito Juarez, the nationalist and patriot of Mexico, but it was not enough when Napoleon III withdrew French troops in 1866. The assignment of USCT regiments in Texas to protect the border against Maximilian was thus unnecessary; tragically, many African Americans died from disease in Texas during this French adventure. Maximilian was captured and executed by the forces of Juarez in spite of the pleas of monarchists, such as Pope Pius IX, in Europe. The United States had been aiding Juarez in his war and Juarez wanted to send a message to foreign nations that their intrusion in Mexican affairs would not be tolerated. The United States lodged no objection to the execution of Maximilian as he faced his firing squad in 1867. His wife Carlota never returned to Mexico and went insane shortly thereafter. Maximilian paid gold to the execution squad to avoid being shot in the face, since he wanted his mother to be able to recognize his corpse, it did not work — they shot him in the face anyway. The gold might have been better spent on engineering his escape, but apparently he never thought of that.

John McArthur who commanded a Union division at Nashville, was born on 17 November 1826 on the Clyde River in Renfrewshire, Scotland. At the age of twenty-three he emigrated to the United States and settled in Chicago, where he was the successful proprietor of the Excelsior Iron Works. He enlisted in a militia company and at the start of the war was appointed colonel of the 12th Illinois Infantry. He was later promoted to general and was cited for gallantry at the Battle of Nashville. After the war, however, he was plagued by misfortune. The iron works failed and he was the commissioner of public works when the great fire of 1871 occurred in Chicago. A bank failure also occurred for which he was held personally responsible. McArthur died in Chicago, Illinois, on 15 May 1906 and is buried in Rosehill Cemetery.[16]

James Monroe ("The Last Cocked Hat") who intervened during the West Point scandal, was the fifth president of the United States. He was born in Westmoreland County, Virginia, on 28 April 1758. He served in the American Revolution and was wounded at Trenton. After the war he entered national politics and was a senator from Virginia, and then secretary of war from September 1814 to March 1815. Monroe was the last of the founding fathers to serve as president. He was elected in 1816 and served two terms. Monroe died in New York City on 4 July 1831, the third president to die on the anniversary of the Declaration of Independence. Monroe was buried in Richmond, Virginia, in Hollywood Cemetery.[17]

Alden Partridge ("Old Pewter") who indirectly caused the "Cadet Mutiny" at West Point, was born in Norwich, Vermont, on 12 February 1785. He graduated from West Point, fifth in a class of fifteen, in 1806. He was assigned as acting superintendent of the Military Academy from 1815 to 1817. He resigned in 1817 following allegations of misconduct. It was during his tenure that the gray uniform for cadets was introduced. This was in honor of an American victory in the War of 1812, in which the troops wore gray rather than the usual blue. Gray material was also cheaper than blue. As a civilian, he continued as an educator and founded several schools, including Norwich University. Partridge died in Norwich, Vermont, on 17 January 1854.[18]

John Wolcott Phelps who tried to arm African American troops, was born on 13 November 1813 in Guilford, Vermont. He graduated from the U.S. Military Academy in the Class of 1836. He took part in the Florida war against the Seminoles in 1836–1839, and he also fought in the Mexican War. As an abolitionist, he resigned from the army in 1859 and spent the next two years arguing in print against the institution of slavery. At the start of the Civil War he was appointed as colonel of the 1st Vermont and was later promoted to general. After his attempt to arm African American troops was repudiated by the government, he resigned in disgust. He then moved to Brattleboro, Vermont. He died at Guilford on 2 February 1885 and is buried there.[19]

James Knox Polk who promoted war with Mexico, was the eleventh president of the United States. He was born in Mecklenburg County, North Carolina, on 2 November 1795. He was elected president and served from 1845 to 1849. During his presidency the size of the United States was greatly expanded. He died in Nashville, Tennessee, on 15 June 1849, shortly after he left office.

Sterling Price ("Old Pap") was born in Prince Edward County, Virginia, on 20 September 1809. He was a Missouri politician and Southern general who lost at the battles of Pea Ridge and Westport. Rather than surrender at the end of the war, he took some of his troops to Mexico, hoping to enlist in the service of Maximilian. When this failed, he returned to St. Louis, Missouri, where he died in poverty on 29 September 1867. He was buried in St. Louis in Bellefontaine Cemetery.

John Riley (also known as Jon Riley) the deserter who led the San Patricio Battalion in Mexico, was born in 1818 in County Galway, Ireland. After serving in the British Army, he emigrated to the United States in 1843, where he settled in Mackinac, Michigan. In 1845, Riley enlisted in the 5th Regiment of the U.S. Army. The regiment was moved to join Zachary Taylor's campaign in Texas. A Pennsylvanian infantryman wrote to a friend, "We are under very strict discipline here, [some of] our officers are very good men, but the balance of them are very tyrannical and brutal toward the men. They strike the men with swords and abuse them in the most brutal manner possible for a human being to be treated. And if a poor soldier should be caught drinking a glass of liquor, he is bound and gagged, and if he says one word protesting his innocence, they have him taken to the lake and water thrown in his face by pails full until he is nearly drowned. Many a poor soldier has been discharged after a long and severe illness [caused] by this water being thrown on him."[20] It was this sort of abuse and the pervasive prejudice against Catholics that caused Riley to desert in April 1846. He found his way to the Mexican Army lines and enlisted to fight for Mexico. After his capture by American forces, he was whipped and branded, escaping execution because he had joined the Mexicans before the war started. He continued in the Mexican Army after the war. Some thought that he settled in Mexico and died there, but author Peter F. Stevens maintains that he returned to Ireland, where he died in Clifden, County Galway.[21]

Ira Russell the Massachusetts surgeon, was born in 1815. He is best known for his attempts to improve medical treatment of African American soldiers and his efforts at Benton Barracks to lower the mortality rate of the patients. He became director of hospitals in the Army of the Frontier. After the war he returned to the practice of medicine in Massachusetts, where he died in 1888.

Antonio Lopez de Santa Anna ("The Napoleon of the West") was born in Xalapa, Veracruz, Mexico, on 21 February 1794 to a respected Spanish colonial family. He fought for and won Mexico's independence from Spain in

1821. Over the next forty years he served as president of Mexico in eleven non-consecutive terms. His brutal repression of Texans fighting for independence earned him the enmity of the United States, especially for his murder of Texan prisoners at Goliad and the execution of survivors at the Alamo. His defeat by Sam Houston at San Jacinto in 1836 temporarily stopped his career but he returned to fight the U.S. Army during the Mexican-American War. His defeat at the Buena Vista, Cerro Gordo and other battles caused his fall from power and he was forced into exile. He returned and ruled again until he was driven from power by Benito Juarez. He lived in exile after that but was allowed to return, crippled and nearly blind, in 1874. He died in Mexico City on 21 June 1876 and was buried in Panteon del Tepeyac Cemetery.

Rufus Saxton recruited and armed African Americans in South Carolina. He was born in Greenfield, Massachusetts, on 19 October 1824. He graduated from the U.S. Military Academy in the Class of 1849. He was appointed a general of volunteers in 1862 and commanded the defense of Harper's Ferry. Later he served in various roles in the Union Army, the most important of which was recruiting African Americans to serve in the army. After the war, he worked in the Freedman's Bureau. After his retirement in 1888 he moved to Washington, where he died on 23 February 1908. He was buried in Arlington National Cemetery.[22]

John McAllister Schofield who devastated Hood's army at Franklin, Tennessee, was born on 29 September 1831 in Gerry, Pennsylvania. He graduated from the U.S. Military Academy with the Class of 1853. He inflicted a disastrous defeat on the Confederate Army under John Bell Hood at the Battle of Franklin and commanded the XXIII Corps at the Battle of Nashville in December 1864. After the war, he served as secretary of war in 1868 but resigned after Grant became president. Schofield later became the superintendent of the U.S. Military Academy (1876–1881) and commanded the U.S. Army after the death of General Sheridan in 1888. Schofield died in Saint Augustine, Florida, on 4 March 1906 and is buried in Arlington National Cemetery.[23]

Carl Schurz who traveled in the post-war South reporting atrocities committed by the whites, was born in Liblar, Germany, on 2 March 1829. He was a revolutionary in Germany and escaped after the liberal revolution failed. He moved to the United States in 1852, settling in Wisconsin, where he practiced law and became an abolitionist supporting Lincoln's campaign for the presidency. Lincoln appointed him a brigadier general and Schurz fought at the Second Battle of Manassas and commanded a division at Chancellorsville and Gettysburg. After the war and his effort to improve the living conditions of African Americans in the South, he was elected to the U.S. Senate from Missouri. In 1876 he was named secretary of the interior, where he was committed to cleaning up department corruption. He left the Department of the Interior in 1881 and moved to New York City, where he was active in national political affairs. Schurz died in New York City on 14 May 1906, and was buried in Sleepy Hollow Cemetery in Sleepy Hollow, New York.

Winfield Scott ("Old Fuss and Feathers") devised the plan to defeat the South. He was a Virginian born in 1786. He served longer as a general than any other person in U.S. history, with a career of forty-seven years. He commanded forces from the War of 1812 through the start of the Civil War. By then he was too old and sick to sit on a horse, but had the knowledge and experience to chart a course for the Union Army. He developed the "Anaconda Plan," proposed to strangle the Confederacy through a naval blockade of the South and also cut it in two by controlling the Mississippi River. Scott's plan was not initially accepted, but became the template for Union success later in the war. The Anaconda Plan was never a top-priority strategy, but as warfare in the West along the Mississippi continued at a slow pace, it finally started to succeed in the way originally planned by Scott. To African Americans, the blockaded ports on the Atlantic coast provided an escape route to the Union.[24] Scott was replaced as commander of the army early in the war and he died in 1866.

Robert Gould Shaw commander of the 54th Massachusetts, was born on 10 October 1837 in Boston, Massachusetts, of a wealthy family. He attended Harvard University but did not graduate. He was a second lieutenant in the 2nd Massachusetts Infantry before his appointment as colonel of the all-black 54th Massachusetts Infantry in 1862. Shaw was killed in action while leading the 54th Massachusetts Infantry at Battery Wagner, Morris Island, South Carolina, on 18 July 1863. He was buried there in a mass grave with his troops. His wife moved to Europe and did not remarry.

William Tecumseh Sherman ("Cump") famous for his march to the sea, was born on 8 February 1820 in Lancaster, Ohio. His father, a justice of the Ohio supreme court, died suddenly in 1829, leaving the family in poverty. Sherman received an appointment to the U.S. Military Academy, graduating sixth in his class in 1840. His classmates included George Henry Thomas, the Union commander at the Battle of Nashville, and General Richard Ewell, a senior commander in the Confederate Army. After the war he commanded the U.S. Army starting in 1869 and retired in 1884. Sherman died in New York City on 14 February 1891 and was buried in Calvary Cemetery, St. Louis, Missouri.[25]

Robert Smalls the African American hero who seized the Confederate ship *Planter*, returned to South Carolina after the war and entered politics. He was a state representative from 1868 to 1870 and state senator from 1870 to 1874. In 1874 he was elected to the U.S. House of Representatives and served intermittently until 1886. In 1889 President Benjamin Harrison appointed Smalls the U.S. collector of customs for the port in Beaufort, an office he held until 1913. Smalls died on 22 February 1915.

Andrew Jackson Smith ("Whiskey") who commanded the XVI Corps at Spanish Fort, was born in Bucks County, Pennsylvania, on 28 April 1815. He attended the U.S. Military Academy at West Point, graduating with the Class of 1838. He ranked thirty-six in a class of forty-five. Smith later served in the Mexican War. He rose in rank to command a corps during the Civil War and is best remembered for his defeat of the Confederate Army at Tupelo, Mississippi, which included one of the few defeats of Nathan Bedford Forrest. Smith was admired by his troops because he shared their hardships. They called themselves "A.J.'s Guerillas." Smith resigned his volunteer commission in 1866 and became a colonel of the U.S. 7th Cavalry Regiment. He retired from the military service in April 1869 to become postmaster at St. Louis, Missouri. Smith died on 30 January 1897 and is buried in St. Louis.

Edmund Kirby Smith who surrendered the last military force of the Confederacy, was born in St. Augustine, Florida, on 16 May 1824. He was a graduate of the West Point Class of 1845, with a class standing of twenty-five out of forty-one. After graduation he taught mathematics at West Point but resigned from the Union Army in 1861 in order to fight for the Confederacy. For most of the war he fought in the West. After the war he was chancellor at the University of Nashville and president of the Atlantic and Pacific Telegraph Company. He died in Sewanee, Tennessee, on 28 March 1893.[26]

Edwin McMasters Stanton the secretary of war, was born on 19 December 1814 in Steubenville, Ohio. Throughout his life he suffered from asthma, which may have contributed to his death. He was the 25th United States attorney general, serving in the Buchanan administration. Soon after the start of the war he was appointed secretary of war after Lincoln fired Stanton's predecessor, Simon Cameron. Stanton's policies did not always agree with Lincoln's, in which case Lincoln, in his words, "plowed around him." Stanton was too valuable to fire. After the death of Lincoln, Stanton, as a Radical Republican, did not support the lenient polices toward the South of Andrew Johnson, the new president, who tried to fire Stanton. This led to a confrontation between the Radical Republicans in Congress and Johnson, leading to the latter's impeachment. Soon after impeachment failed, Stanton was removed from his position as secretary of war. Stanton died in Washington, D.C., on 24 December 1869.

James Steedman ("Old Steady") led African American troops at Nashville. He was born on 29 July 1817 in Northumberland County, Pennsylvania. Steedman was a self-made man who inspired confidence among his troops. He had very little formal education but learned the trade of a printer and advanced to the position of public printer of the U.S. government in 1857. At the start of the war he was selected as colonel of the 14th Ohio and was promoted to general in 1862. He led his troops to several victories; perhaps the best known was his successful attack on Hood's right flank at the Battle of Nashville in 1864. After the war he became a collector of internal revenue in New Orleans. Later, he served in the Ohio state senate and became chief of police in Toledo, Ohio, in 1883. Steedman died on 18 October 1883 in Toledo, and was buried in Woodlawn Cemetery.[27]

Thaddeus Stevens the Republican leader in the House who led the effort to impeach Andrew Johnson, was born on 4 April 1792 in Danville, Vermont. He was born with a clubfoot and an alcoholic father who kept his family at the poverty level. Stevens overcame disadvantages to graduate from Dartmouth College and practice law. He was first elected to the U.S. House of Representatives in 1849 and became one of the most powerful men in Congress during the Civil War. As the leader of the Radical Republicans in the House after the war, he directed the course of Reconstruction. After his failed effort to impeach Andrew Johnson, he died in Washington, D.C., on 11 August 1868. He was buried in Lancaster, Pennsylvania.

Charles Sumner who led the effort to convict Andrew Johnson in the Senate impeachment trial, was born in Boston, Massachusetts, on 6 January 1811. He was an attorney who was elected to the Senate and nearly killed there when he was attacked in 1856 by South Carolina representative Preston Brooks. Sumner had accused one of Brook's relatives of being a "pimp for slavery." Sumner was champion of equal rights, especially voting rights for African Americans. As a Radical Republican he defeated Andrew Johnson's reconstruction plans, which some say would have continued to enslave African Americans. After the failure of the Senate to convict Andrew Johnson, Sumner continued his support for African American equal rights and was co-author of the Civil Rights Act of 1875, which was enacted a year after his death. The act was later declared unconstitutional by the U.S. Supreme Court and was the last significant effort on civil rights until Lyndon Johnson's Civil Rights Act of 1964. Sumner died in Washington, D.C., on 11 March 1874. He was buried in Cambridge, Massachusetts.

Zachary Taylor ("Old Rough and Ready") achieved his greatest victory over Santa Anna at the Battle of Buena Vista. He was born in Barboursville, Virginia, on 24 November 1784. Taylor had a forty-year career in the army. He served in the War of 1812, the Black Hawk War, the Seminole War, and the Mexican-American War. Taylor became the twelfth president of the United States and served from 4 March 1849 to 9 July 1850. He died in office after sixteen months as president. The cause of his death was not clear, but it appears that he died of digestive complications following a 4th of July ground-breaking ceremony for the Washington Monument. He is buried in Louisville, Kentucky, in the Zachary Taylor National Cemetery.[28]

Sylvanus Thayer   ("The Father of the Military Academy") who reorganized West Point after the disastrous tenure of Alden Partridge, was born in Braintree, Massachusetts, on 9 June 1785. He graduated from the Military Academy in the Class of 1808 with a class standing of third out of fifteen. He served in the War of 1812, where he directed the fortification of Norfolk, Virginia. He was appointed superintendent of the U.S. Military Academy in 1817, replacing Alden Partridge. During his long service he reorganized the Military Academy and resigned from that position in 1833. Thayer also served in the Union Army, retiring in 1863. He donated funds to establish the Thayer School of Engineering at Dartmouth College and for a time was the oldest living graduate of the Military Academy (1871–1872). Thayer died in Braintree, Massachusetts, on 7 September 1872 and was buried at West Point.[29]

Evan Thomas   the son of Lorenzo Thomas, served in the Civil War and was a career army officer like his father. At Gettysburg, he commanded his artillery battery with great skill. When the Union line was broken and the First Minnesota moved to block the Confederates, Thomas delivered devastating fire on the Confederates and helped save the day for the Union.[30] He continued to serve after the war and was killed in the Modoc Indian War in California on 26 April 1873. This was two weeks after the murder of General Canby and other members of the Peace Commission, who were trying to negotiate an end to the Modoc War. In an engagement with the Modocs at the Lava Beds, Thomas was trapped and killed with his men. His last stand is described below by one of the survivors:

> Thomas, Harris, Howe, Semig, and a handful of men also withdrew toward the west, following after Lieutenant Wright and the few who had stayed with him. Tickner, the guide, had seen enough; he ran after the fleeing soldiers toward Gillem's Camp. Semig bravely haulted on open ground, dressed the wounds of two soldiers, then hurried on to catch up with Thomas, overtaking him "'in a hollow' with some small rocks and sage bushes, not over fifty yards from the ridge which Wright's command had been ordered to take." Thomas, believing that Wright had taken the ridge, shouted for him "and as a reply received several shots." Defending themselves as best they could in the depression, Thomas and all his command, now reduced to the officers and twenty men, fought until all were killed or severely wounded. Wright and his small group suffered the same fate. Corporal Noble from Battery A reported that "Wright was first shot through the groin, dangerously wounded." He buried his watch so that the enemy could not have it, then "a second bullet passed through his heart and he shortly afterwards breathed his last." A lieutenant, not at the scene, wrote soon after, "Wright was severely wounded on the way to the heights, and his company, with one or two exceptions, deserted

him and fled like a pack of sheep; then the slaughter began." Wright's replacement later declared that the infantry had not run away faster or farther than the artillery.³¹

George Henry Thomas ("The Rock of Chickamauga") was born on 31 July 1816 in Southampton County, Virginia, and was one of the few Virginians to fight for the North as a general officer. He was born in the area that was the center of Nat Turner's slave rebellion in 1831, from which his family was forced to flee. The sisters of Thomas would disavow him to the end of their days because he fought for the Union. Thomas graduated from the U.S. Military Academy with the Class of 1840, which included William T. Sherman. His victory at Nashville destroyed the army of John Bell Hood and is considered one of the most decisive battles of the war. There was always antipathy between Thomas and Grant, which was never reconciled. Perhaps Grant did not trust him because he was a Southerner. After the war he commanded the Division of the Pacific and died in San Francisco on 28 March 1870. He was buried in Troy, New York.

Edward Davis Townsend took over the duties of the U.S. Army adjutant general when Lorenzo Thomas headed West to recruit. Stanton preferred Townsend over Thomas. Townsend was born on 22 August 1817 and was a graduate of the 1837 class of the U.S. Military Academy. After the war, he was promoted to general in 1869 and became adjutant general. He retired in 1880 and died in Washington, D.C., in 1893 after an accidental shock from a cable car. He was buried in Rock Creek Cemetery.

Nathaniel ("Nat") Turner who led the 1831 slave rebellion in Virginia, was born on 2 October 1800. After the rebellion failed, Turner was captured and hanged on 11 November 1831. Approximately sixty whites and at least one hundred African Americans died during and after the revolution. While fifty-six African Americans were executed by the state, many others were lynched by white mob violence after the rebellion failed.

Daniel Ullmann who accepted Lincoln's offer to command African American troops, was born on 28 April 1810 in Wilmington, Delaware. He graduated from Yale in 1829 and moved to New York City, where he practiced law. At the start of the war, he helped recruit the 78th New York Regiment and was commissioned as a colonel of that regiment. In 1863 he was promoted to general and sent to New Orleans to raise five regiments of African Americans. After the war he retired to Nyack, New York, where he spent his time in scientific and literary studies. He died in Nyack on 20 September 1892 and is buried there.³²

Ben Wade was the Radical Republican who would have been president if Andrew Johnson had been removed from office. He was born in Feeding Hills,

Massachusetts, on 27 October 1800. He was admitted to the bar in 1828. He joined the Republican Party and was elected to the Senate in 1851. He supported civil rights bills and became president pro tempore of the Senate. After the Senate failed to convict Andrew Johnson, Wade was defeated in the 1868 elections and returned to his Ohio law practice. He died in Jefferson, Ohio, on 2 March 1878.

Edward Augustus Wild organized two African American regiments for Massachusetts Governor Andrew. Wild was born in Brookline, Massachusetts, on 25 November 1825. He graduated from Harvard in 1844 and from the Jefferson Medical College soon after. He served as a surgeon until the start of the Civil War. He is famous for forming Wild's African Brigade, which he commanded until the end of the war. He was wounded at South Mountain and his arm was amputated. After the war he was unable to practice medicine and engaged in several other pursuits, including superintendent of a Nevada silver mine. He moved south to Colombia, where he died in Medellin on 28 August 1891. He was buried in the Cementerio de San Pedro.[33]

James Harrison Wilson the Union cavalry leader at Nashville, was born near Shawneetown, Illinois, on 2 September 1837. He graduated from the U.S. Military Academy, sixth in the Class of 1860. He was instrumental in destroying the army of John Bell Hood. He survived the war and resigned as a major general in 1870. He returned to the army in 1898 to fight in the Spanish-American War as a major general of volunteers. Wilson died in Wilmington, Delaware, on 23 February 1925 and was buried in Old Swedes Churchyard. He was the last surviving member of the West Point Class of 1860.[34]

Appendix A

Family History of Lorenzo Thomas[1]

First Generation in America

Evan Thomas: Born in Wales, 1763. Married Elizabeth Sherer on 7 January 1796 in Philadelphia. Died in New Castle, Delaware, in 1836.

Children:
Theodore Thomas
Evan Thomas (1799–1850)
Lorenzo Thomas (1804–1875) (see below)
+ others (names not known)

Second Generation

Lorenzo Thomas (1804–1875): Married Elizabeth Brindley Colesberry (1806–1879) in New Castle, Delaware, on 4 December 1832.

Children:
S. B. Thomas, born circa 1832
Henry Colesberry Thomas (1833–1909): Married Sallie Brindley (1828–1885); Henry worked as a clerk in the War Department his entire life
Lorenzo ("Lo") Thomas (1837–1912): Served in the Civil War in the First U.S. Artillery
Mary B. Thomas (1838–1918)
Evan ("Ev") Thomas (1843–1873) (see below)
Anna Thomas, born 1848
Randolph Thomas (c. 1850–1861)
Elizabeth Thomas, born 1852
J. J. B. Thomas, born circa 1858

Third Generation

Evan Thomas (1843–1873): Married Josephine Foster (1847–1897) on 25 November 1868. Evan was a veteran of the Civil War who remained in the army and was killed in the Modoc Indian War on 26 April 1873 at Lava Beds, California.

Children:
Florence Voohees Thomas (1869–1937)
Marion Josephine Thomas (1871–1954)

Appendix B

Early Recruiting Efforts

The African American Civil War Memorial in Washington, D.C., commemorates their service, which started in 1861.[1] At that time, the African Americans in the North were told when they tried to enlist that this was a white man's fight and they had nothing to do with it.[2] Their service was not wanted. By 1862, however, the U.S. Army needed more recruits and several events occurred that would satisfy the need.

In the South the cause was states' rights and the specter of armed African Americans terrified the public, reviving memories of blacks butchering the whites on plantations (as had occurred in the Nat Turner uprising). In a speech on 21 March 1861, Alexander Stephens, vice president of the Confederate States of America, stated:

> The new [Confederate] constitution has put at rest all questions relating to African slavery as it exists among us — the proper "status" of the Negro in our form of civilization. The prevailing ideas at the time of the formation of the old constitution were that the enslavement of the African was in violation of the laws of nature; that it was wrong in "principle," socially, morally and politically. Those ideas were fundamentally wrong. They rested upon the assumption of the equality of the races. This was an error.... Our new government is founded upon exactly the opposite ideas; its foundations are laid, its cornerstone rests upon the great truth, that the negro is not equal to the white man; that slavery — subordination to the superior race — is his natural and normal condition. This, our new government, is the first, in the history of the world, based on this great physical and moral truth.[3]

In both the South and the North the view expressed by Stephens (that African Americans were inferior to whites) led many to believe that they could not be trusted as soldiers. At the start of the war, the United States Army numbered 1,108 officers and 15,259 soldiers organized into nineteen regiments. Twenty-nine percent of the officers left the army to join the Confederacy, but few enlisted men left.[4] There is no record of any African Americans in the army at the start of the war. The Union raised an army of 714,231 men in the first year of the war. None were African Americans.[5]

As the war continued and African Americans were enlisted, there were fundamental differences in the service of African Americans in the Confederate and Union armies. In the North, nearly all African Americans were enlisted in regiments of U.S. Colored Troops. In the Confederate Army, however, free African Americans were integrated into white units. As a consequence, in the Confederacy, African Americans enlisted in state militia or home guard units.[6] The result of all of this was that the Union Army was segregated, whereas the African Americans in the South were integrated. More-over, the South used tens of thousands of African American slaves, with the consent of their owners, as laborers to build fortifications and so forth.

During the course of the war there were dozens of engagements fought by the Union Army that featured African American units who behaved with incredible valor, and much was written then and now about these units. In the South the participation of African Americans in Confederate units was invisible. There is no evidence that African Americans in the South fought as a large group in any engagement.[7] As a result, when writing of successes in battle of African American units in the North, it is standard to describe the valor of African Americans fighting for the Union at battles such as Fort Wagner (which featured the 54th Massachusetts Infantry), but there is no counterpart to this when writing about African Americans in the Confederate Army.

Years after the war, when many Northern African Americans were receiving pensions for service with their white colleagues, Southern African Americans received very little. Pensions were offered by the Southern states many years after the war, and the pension applications are one of the few surviving records that provide names of African Americans fighting for the South. Unfortunately, in most cases, the Southern states denied the pension applications of African Americans.

Both the North and the South recognized, as the war progressed and both sides became desperate for manpower, that the use of African Americans could decide the outcome of the war.[8] In early 1865, General Robert E. Lee continued to press for the enlistment of African Americans in the Confederate Army.[9] And prior to that, Lincoln reported to Judge Mills of Wisconsin, "The slightest knowledge of arithmetic will prove to any man that the rebel armies cannot be destroyed with the Democratic [Party] strategy [disbanding African American units]. It would sacrifice all of the white men of the North to do it. There are now in the service of the United States near two hundred thousand able-bodied colored men, most of them under arms, defending and acquiring Union territory."[10] The problem both sides had was bringing the public and their respective Congresses on board to arm the blacks to fight.

As Lincoln said, the slightest knowledge of arithmetic proved the case. The South had nearly four million African American slaves. Most slaves would serve the Confederacy as body servants or laborers, with few armed to fight except within the Confederate Navy, which had an established practice of enlisting African Americans[11] (this practice continued and expanded as more ships were launched to fight the war). The North had over 200,000 African Americans, nearly all free. On both sides, however, the numbers are deceiving. In the North, African Americans were armed to fight in USCT regiments, but initially their service was mostly that of laborers so as "to free up white soldiers to fight." As will be seen, this practice was ended later in the war to allow these African American soldiers to train and fight as infantry, requiring the white soldiers to pull their fair share of duty building fortifications and other fatigue duty (labor unrelated to combat).

South

For the South, the arithmetic problem was different. Throughout the war, half a million slaves deserted the South to serve the Union. Of the remaining three and a half million slaves, the vast majority kept the war effort going by serving on the farms and in other functions, just as they had always done. Exact numbers of those serving the Confederate cause in uniform (except for the navy) are not known. The number of slaves, or "body servants," who served with their masters is quoted by several sources as 30,000 and some of these were armed and would fight.[12] Dr. Lewis Steiner of the U.S. Sanitary Commission (USSC) recorded in his diary what he observed shortly before the Battle of Antietam. Steiner estimated that 5 percent of the Confederate Army was black:

> Wednesday, September 10
>
> At 4 o'clock this morning the Rebel army began to move from our town, Jackson's force taking the advance. The movement continued until 8 o'clock P.M., occupying 16 hours. The most liberal calculation could not give them more than 64,000 men. Over 3,000 Negroes must be included in the number.... They had arms, rifles, muskets, sabers, bowie-knives, dirks, etc. They were supplied, in many instances, with knapsacks, haver-sacks, canteens, etc., and they were manifestly an integral portion of the Southern Confederacy army. They were seen riding on horses and mules, driving wagons, riding on caissons, in ambulances, with the staff of generals and promiscuously mixed up with all the Rebel horde.[13]

Unfortunately, body servants were not mustered into the Confederate Army, so the exact number is not known since they were not on rosters, but African American pension applications that were submitted to the Southern states half a century after the war numbered into the thousands.[14] Of course, nearly all of the slaves, such as body servants, were compelled to serve and had no choice.

Arming African Americans in the South was an enduring problem that hampered their use in fighting the North. Southern whites lived in a state of paranoia throughout the war. The fear was that if the slaves were armed to fight against the North, they could use the weapons for a bloody rebellion. On any given plantation, whites felt comfortable with their own slaves, who were considered loyal, trustworthy, and so on, but it was those "other slaves" outside of the plantation who would supposedly murder the whites in their beds. The discomfort increased as more and more whites moved north to fight the Yankees. This meant that there were fewer whites on the plantations to defend against an African American uprising. Would this loss of white manpower in the South encourage an insurrection? In the end, African Americans remained loyal on the plantations and no African American insurrection occurred during the war.[15] Nevertheless, the fear of this prevented the arming of the slaves until the end of the war.

There were other problems as well. Joseph T. Wilson, a Union soldier, summarized it best in his history of the Civil War:

> An innate reasoning taught ... that slaves could not be relied upon to fight for their own enslavement. To get to the breastworks was but to get a chance to run to the Yankees; and thousands of those whose elastic step kept time with the martial strains of the drum and fife, as they marched on through city and town, enroute to the front, were not elated with the hope of Southern success, but were buoyant with the prospects of reaching the North. The confederates found it no easy task to watch the negroes and the Yankees too; their attention could be given to but one at a time; as a slave expressed it, "when marsa watch the Yankee, nigger go; when marsa watch the nigger, Yankee come." But the Yankees did not always receive him kindly during the first year of the war.[16]

While Lincoln hesitated to enlist African Americans at the start of the war, the South acted. While there was no official Confederate policy of enlisting African Americans to fight until 1865, the states took action even before Fort Sumter. In Louisiana three regiments were formed in 1861 with officers of their own race.[17] In Tennessee on 28 June 1861, the legislature authorized the governor "at his discretion, to receive into the military service of the state all male free persons of color between the ages of 15 and 50."[18] The African Americans enlisted would receive $8 a month,[19] and would be used to accomplish manual labor.[20] Everyone in both the North and the South realized that once a slave was equipped with a firearm and trained to use it, he would never be a slave again.

Aside from serving as labor battalions and body servants, African Americans also provided service to the South on the home front. Slavery was the "tower of strength" for the Confederacy, the foundation of the Southern society. To counter the flow of slaves to Union lines, all sorts of lies were invented by the plantation owners, the Southern press and the government. They did little good. Mrs. Taylor recalled, "The whites would tell their colored people not to go to the Yankees, for they would harness them to carts and make them pull carts around in place of horses."²¹ But lies were not always necessary. When the New York City draft rioters of July 1863 targeted African Americans to be killed, the Southern press gleefully reported details to their readers. What started as a riot against the draft in New York City turned into a riot against African Americans because they were competing for white jobs.

Despite the lies and events such as the draft riots, many African Americans in the South were eager to join the fight against slavery. Others were not. *The Providence (R. I.) Post* reported, "Negroes as a mass have shown no friendship to the Union.... The few thousands who have come into our lines to live at the expense of the whites seek rather a life of laziness than self-dependence.... Their sympathies are with the Rebels."²² Elizabeth Keckley, a companion of Mary Todd Lincoln, recalled, "Often I heard them [the African Americans] declare that they would rather go back to slavery in the South and be with their old masters than to enjoy freedom of the North."²³

As stated, thousands of African Americans in the South accompanied their masters to war as body servants (cooks, valets, bodyguards, etc.) but their service was frequently far beyond that. Many were armed and fought with their masters in battle.²⁴ Numerous stories are told of Confederate African Americans who were wounded or separated from their Confederate units and eventually found their way back to their organization. They gave no thought to joining the Union forces. Those who did occasionally join Union forces were faced with a dilemma. For example, one African American Union soldier refused to fire on a Confederate unit: "My young master is thar [*sic*]; and I played with him all my life and he has saved me from getting a many whippings I would have got, and I can't shoot thar [*sic*], for I loves my young master still."²⁵

In November 1864 Jefferson Davis continued his resistance to allowing African Americans to enlist in the Confederate Army to fight "until our white population shall prove insufficient for the armies we require." Apparently, President Davis had not gotten the news: the Confederacy was surrounded, cut into pieces and on the verge of collapse. General Robert E. Lee summed up the situation in a letter to Senator Andrew Hunter: "I think we must decide whether slavery shall be extinguished by our enemies and the slaves be used against us, or use them ourselves at the risk of the effects which may be produced upon our social institutions."²⁶ In other words, once you arm the slaves and offer them freedom for their enlistment, the society in the South that was based upon slavery would collapse (which it did). Lee, Davis and others may have wanted to end slavery much earlier, but the citizens of the South and their representatives in the Confederate Congress would not allow it. Some say that lack of unity in the Confederacy caused its demise or, put another way, "States' rights killed the Confederacy."

It was not until 13 March 1865, a few weeks before the Confederacy collapsed, that the Confederate Congress enacted legislation authorizing the enrollment of African Americans in the Confederate Army.[27] "Of course the negro people about the city of Richmond heard of the proposition to arm and emancipate them if they would voluntarily fight for their old masters. They discussed its merits with a sagacity wiser than those who proposed the scheme, and it is safe to say that they concluded in the language of one of them who spoke on the matter 'It too late, de Yankees am coming.'" [28]

In a measure detached from reality, the legislature stated that each Confederate state was *required* to furnish 300,000 men for duty.[29] If one does the math, it becomes clear that the total requirement would exceed the African American population and the remaining available whites in the South. Several African American units were actually formed before the end of the war, but none fired a shot.[30]

Fragmentary records of African Americans in the Confederate Army have survived. Author Charles Kelly Barrow has assembled African American records from Georgia, Virginia, and North Carolina.[31] The total number listed by Barrow is 120. Most of these African American records list occupations such as cooks, musicians, body servants or teamsters. Many of these soldiers also fought as infantry but that does not show in the records. Pension applications from African Americans tell more about their duties and units.

General William T. Sherman recorded in his memoirs sights that he saw during his march to the sea: "The negroes were simply frantic with joy. Whenever they heard my name, they clustered around my horse, shouted and prayed in their particular style."[32] This same general refused to allow African American regiments to join his column in his march to the sea because he did not trust them to fight.

North

Frederick Douglass pressed the Union to enlist African Americans: "Once let the black man get upon his person the brass letters, U.S., let him get an eagle on his button, and a musket on his shoulder and bullets in his pocket, and there is no power on earth which can deny that he has earned the right to citizenship in the United States."[33]

In the months that followed Fort Sumter, nothing of note happened in the White House or Congress regarding the enlistment African Americans to fight for the Union. While rumors were circulating in both the North and South that the other side was raising African American regiments, in fact nothing was happening. The urging of Frederick Douglass and others went unheeded: "Would to god you would let us do something. We lack nothing but your consent. We are ready and would go, counting ourselves happy in being permitted to serve and suffer for the cause of freedom and free institutions. But you won't let us go."³⁴

William Lloyd Garrison suggested that slave insurrections be promoted in the South, but few backed this proposal.³⁵ The Lincoln administration made it clear that this was not an abolitionist war and servile insurrection had no part in it.³⁶ The war was to preserve the Union, not free the slaves, or so Lincoln said at that time.³⁷

On 30 August 1861 General John C. Frémont, commander in the West, challenged this policy when he declared martial law in Missouri and freed the slaves of every rebel in the state. Lincoln modified the Frémont order to indicate that only those rebels who had directly aided the Confederate war effort would lose their slaves.³⁸

In May 1861, General George McClellan, on campaign in what is now West Virginia, made his sentiments clear: "See that the rights and property of the people are respected, and repress all attempts at Negros insurrection."³⁹ In July, Frederick Douglass assailed Lincoln and McClellan because they were seen as not respecting the human rights of the African Americans.

> ABRAHAM LINCOLN is no more fit for the place he holds than was JAMES BUCHANAN, and the latter was no more the miserable tool of traitors and rebels than the former is allowing himself to be. As to McClellan he still leaves us in doubt as to whether he is a military imposter, or a deliberate traitor. The country is destined to become sick of both McClellan and Lincoln, and the sooner the better.... The signs of the times indicate that the people will have to take this war into their own hands and dispense with the services of all who by their incompetency give aid and comfort to the destroyers of the country.⁴⁰

It was Gideon Wells, the secretary of the navy, who reversed the policy (for the navy). Contraband (escaped slaves from the South) had been collected by navy vessels as they cruised the Rappahannock River in Virginia. What to do with these blacks? At the same time, the navy was short of manpower. Wells solved both problems with his order on 15 September 1861: "The Department finds it necessary to adopt a regulation with respect [to] the large number of persons of color, commonly known as contrabands, now subsisted at the navy yard and on board ships of war.... You are authorized ... to enlist them for the naval service, under the same forms and regulations as apply to other enlistments."⁴¹ While they would be enlisted in the navy, the African Americans would receive a lesser wage than whites ($10 versus $13 a month), although they would man the guns on warships and perform all other duties accomplished by whites.⁴²

The Wells order was not reversed, but when the secretary of the war, Simon Cameron, tried to move in the same direction, he lost his job.⁴³ It seemed logical and a good idea at the time: In November 1861, General Thomas W. Sherman was given the task of invading the coast of South Carolina. As he invaded, he was given authority to "avail yourself of the service of any persons ... as you may deem most beneficial to the service."[44] This meant that Sherman could use African Americans to fight, but then a clause was added, some say by Lincoln, that no arming of "them" was authorized. With this hodgepodge of instructions, Sherman moved inland, but did not take advantage of his opportunity to enlist African Americans.[45] The end came for Cameron when he joined a speaking tour, the theme of which was to arm and equip the slaves of the rebels. He followed this up with his annual report as secretary of war, which emphasized the same goal. He sealed his fate when he released his report to the press before submitting it to Lincoln. Cameron soon found himself the new ambassador to the czar.[46]

In May 1861, General Benjamin Butler, the Union commander at Fort Monroe, refused to return three runaway slaves to their owner. This had been an issue since the war started. The Rev. J. Sella Martin, pastor of Joy Street Baptist Church in Boston, wrote to Frederick Douglass: "They [Union officers] refuse to let white men sell the Southerners food, and yet they return slaves to work on plantations to raise all the food that the Southerners want. They arrest traitors, and yet make enemies of the colored people, North and South."[47] Butler viewed the escaped slaves as "contraband of war" and the U.S. Congress endorsed Butler's decision through the First Confiscation Act, which was signed by Lincoln on 6 August 1861. This law authorized the federal government to seize property (including slaves) of all those participating directly in the revolution. These African American "contrabands" could be freed at locations occupied by the U.S. Army, but they were prohibited from joining Union forces.[48] Clearly, this was a way to punish Southern slave owners, but did not help the Union's war-fighting capability. It was not until July 1862 that the U.S. Army was allowed to hire African Americans but as laborers only. They were not allowed to fight. Wages were one ration a day and $10 a month, $3 of which was to be provided as clothing.[49]

While Lincoln and Congress backed away from allowing African Americans in combat, commanders in the field saw the advantages and started recruiting African Americans to fight. General David Hunter, the successor to General Thomas Sherman, recruited a regiment of runaway slaves in South Carolina in April 1862. Hunter was one of the oldest officers in the field at that time. He was an 1822 graduate of West Point and his standing was 25th in a class of 40. Hunter had a long record of army service and was nearly 59 years old at the start of the Civil War. He had repeatedly asked the War Department for reinforcements and had received none. In addition to his other problems, rumors were circulating that the African Americans would be collected and shipped to Cuba, Africa and the West Indies.[50] This hindered enlistments.

His reaction was to enlist African Americans to fight and he formed African American regiments. Lincoln wanted to distance himself from Hunter's order and on 19 May announced:

> I, Abraham Lincoln, President of the United States, proclaim and declare, that the government of the United States, had no knowledge, information, or belief, of an intention on the part of General Hunter to issue such a proclamation; nor has it any authentic information that the document is genuine. And, further, that neither General Hunter, nor any other commander, or person, has been authorized by the Government of the United States, to make proclamations declaring the slaves of any State free; and that the supposed proclamation, now in question, whether genuine or false, is altogether void.[51]

Hunter would eventually see his policies vindicated when Lorenzo Thomas was ordered west to recruit. Hunter's problem was that his policy was right, but his timing was wrong.[52] Lincoln and his administration were changing their view. Some of Lincoln's cabinet supported arming the African Americans, but in July 1862, Lincoln would not go that far. At this point, without any backing from Washington, Hunter disbanded the regiment[53] except for one company. However, even after this, there were aftershocks. The Confederacy reacted violently, suggesting that Hunter was promoting a slave insurrection throughout the South by arming the African Americans in his region.[54] Jefferson Davis wrote to Robert E. Lee:

> The newspapers, received from the enemy country, announce as a fact that Major-General Hunter has armed slaves for the murder of their masters and has done all in his power to inaugurate a servile war which is worse than that of the savage, insomuch as it superintends other horrors to indiscriminate slaughter of all ages, sexes and conditions.[55]

The South's paranoia over the possibility of an African American uprising was always in the background. Further, the Confederacy decided that any white Union officer commanding an African American unit would be executed if captured for "inciting negro insurrections."[56]

The result of the Confederate proclamation was an uproar in the U.S. Congress, with the abolitionists winning. On 17 July 1862, the Second Confiscation Act of 1862 was signed into law. It attempted to broaden the authority of the federal government to seize property of anyone giving aid and comfort to the enemy. All slaves entering Union lines would be "forever free."[57] The Second Confiscation Act also provided a special authority allowing the arming of Negroes,[58] but it passed authority to the president, not Hunter, and the president at this point had no intention of arming the African Americans. Lincoln's concern was that if he armed the African Americans, he would lose the border slave states, such as Kentucky, to the Confederacy. The *Times* reported his belief "that the nation could not afford to lose Kentucky at this crisis, and gave it as his opinion that to arm the Negroes would turn 50,000 bayonets from the loyal Border States against that were now for us."[59] In other words, the Union troops in the border states would change sides and fight for the South. In practice, neither confiscation act had much effect on the war and very little property was seized.[60] In the same month, the Militia Act was passed, authorizing the president to receive into the service of the United States "for the purpose of construction entrenchments, or performing camo [sic] duties, or any other labor, or any military or naval ... persons of African descent."[61]

Benjamin Butler, formerly of the House of Representatives, had by this time become a Union general. He started the campaign to recruit and mustered tens of thousands of African Americans to fight for the Union in spite of prejudice in the North.[62] A Civil War officer described Butler as follows:

> With his head set immediately on a stout shapeless body, his very squinting eyes, and a set of legs and arms that look as if made for somebody else, and hastily glued to him by mistake, [Butler] presents a combination of Victor Emanuel [King of Savoy], Aesop, [and] Richard III, which is very confusing to the mind.[63]

The summer of 1862 found General Butler in New Orleans. In April he had moved up the Mississippi River with Admiral Farragut to seize New Orleans. While Butler commanded at New Orleans, one of his subordinates, General John W. Phelps, was located nearby at Fort Parapet. Phelps was an abolitionist determined to arm African Americans to fight for the Union. Complaints started to arrive about Phelps' activities. He was enticing the slaves to leave their plantations and cross lines into his camp. He then started organizing five companies of African Americans. On 30 July 1862, he sent a requisition to Butler for arms and equipment for three regiments that he was forming. Phelps presented a very interesting case to Butler:

> Society in the South seems to be on the point of dissolution; and the best way of preventing the African Americans from becoming instrumental in a general state of anarchy, is to enlist him in the cause of the Republic. If we reject his services, any petty military chieftain by offering him freedom, can have them for the purpose of robbery and plunder. It is for the interests of the South, as well of the North, that the African should be permitted to offer his block for the temple of freedom. Sentiments unworthy of the man of the present day — worthy only of another Cain — could alone prevent such an offer from being accepted.[64]

Nevertheless, Butler refused and Phelps submitted his resignation.[65]

At this point, Butler, a clever Massachusetts politician before he became a general, decided to out–Phelps Phelps. He realized that the Confederate Army had raised three regiments of free African Americans to defend New Orleans and the regiments had been disbanded. Why not recall them to fight for the Union? On 22 August he published his General Order Number 63. It called for free colored militia men to volunteer for the Union.[66] Butler raised three regiments of African Americans, cleverly stating that he was merely recommissioning Confederate regiments that already existed and had surrendered in New Orleans. He got away with it, although his claim was a real stretch: less than 10 percent were members of the original Confederate regiments.[67] The Confederate government that had condemned Hunter and Phelps "for having organized and armed negro slaves against their masters" did not have a word to say about Butler.[68]

Also, by the summer of 1862, war weariness was setting in after a series of Union defeats. The realization that the North needed more manpower to prosecute the war led to acceptance that African Americans should be brought into the Union Army. As mentioned earlier, the Militia Act had already been passed, removing the restrictions of the 1792 law that banned African Americans from serving. This act authorized the employment of free African Americans as soldiers.[69]

West of the Mississippi River arming of African Americans for the Union had started with far less pain than in the South and East. Senator James H. Lane began enlisting African Americans in Kansas. Lane was a lawyer born in Indiana who moved to Kansas in 1855. He was a Jayhawker (Union guerrilla) who committed more than his fair share of atrocities, but was respectable enough to have a university named for him later. Lincoln also had enough confidence in him to direct that he be promoted to brigadier general.[70] In August 1862, Lane started recruiting whites and African Americans at Lawrence, Kansas. African Americans would be laborers and would not be armed. Lane sent glowing reports back to Washington: "Recruiting opened beautifully good for four regiments of whites and two of blacks."[71] Secretary of War Stanton telegraphed Lane on 23 September 1862: "You are not authorized to organize Indians, nor any but loyal white men."[72]

Things seemed to get out of hand. There were complaints of African American troops moving into Missouri and attacking the state militia. These were followed by a pitched battle between five companies of African Americans and a large guerrilla force in Missouri: "The first engagement of the war in which colored troops were engaged [they won]."[73] This was great publicity for the African American troops, but complaints flowed in to Washington. Stanton continued to protest the arming of African Americans, but was ignored.

Policy in Washington was about to change and Lane sensed that. The 1st Kansas Colored Volunteers Regiment was formed and became the fourth African American regiment activated after Ben Butler's three regiments in Louisiana.

When General Hunter failed and left the Sea Islands of South Carolina, General Rufus Saxton took over. The disbanded 1st South Carolina Colored Volunteers was about to rise from the ashes.

After nearly eighteen months of war, the manpower pinch in both North and South was starting to drive policy. On 25 August 1862, Secretary of War Stanton directed Saxton to recruit no more than 5,000 African American troops. They would be armed. This was a turning point for the Lincoln administration, and while Lincoln had not entirely decided to arm African Americans, Stanton told Saxton to do it. It was not long before the African Americans were fighting and winning against the Confederate Army in a series of raids along the coast. With every raid, they brought in more African Americans to fight.[74] White acceptance of African American soldiers was also growing. When asked about African American troops, one white soldier commented, "They've as much right to fight for themselves as I have to fight for them."[75] On 31 January 1863, the 1st Carolina was made a part of the Union Army. This was the fifth African American regiment to be mustered.

The Emancipation Proclamation of 1 January 1863 established Lincoln's commitment to the use of African Americans as soldiers: "And I further declare and make known, that such persons of suitable condition, will be received into the armed service of the United States to garrison forts, positions, stations, and other places, and to man vessels of all sorts in said service."[76] Lincoln was concerned about the reaction of the border states and Southern plantation owners who might view the document as encouraging slave insurrections and attacks on whites. For this reason, his proclamation stressed the use of African Americans in defensive situations such as garrison forts.[77] Also, it applied only to the Confederate states and not the border states; parts of Virginia and Louisiana were also exempted.[78] Once enlisted to fight, however, the African Americans would go and do what was required in all situations, not just defensive positions. By March authorization had been granted to form eight new regiments of African Americans.[79] Henry M. Turner, the pastor of the Israel Bethel Church in Washington, recalled the events of 1 January 1863: "I went to the office of the *Evening Star* and got the proclamation.... Great processions of colored and white men marched to and from the White House and congratulated President Lincoln on his proclamation. ... Nothing like that will be seen again in this life."[80] Two years later, on 31 January 1865, Congress adopted the Thirteenth Amendment to the Constitution, which abolished slavery throughout the United States.[81]

Daniel Ullmann, a politician from New York, had commanded the 78th New York Volunteers during the Peninsular Campaign and visited Lincoln to urge the enlistment of African Americans. Lincoln simply asked, "Ullmann, would you be willing to command black soldiers?" After recovering from the surprise, Ullmann agreed and what followed was a very strange arrangement.

Ullmann would raise a white cadre in New York City and then enlist African Americans in Louisiana.[82] Since New York society was not enthusiastic about providing officers for an African American brigade, no progress was made on recruiting whites (by July the New York City draft riots that targeted African Americans for murder were in full swing). Vice President Hamlin came to Ullmann's assistance and was successful in obtaining support from the governor of Maine, who agreed to find white officers for Ullmann's new brigade. One of the new regimental commanders would be Cyrus Hamlin, the vice president's son. So with white officers from Maine and the new General Ullmann from New York, the entourage cast off on 10 April 1863 for New Orleans to raise an African American brigade.[83] The reason for the odd arrangement was that recruiters had to go where recruits were plentiful and New York was unlikely to enlist enough African Americans to fill the new brigade. On the other hand, New Orleans had a large population of African Americans and Ben Butler had already enlisted three regiments.

In January 1863, Governor John Andrew of Massachusetts asked Stanton for permission to form a new African American regiment, which was approved. Andrew first planned to raise the regiment from African Americans in North Carolina, where many recruits were available. He planned to use Ben Butler to accomplish this, but when permission to use Butler was denied, he proceeded to recruit in Massachusetts. This would be difficult, since the last census indicated that out of a total of 1,973 African Americans, only 394 could be counted upon to enlist in Massachusetts (based upon the ratio of those who enlisted from the white population), which was hardly enough to raise a regiment.[84] This was the first African American regiment raised in the North. In this way, the 54th Massachusetts Infantry Regiment was born.[85] It would become the most famous of the African American regiments and was the subject of the motion picture *Glory* and two books: *One Gallant Rush* and *Lay this Laurel*. With the help of abolitionists, recruits were soon flowing in from other states. By March, four companies had been formed and recruits were following at a rate of one hundred a week. Andrew then moved to form another new Massachusetts African American regiment, the 55th.

Soon changes would arrive that would cause the formation of new African American regiments on a massive scale in the captured territories of the South. But while recruiting of African Americans in the South was blossoming, recruiting in the North was drying up. There were three reasons. First, by 1863, free African Americans in the North were enjoying a booming wartime economy that meant better wages. Second, news was spreading throughout the North of Confederates murdering African American soldiers or sending them into slavery.[86] (This point is contested among historians today. Some say it strengthened resolve and aided recruitment; others, not). Third, the requirement that all officers of African American regiments be white deterred recruitment (see Chapter 3). In addition, Washington, D.C., a Southern city, was not a good place to enlist. Recruits were attacked by mobs. A reporter for the *Christian Recorder* wrote, "I saw an excited rabble pursuing a corporal of the 1st Colored Regiment. Such taunts as 'Kill the Black ... strip him ... we'll stop this negro enlistment' ... the corporal received some pretty severe bruises."[87] But in spite of discouragement, recruiting continued. An African American private from the 54th Massachusetts penned the following song:

> Fremont told them, when it first began,
> How to save the Union, and the way it should be done;
> But Kentucky swore so hard, and old Abe he had his fears
> Till every hope was lost but the colored volunteers.
>
> McClellan went to Richmond with two hundred thousand brave;
> He said, "keep back the niggers," and the Union he would save.
> Little Mac he had his way — still the Union is in tears —
> *Now* they call for the help of the colored volunteers.
>
> So rally, boys, rally, let us never mind the past;
> We had a hard road to travel, but our days are coming fast, —
> For God is for the right, and we have no need to fear, —
> The Union must be saved by the colored volunteer.[88]

In December 1862, General Nathan P. Banks replaced Butler and found that the condition of the contrabands was deplorable. They were living in huts on substandard food. Banks encouraged them to return to their old plantations and work there at a wage of ten dollars a month.[89] Frederick Douglass complained, "It practically enslaves the negro, and makes the Proclamation of 1863 a mockery and delusion."[90] Banks' approach did, however, improve the living conditions of the African Americans and included one provision supported by all: a school board was set up to educate African Americans.[91] This was perhaps Banks' greatest contribution to the war. His next step was a disaster. He replaced the African American officers of the Louisiana regiments with whites. The African Americans stopped enlisting, so Banks was forced to use conscription to fill new regiments.[92]

By the time the Ullmann entourage arrived from New York, Banks had received his orders from Washington to cooperate. On 1 May 1863, Banks launched his own program to recruit African Americans. He planned to form "Corps d'Afrique" composed of eighteen regiments of African American troops.[93] In June, Banks merged the regiments being created by Ullmann into his own "Corps d'Afrique." The French-English African American newspaper sounded the call: "To arms! It is our duty. The nation counts on the devotion and the courage of its sons.... We are the sons of Louisiana, and when Louisiana calls, we march."[94] In mid–August, Banks reported to Lincoln that he had raised 10,000 or 12,000 men.[95] Changing from slaves to soldiers was not a pleasant experience. Robert Cowden described the recruits.

Early Recruiting Efforts 135

The average plantation negro was a hard-looking specimen, with about as little of the soldier to be seen in him as there was of the angel in Michael Angelo's block of marble before he had applied his chisel. His head covered with a web of knotted cotton strings that had once been white, braided into his long, black, curly wool; his dress a close-fitting wool shirt, and pantaloons of homespun material, butternut brown, worn without suspenders, hanging slouchily [*sic*] upon him, and generally too short in the legs by several inches.... He had a rolling, dragging, moping gait and a cringing manner, with a downcast thievish glance that dared not look you in the eye.[96]

Edward A. Wild was a graduate of Harvard and the Jefferson Medical College. At the start of the Civil War, he gave up his medical practice in order to fight for the Union. After two years of campaigning, he had lost his left arm and part of his right hand, ending any hope of resuming his career as a surgeon after the war. While Wild was recuperating in Boston, Governor Andrew asked him to help organize two African American regiments, the 54th and 55th Massachusetts. He was successful. Andrew next asked him to organize and lead an African American brigade of four regiments. In May 1863, he freed hundreds of slaves in North Carolina, resettled them safely and then recruited many of them to join the military.[97] Wild took command of a brigade of black infantry that soon became known as "Wild's African Brigade." The brigade comprised the 55th Massachusetts Infantry and the 2nd and 3rd North Carolina Colored Volunteers (which were later renumbered as the 36th and 37th U.S. Colored Troops, respectively).[98] Wild led his brigade for the remainder of the war and it occupied Richmond, Virginia. The brigade was there to observe Abraham Lincoln as he visited the home of the defeated Confederacy.

In the fall of 1862 reality had set in: hardly anyone in the North or South believed that this bloody war was primarily intended to preserve the Union or protect the South's states' rights. The issue was the abolition of slavery, and with the Emancipation Proclamation effective on 1 January 1863, Northern states were clamoring for permission to raise African American regiments. Hunter's original regiment was reorganized as the 1st South Carolina (Colored) Regiment.[99] By the end of 1863, over 50,000 African Americans had been enlisted to fight for the North; by the end of the war, the number was over 200,000.[100] Recruitment was spurred by offers of freedom and pay. Enlistment was voluntary in loyal slave states such as Maryland, Delaware, Missouri and Kentucky,[101] but in Northern states, African Americans could be conscripted alongside whites. Kansas, Louisiana and the Carolinas used conscription and could draw on those African Americans who were contraband.[102]

Appendix C

The Impeachment Articles[1]

Article I

That said Andrew Johnson, President of the United States, on the 21st day of February, in the year of our Lord, 1868, at Washington, in the District of Columbia, unmindful of the high duties of his office, of his oath of office, and of the requirement of the Constitution that he should take care that the laws be faithfully executed, did unlawfully and in violation of the Constitution and laws of the United States issue and order in writing for the removal of Edwin M. Stanton from the office of Secretary for the Department of War, said Edwin M. Stanton having been theretofore duly appointed and commissioned, by and with the advice and consent of the Senate of the United States, as such Secretary, and said Andrew Johnson, President of the United States, on the 12th day of August, in the year of our Lord 1867, and during the recess of said Senate, having suspended by his order Edwin M. Stanton from said office, and within twenty days after the first day of the next meeting of said Senate, that is to say, on the 12th day of December, in the year last aforesaid, having reported to said Senate such suspension, with the evidence and reasons for his action in the case and the name of the person designated to perform the duties of such office temporarily until the next meeting of the Senate, and said Senate there afterward, on the 13th day of January, in the year of our Lord 1868, having duly considered the evidence and reasons reported by said Andrew Johnson for said suspension, and did refuse to concur in said suspension, whereby and by force of the provisions of an act entitled "An act regulating the tenure of certain civil offices," passed March 2, 1867, said Edwin M. Stanton did forthwith resume the functions of his office, whereof the said Andrew Johnson had then and there due notice, and said Edwin Stanton, by reason of the premises, on said 21st day of February, being lawfully entitled to hold said office of Secretary for the Department of War, which said order for the removal of said Edwin M. Stanton is, in substance, as follows, that is to say:

Executive Mansion, Washington, D.C., *February* 1, 1868

SIR: By virtue of the power and authority vested in me, as President by the Constitution and laws of the United States, you are hereby removed from the office of Secretary for the Department of War; and your functions as such will terminate upon receipt of their communication. You will transfer to Brevet Major-General L. Thomas, Adjutant-General of the Army, who has this day been authorized and empowered to act as Secretary of War ad interim, all books papers and other public property now in your custody and charge.

Respectfully yours, ANDREW JOHNSON.

Hon. E. M. Stanton, Secretary of War

Which order was unlawfully issued, and with intent then and there to violate the act entitled "An act regulating the tenure of certain civil offices," passed March 2, 1867; and, with the further intent contrary to the provisions of said act, and in violation thereof, and contrary to the provisions of the Constitution of the United States, and without the advice and consent of the Senate of the United States, the said Senate then and there being in session, to remove said Edwin M. Stanton from the office of Secretary for the Department of War, the said Edwin M. Stanton being then and there Secretary for the Department of War, and being then and there in the due and lawful execution of the duties of said office, whereby said Andrew Johnson, President of the United States, did then and there commit, and was guilty of a high misdemeanor in office.

Article II

That on the 21st day of February, in the year of our Lord 1868, at Washington, in the District of Columbia, said Andrew Johnson, President of the United States, unmindful of the high duties of his office, of his oath of office, and in violation of the Constitution of the United States, and contrary to the provisions of an act entitled "An act regulating the tenure of certain civil offices," passed March 2, 1867, without the advice and consent of the Senate of the United States, said Senate then and there being in session, and without authority of law, did, with intent to violate the Constitution of the United States and the act aforesaid, issue and deliver to one Lorenzo Thomas a letter of authority, in substance as follows, that is to say:

Executive Mansion, Washington, D.C., *February* 21, 1868

SIR: The Hon. Edwin M. Stanton having been this day removed from office as Secretary for the Department of War, you are hereby authorized and empowered to act as Secretary of War *ad interim*, and will immediately enter upon the discharge of the duties pertaining to that office.

Mr. Stanton has been instructed to transfer to you all the records, books, papers and other public property now in his custody and charge.

Respectfully yours, ANDREW JOHNSON

To Brevet Major-General Lorenzo Thomas, *Adjutant General United States Army, Washington, D.C.*

Then and there being no vacancy in said office of Secretary for the Department of War: whereby said Andrew Johnson, President of the United States, did then and there commit, and was guilty of a high misdemeanor in office.

Article III

That said Andrew Johnson, President of the United States, on the 21st day of February, in the year of our Lord 1868, at Washington, in the District of Columbia, did commit, and was guilty of a high misdemeanor in office, in this, that, without authority of law, while the Senate of the United States was then and there in session, he did appoint one Lorenzo Thomas to be Secretary for the Department of War, *ad interim*, without the advice and consent of the Senate, and with intent to violate the Constitution of the United States, no vacancy having happened in said office of Secretary for the Department of War during the recess of the Senate, and no vacancy existing in said office at the time, and which said appointment, so made by Andrew Johnson, of said Lorenzo Thomas is in substance as follows, that is to say:

Executive Mansion, Washington, D.C., *February* 21, 1868

SIR: The Hon. Edwin M. Stanton having been this day removed from office as Secretary for the Department of War, you are hereby authorized and empowered to act as Secretary of War *ad interim*, and will immediately enter upon the discharge of the duties pertaining to that office.

Mr. Stanton has been instructed to transfer to you all the records, books, papers and other public property now in his custody and charge.

Respectfully yours, ANDREW JOHNSON

To Brevet Major-General Lorenzo Thomas, *Adjutant General United States Army, Washington, D.C.*

Article IV

That said Andrew Johnson, President of the United States, unmindful of the high duties of his office, and of his oath of office, in violation of the Constitution and laws of the United States, on the 21st day of February, in the year of our Lord 1868, at Washington, in the District of Columbia, did unlawfully conspire with one Lorenzo Thomas, and with other persons of the House of Representatives unknown, with intent by intimidation and threats unlawfully to hinder and prevent Edwin M. Stanton, then and there, the Secretary for the Department of War, duly appointed under the laws of the United States, from holding said office of Secretary for the Department of War, contrary to and in violation of the Constitution of the United States, and of the provisions of an act entitled "An act to define and punish certain conspiracies," approved July 31, 1861, whereby said Andrew Johnson, President of the United States, did then and there commit and was guilty of a high crime in office.

Article V

That said Andrew Johnson, President of the United States, unmindful of the high duties of his office and of his oath of office, on the 21st of February, in the year of our Lord 1868, and on divers other days and times in said year before the 2d day of March, A.D. 1868, at Washington, in the District of Columbia, did unlawfully conspire with one Lorenzo Thomas, and with other persons to the House of Representatives unknown, to prevent and hinder the execution of an act entitled "An act regulating the tenure of certain civil offices," passed March 2, 1867, and in pursuance of said conspiracy, did unlawfully attempt to prevent Edwin M. Stanton, then and there being Secretary for the Department of War, duly appointed and commissioned under the laws of the United States, from holding said office, whereby the said Andrew Johnson, President of the United States, did then and there commit and was guilty of a high misdemeanor in office.

Article VI

That said Andrew Johnson, President of the United States, unmindful of the high duties of his office and of his oath of office, on the 21st day of February, in the year of our Lord 1868, at Washington, in the District of Columbia, did unlawfully conspire with one Lorenzo Thomas, by force to seize, take, and possess the property of the United States in the Department of War, and then and there in the custody and charge of Edwin M. Stanton, Secretary for said Department, contrary to the provisions of an act entitled "An act to define and punish certain conspiracies," approved July 31, 1861, and with intent to violate and disregard an act entitled "An act regulating the tenure of certain civil offices," passed March 2, 1867, whereby said Andrew Johnson, President of the United States, did then and there commit a high crime in office.

Article VII

That said Andrew Johnson, President of the United States, unmindful of the high duties of his office, and of his oath of office, on the 21st day of February, in the year of our Lord 1868, at Washington, in the District of Columbia, did unlawfully conspire with one Lorenzo Thomas with intent unlawfully to seize, take, and possess the property of the United States in the Department of War, in the custody and charge of Edwin M. Stanton, Secretary of said Department, with intent to violate and disregard the act entitled "An act regulating the tenure of certain civil offices," passed March 2, 1867, whereby said Andrew Johnson, President of the United States, did then and there commit a high misdemeanor in office.

Article VIII

That said Andrew Johnson, President of the United States, unmindful of the high duties of his office and of his oath of office, with intent unlawfully to control the disbursements of the moneys appropriated for the military service and for the Department of War, on the 21st day of February, in the year of our Lord 1868, at Washington, in the District of Columbia, did unlawfully and contrary to the provisions of an act entitled "An act regulating the tenure of certain civil offices," passed March 2, 1867, and in violation of the Constitution of the United States, and without the advice and consent of the Senate of the United States, and while the Senate was then and there in session, there being no vacancy in the office of Secretary for the Department of War, with intent to violate and disregard the act aforesaid, then and there issue and deliver to one Lorenzo Thomas a letter of authority in writing, in substance as follows, that is to say:

Executive Mansion, Washington, D.C., *February* 21, 1868

SIR: The Hon. Edwin M. Stanton having been this day removed from office as Secretary for the Department of War, you are hereby authorized and empowered to act as Secretary of War *ad interim*, and will immediately enter upon the discharge of the duties pertaining to that office.

Mr. Stanton has been instructed to transfer to you all the records, books, papers and other public property now in his custody and charge.

Respectfully yours, ANDREW JOHNSON

To Brevet Major-General Lorenzo Thomas, *Adjutant General United States Army, Washington, D. C.*

Whereby said Andrew Johnson, President of the United States, did then and there commit and was guilty of a high misdemeanor in office.

Article IX

That said Andrew Johnson, President of the United States, on the 22nd day of February, in the year of our Lord 1868, at Washington, in the District of Columbia, in disregard of the Constitution and the laws of the United States, duly enacted, as Commander-in-Chief of the Army of the United States, did bring before himself, then and there William H. Emory, a Major-General by brevet in the Army of the United States, actually in command of the department of Washington, and the military forces thereof, and did then and there, as such Commander-in-Chief, declare to, and instruct said Emory, that part of a law of the United States, passed March 2, 1867, entitled "An act for making appropriations for the support of the army for the year ending June 30, 1868, and for other purposes," especially the second section thereof, which provides, among other things, that "all orders and instructions relating to military operations issued by the President or Secretary of War, shall be issued through the General of the Army, and, in case of his inability, through the next in rank," was unconstitutional, and in contravention of the commission of said Emory, and which said provision of law had been theretofore duly and legally promulgated by general order for the government and direction of the Army of the United States, as the said Andrew Johnson then and there well knew, with intent thereby to induce said Emory, in his official capacity as Commander of the department of Washington, to violate the provisions of said act, and to take and receive, act upon and obey such orders as he, the said Andrew Johnson, might make and give, and which should not be issued through the General of the Army of the United States, according to the provisions of said act, and with the further intent thereby to enable him, the said Andrew Johnson, to prevent the execution of an act entitled "An act regulating the tenure of certain civil offices," passed March 2, 1867, and to unlawfully prevent Edwin M. Stanton, then being Secretary for the Department of War, from holding said office and discharging the duties thereof, whereby said Andrew Johnson, President of the United States, did then and there commit, and was guilty of a high misdemeanor in office.

Article X

That said Andrew Johnson, President of the United States, unmindful of the high duties of his office and the dignity and proprieties thereof, and of the harmony and courtesies which ought to exist and be maintained between the executive and legislative branches of the Government of the United States, designing and intending to set aside the rightful authorities and powers of

Congress, did attempt to bring into disgrace, ridicule, hatred, contempt and reproach the Congress of the United States, and the several branches thereof, to impair and destroy the regard and respect of all the good people of the United States for the Congress and legislative power thereof, (which all officers of the government ought inviolably to preserve and maintain,) and to excite the odium and resentment of all good people of the United States against Congress and the laws by it duly and constitutionally enacted; and in pursuance of his said design and intent, openly and publicly and before divers assemblages of citizens of the United States, convened in divers parts thereof, to meet and receive said Andrew Johnson as the Chief Magistrate of the United States, did, on the 18th day of August, in the year of our Lord 1866, and on divers other days and times, as well before as afterward, make and declare, with a loud voice certain intemperate, inflammatory, and scandalous harangues, and therein utter loud threats and bitter menaces, as well against Congress as the laws of the United States duly enacted thereby, amid the cries, jeers and laughter of the multitudes then assembled and in hearing, which are set forth in the several specifications hereinafter written, in substance and effect, that is to say:

Specification First. In this, that at Washington, in the District of Columbia, in the Executive Mansion, to a committee of citizens who called upon the President of the United States, speaking of and concerning the Congress of the United States, heretofore, to wit: On the 18th day of August, in the year of our Lord, 1866, in a loud voice, declare in substance and effect, among other things, that is to say:

"So far as the Executive Department of the government is concerned, the effort has been made to restore the Union, to heal the breach, to pour oil into the wounds which were consequent upon the struggle, and, to speak in a common phrase, to prepare, as the learned and wise physician would, a plaster healing in character and co-extensive with the wound. We thought and we think that we had partially succeeded, but as the work progressed, as reconstruction seemed to be taking place, and the country was becoming reunited, we found a disturbing and marring element opposing us. In alluding to that element, I shall go no further than your Convention, and the distinguished gentleman who has delivered the report of the proceedings. I shall make no reference that I do not believe the time and the occasion justify.

"We have witnessed in one department of the government every endeavor to prevent the restoration of peace, harmony and union. We have seen hanging upon the verge of the government, as it were, a body called or which assumes to be the Congress of the United States, while in fact it is a Congress of only a part of the States. We have seen this Congress pretend to be for the Union, when its every step and act tended to perpetuate disunion and make a disruption of the States inevitable.

"We have seen Congress gradually encroach, step by step, upon constitutional rights, and violate day after day, and month after month fundamental principles of the government. We have seen a Congress that seemed to forget that there was a limit to the sphere and scope of legislation. We have seen a Congress in a minority assume to exercise power which, if allowed to be consummated, would result in despotism or monarchy itself."

Specification Second. In this, that at Cleveland, in the State of Ohio, heretofore to wit: On the third day of September, in the year of our Lord 1866, before a public assemblage of citizens and others, said Andrew Johnson, President of the United States, speaking of and concerning the Congress of the United States, did, in a loud voice, declare in substance and effect, among other things, that is to say:

"I will tell you what I did do? I called upon your Congress that is trying to break up the Government...."

"In conclusion, beside that, Congress had taken much pains to poison their constituents against him. But what has Congress done? Have they done anything to restore the union of the States? No: On the contrary, they had done everything to prevent it: and because he stood now where he did when the rebellion commenced, he had been denounced as a traitor. Who had run greater risks or made greater sacrifices than himself? But Congress, factious and domineering, had undertaken to poison the minds of the American people."

Specification Third. In this case, that at St. Louis, in the State of Missouri, heretofore to wit: On the 8th day of September, in the year of our Lord 1866, before a public assemblage of citizens and others, said Andrew Johnson, President of the United States, speaking of acts concerning the Congress of the United States, did, in a loud voice, declare in substance and effect, among other things, that is to say:

"Go on. Perhaps if you had a word or two on the subject of New Orleans you might understand more about it than you do, and if you will go back and ascertain the cause of the riot at New Orleans, perhaps you will not be so prompt in calling out 'New Orleans.' If you will take up the riot of New Orleans and trace it back to its source and its immediate cause, you will find out who was responsible for the blood that was shed there. If you will take up the riot at New Orleans and trace it back to the Radical Congress, you will find that the riot at New Orleans was substantially planned. If you will take up the proceedings in their caucuses you will understand that they knew that a convention was to be called which was extinct by its powers having expired; that it was said that the intention was that a new government was to be organized, and on the organization of that government the intention was to enfranchise one portion of the population, called the colored population, who had been emancipated, and at the same time disfranchise white men. When you design to talk about New Orleans you ought to understand what you are talking about. When you read the speeches that were made, and take up the facts on the Friday and Saturday before that convention sat, you will find that speeches were made incendiary in their character, exciting that portion of the population, the black population, to arm themselves and prepare for the shedding of blood. You will also find that convention did assemble in violation of law, and the intention of that convention was to supersede the organized authorities in the State of Louisiana, which had been organized by the government of the United States, and every man engaged in that rebellion, in the convention, with the intention of superseding and upturning the civil government which had been recognized by the Government of the United States, I say that he was a traitor to the Constitution of the United States, and hence you find that another rebellion was commenced, having its origin in the Radical Congress.

"So much for the New Orleans riot. And there was the cause and the origin of the blood that was shed, and every drop of blood that was shed is upon their skirts and they are responsible for it. I could test this thing a little closer, but will not do it here to-night. But when you talk about the causes and consequences that resulted from proceedings of that kind, perhaps, as I have been introduced here and you have provoked questions of this kind, though it does not provoke me, I will tell you a few wholesome things that have been done by this Radical Congress in connection with New Orleans and the extension of the elective franchise.

"I know that I have been traduced and abused. I know it has come in advance of me here, as elsewhere, that I have attempted to exercise an arbitrary power in resisting laws that were intended to be forced upon the government; that I had exercised that power; that I had abandoned the party that elected me, and that I was a traitor, because I exercised the veto power in attempting, and did arrest for a time, that which was called a 'Freedmen's Bureau' bill. Yes, that I was a traitor. And I have been traduced; I have been slandered; I have been maligned. I have been called Judas Iscariot, and all that. Now, my countrymen, here to-night, it is very easy to indulge in epithets; it is easy to call a man a Judas, and cry out traitor, but when he is called upon to give arguments and facts he is very often found wanting. Judas Iscariot? Judas! There was a Judas, and he was one of the twelve Apostles. Oh, yes, the twelve Apostles had a Christ, and he never could have had a Judas unless he had twelve Apostles. If I have played the Judas who has been my Christ that I have played the Judas with? Was it Thad. Stevens? Was it Wendell Phillips? Was it Charles Sumner? They are the men that stop and compare themselves with the Savior, and everybody that differs with them in opinion, and tries to stay and arrest their diabolical and nefarious policy is to be denounced as a Judas.

"Well, let me say to you, if you will stand by me in this action, if you will stand by me in trying to give the people a fair chance — soldiers and citizens — to participate in these offices, God be willing, I will kick them out. I will kick them out just as fast as I can. Let me say to you, in concluding, that what I have said is what I intended to say; I was not provoked into this, and care not for their menaces, the taunts and the jeers. I care not for threats, I do not intend to be bullied by enemies, nor overawed by my friends. But, God willing, with your help, I will veto their measures whenever any of them come to me."

Which said utterances, declarations, threats and harangues, highly censurable in any, are peculiarly indecent and unbecoming in the Chief Magistrate of the United States, by means whereof the said Andrew Johnson has brought the high office of the President of the United States into contempt, ridicule and disgrace, to the great scandal of all good citizens, whereby said Andrew Johnson, President of the United States, did commit, and was then and there guilty of a high misdemeanor in office.

Article XI

That the said Andrew Johnson, President of the United States, unmindful of the high duties of his office and of his oath of office, and in disregard of the Constitution and laws of the United States, did, heretofore, to wit: On the 18th day of August, 1866, at the city of Washington, and in the District of Columbia, by public speech, declare and affirm in substance, that the Thirty-Ninth Congress of the United States was not a Congress of the United States authorized by the Constitution to exercise legislative power under the same; but, on the contrary, was a Congress of only part of the States, thereby denying and intending to deny, that the legislation of said Congress was valid or obligatory upon him, the said Andrew Johnson, except in so far as he saw fit to approve the same, and also thereby denying the power of the said Thirty-Ninth Congress to propose amendments to the Constitution of the United States. And in pursuance of said declaration, the said Andrew Johnson, President of the United States, afterwards, to wit: On the 21st day of February, 1868, at the city of Washington, D.C., did, unlawfully and in disregard of the requirements of the Constitution that he should take care that the laws be faithfully executed, attempt to prevent the execution of an act entitled "An act regulating the tenure of certain civil offices," passed March 2, 1867, by unlawfully devising and contriving and attempting to devise and contrive means by which he should prevent Edwin M. Stanton from forthwith resuming the functions of the office of Secretary for the Department of War, notwithstanding the refusal of the Senate to concur in the suspension therefore made by the said Andrew Johnson of said Edwin M. Stanton from said office of Secretary for the Department of War; and also by further unlawfully devising and contriving, and attempting to devise and contrive, means then and there to prevent the execution of an act entitled "An act making appropriations for the support of the army for the fiscal year ending June 30, 1868, and for other purposes," approved March 2, 1867. And also to prevent the execution of an act entitled "An act to provide for the more efficient government of the rebel States," passed March 2, 1867. Whereby the said Andrew Johnson, President of the United States, did then, to wit: on the 21st day of February, 1868, at the city of Washington, commit and was guilty of a high misdemeanor in office.

APPENDIX D

The Senate Votes[1]

YEAS (VOTING TO CONVICT) — 35

Henry Anthony (R-Rhode Island), Simon Cameron (R-Pennsylvania), Alexander Cattell (R-New Jersey), Zachariah Chandler (R-Michigan), Cornelius Cole (R-California), Roscoe Conkling (R-New York), John Conness (R-California), Henry Corbett (R-Oregon), Aaron Cragin (R-New Hampshire), Charles Drake (R-Missouri), George Edmunds (R-Vermont), Orris Ferry (R-Connecticut), Frederick Frelinghuysen (R-New Jersey), James Harlan (R-Iowa), Jacob Howard (R-Michigan), Timothy Howe (R-Wisconsin), Edwin Morgan (R-New York), Justin Morrill (R-Vermont), Lot Morrill (R-Maine), Oliver Morton (R-Indiana), James Nye (R-Nevada), James Patterson (R-New Hampshire), Samuel Pomeroy (R-Kansas), Alexander Ramsey (R-Minnesota), John Sherman (R-Ohio), William Sprague (R-Rhode Island), William Stewart (R-Nevada), Charles Sumner (R-Massachusetts), John Thayer (R-Nebraska), Thomas Tipton (R-Nebraska), Benjamin Wade (R-Ohio), Waitman Willey (R-West Virginia), George Williams (R-Oregon), Henry Wilson (R-Massachusetts), Richard Yates (R-Illinois)

NAYS (VOTING TO ACQUIT) — 19

James Bayard (D-Delaware), Charles Buckalew (D-Pennsylvania), Garrett Davis (D-Kentucky), James Dixon (R-Connecticut), James Doolittle (R-Wisconsin), William Fessenden (R-Maine), Joseph Fowler (R-Tennessee), James Grimes (R-Iowa), John Henderson (R-Missouri), Thomas Hendricks (D-Indiana), Reverdy Johnson (D-Maryland), Thomas McCreery (D-Kentucky), Daniel Norton (R-Minnesota), David Patterson (D-Tennessee), Edmund Ross (R-Kansas), Willard Saulsbury (D-Delaware), Lyman Trumbull (R-Illinois), Peter Van Winkle (R-West Virginia), George Vickers (D-Maryland)

APPENDIX E

The Thomas Papers

The Records of the Fourth Infantry[1]

LORENZO THOMAS

Cadet, 1819; Second Lieutenant 4th Infantry, July 1823; in Florida campaign, 1824–1828; Regimental Adjutant, 1828–1831; First Lieutenant, March 1829; on recruiting service, 1831–1833; in Adjutant General's Office at Washington, D.C., 1837–1838; Assistant Quartermaster, 1836–1838; in Florida War, 1836–1837, doing quartermaster duty; Chief of Staff of the Army in Florida, 1839–1840; Brevet Major, Staff, Assistant Adjutant General, July 1838; Assistant Adjutant General at Washington, D.C., 1840–1846; member of the Board of Visitors to the Military Academy, 1844; in War with Mexico as Chief of Staff of Major General Butler, being engaged in the Battle of *Monterrey,* September 1846; Brevet Lieutenant Colonel, September 1846, cited for gallant and meritorious conduct in the several conflicts at Monterrey, Mexico; Major 4th Infantry, January 1848; Assistant Adjutant General at Headquarters of the Army, Washington, D.C., 1848–1858; Lieutenant Colonel, Staff, Assistant Adjutant General, July 1852; Chief of Staff of Lieutenant General Scott, 1853–1861; Colonel, Staff, Assistant Adjutant General, March 1861; Brevet Brigadier General United States Army, May 1861; Brigadier General, Staff, Adjutant General United States Army, August 1861; organizing colored troops, 1863–1865; Brevet Major General, March 1865, cited for faithful and meritorious services during the rebellion; on Military Commission at Washington, D.C., 1865; awaiting orders, 1865–1866; on inspection tour relating to Provost Marshal General's Office, 1866; awaiting orders, 1866–1867; on tour of inspection of National Cemeteries, 1867. *Retired* February 22, 1869.

The Lorenzo Thomas Report on the Battle of Monterrey[2]

The army arrived at their camp in the vicinity of Monterrey about noon, September 19. That afternoon the General [Butler] endeavored by personal observation to get information of the enemy's position. He, like General Taylor, saw the importance of gaining the road to Saltillo, and fully favored the movement of General Worth's division to turn their left, & c. Worth marched Sunday, September 20, for this purpose; thus leaving Twiggs' and Butler's divisions with Gen. Taylor. Gen. Butler was also in favor of throwing his division across the St. John's river, and approaching the town from the east, which was at first determined upon. This was changed, as it would leave but one, and perhaps the smallest division, to guard the camp and attack in front. The 20th, the General also reconnoitered the enemy's position. Early in the morning of the 21st the force was ordered out to create a diversion in favor of Worth, that he might gain his position; and before our division came within long range of the enemy's principal battery, the foot of Twigg's division had been ordered down to the northeast side of the town, to make an armed reconnaissance of the advanced battery, and to take it if it could be done without great loss. The volunteer division was scarcely formed in rear of our howitzer and mortar battery — established the night previous, under cover of a rise of ground before the infantry sent down to the northeast side of the town became closely and hotly engaged; the batteries of that division were sent down, *and we were then ordered to support the attack*. Leaving the Kentucky regiment to support the mortar and howitzer battery, the General rapidly put in march, by a flank movement, the other three regiments, moving for some one and a half or two miles under a heavy fire of round shot. As further ordered, the Ohio regiment was detached from Quitman's brigade, and led by the General (at this time accompanied by General Taylor) into the town. Quitman carried his brigade directly on the battery first attacked, and gallantly carried it. Before this, however, as we entered the suburbs, the chief, engineer came up and advised us to withdraw, as the object of the attack had failed and if we moved on, we must meet with great loss. The General was loath to fall back without consulting with General Taylor, which he did do — the General being but a short distance off. As we were withdrawing, news came that Quitman had carried the battery, and General Butler led the Ohio regiment back to the town at a different point. In the street we became exposed to a line of batteries on the opposite side of a small stream, and also from a *tete de pont* (bridge-head) which enfiladed us. Our men fell rapidly as we moved up the street to get a position to charge the battery across the stream. Coming to a cross street, the General reconnoitered the position, and, determining to charge from that point, sent me back a short distance to stop the firing, and advance the regiment with the bayonet. I had just left him, when he was struck in the leg, being on foot, and was obliged to leave the field.

On entering the town, the General and his troops became at once hotly engaged at short musket range. He had to make his reconnaissance's under heavy fire. This he did unflinchingly, and by exposing his person — on one occasion passing through a large gateway into a yard, which was entirely open to the enemy. When he was wounded, at the intersection of the two streets, he was exposed to a cross-fire of musketry and grape. In battle the General's bearing was truly that of a soldier; and those under him felt the influence of his presence. He had the entire confidence of his men.

When Gen. Taylor went on his expedition to Victoria, in December, he placed General Butler in command of the troops left on the Rio Grande, and at the stations from the river on to Saltillo-Worth's small division of regulars being at the latter place. Gen. Wool's column had by this time reached Parras, one hundred or more miles west of Saltillo. Gen. Butler had so far recovered from his wound as to walk a little and take exercise on horseback, though with pain to his limb. One night (about the 19th December) an express came from Gen. Worth at Saltillo, stating that the Mexican forces were advancing *in* large numbers from San Louis de Potosi. and that he expected to be attacked in two days. His division, all told, did not exceed 1,600 men, if so many, and he asked [for] reinforcements. The General remained up during the balance of the night, sent off the necessary couriers to the rear for reinforcements, and had the 1st Kentucky and the 1st Ohio foot, then encamped three miles from the town in the place by daylight and these two regiments with Webster's battery, were encamped that night ten miles on the road to Saltillo. This promptness enabled the General to make his second day's march of twenty-two miles in good season, and to hold the celebrated pass of Los Muertos, and check the enemy should he have attacked Gen. Worth on that day and obliged him to evacuate the town. Whilst on the next and last day's march, the General received notice that the reported advance of the enemy was untrue. Arriving at the camp-ground, the General suffered intense pain from his wound, and slept not during the night. This journey, over a rugged, mountainous road, and the exercise he took in examining the country for twenty miles in advance of Saltillo, caused the great increase of pain now experienced.

The Lorenzo Thomas account then goes on to relate Gen. Butler's proceedings while in command of all the forces after the junction of Generals Worth and Wool — his disposition to meet the threatened attack of Santa Anna — the defences created by him at Saltillo, and used during the attack at Buena Vista in dispersing Minon's forces — his just treatment of the people of Saltillo, with the prudent and effectual precautions taken to make them passive in the event of Santa Anna's approach. It concludes by stating that all apprehensions of Santa Anna's advance subsiding, Gen. Butler returned to meet Gen. Taylor at Monterrey, to report the condition of affairs; and the latter, having taken the command at Saltillo, transmitted a leave of absence to Gen. Butler, to afford opportunity for the cure of his wound.

Annual Reunion[3]

LORENZO THOMAS.
No. 342. CLASS OF 1823.
Died March 2d, 1875, at Washington, D.C., aged 70.

BREVET MAJOR-GENERAL LORENZO THOMAS was born in New Castle, Delaware, October 26th, 1804. His father, Evan Thomas, was of Welsh extraction. His mother was a descendant from an English family named Randolph, her maiden name being Sherer. She was remotely connected with the Virginia Randolphs. General Thomas belonged to a military family. One of his uncles was a favorite officer of General Washington, and served with distinction in the Revolution, in a number of battles. Members of the Randolph connection were in the same war. The General's father and oldest brother were in a militia organization during the War of 1812-1815 with England.

His early education was received at the academy in New Castle. He was at first destined for mercantile pursuits, for which he had a strong predilection, which exerted a certain influence over his career through life. It was manifest in the performance of his military duties, and was probably the cause of his connection with the Quarter-Master's Department. The Hon. Nicholas Van Dyke, Senator from Delaware, however, ultimately determined his profession by kindly procuring for him an appointment as Cadet at the U.S. Military Academy. This was too tempting an offer for a lad without means, and he accordingly entered the Academy, September 1st, 1819, at the age of nearly fifteen years. He maintained a fair standing throughout the course; graduated in June, 1823, seventeenth in a class of thirty-five, and was assigned as Second Lieutenant to the 4th Infantry.

In the summer of 1821, the Corps of Cadets made an excursion under Major Worth, the Commandant. After encamping three days at Albany, it marched across to Springfield, where it remained three days. In another week it arrived in Boston. During its twelve days' stay in Boston it was entertained with the most distinguished kindness and hospitality, and visited all the places of note in the city and vicinity. On the 11th of August, "The Selectmen of the Town of Boston," presented the Corps with a stand of colors. On the 14th the Corps visited the town of Quincy, to pay honor to the venerable Ex-President John Adams, who received it with a complimentary address, and gave it an elegant breakfast, spread under an awning near his mansion. On its return the Corps marched by way of Dedham, Providence, and New London; took steamboat there for New York via New Haven, and reached West Point the 25th of August. The most hearty welcome was given it at every place through which it passed, the citizens sparing no pains to do it honor. The unexceptionable conduct and bearing of the cadets won for them everywhere a cordial respect and esteem. The subject of this memoir appears as "Private L. Thomas" on the roll of the Fourth Company of the Battalion, in the journal of this march.

Several of the first years of General Thomas' service were in Florida, and he there underwent the ordeal of the yellow fever, being obliged to go North to recover his health. He was on the recruiting service from 1831 to 1833, and more than thirty years afterward a Rochester newspaper, referring to him at that period, bore testimony "that the demeanor of few men were so well calculated to impress the minds of those around him with livelier feelings of kindness and respect."

From the year 1836 to 1838, he was attached to the Quarter-Master's Department in the Florida war, and in the office at Washington. On the organization of the Staff Departments, in 1838, he was appointed Assistant Adjutant General, with the rank of Major. In this capacity he again served in the Florida war. At his own request he was ordered to the army in Mexico, early in the war with that country, and acted as Chief of Staff to Major-General William O. Butler, on both the lines of operation. After the relief of General Scott, General Butler succeeded to the command of the U.S. forces in Mexico, until they were withdrawn The executive ability of General Thomas had full scope during this period, for he was regarded with great confidence by General Butler. The personal esteem which these gentlemen then learned to entertain for each other was never interrupted.

The remainder of General Thomas' service, until he became Adjutant-General in 1861, was chiefly at the Headquarters of the General-in-Chief. Early in 1863, he was sent on duties of the highest responsibility, with unusual powers, to represent the Secretary of War, first in mustering out large bodies of Volunteers whose terms had expired, and then in organizing and putting in the field regiments of colored troops. A few regiments of these men had been raised in the South, and these had demonstrated their efficiency when led by good officers. To General Thomas it was a novel experience; at first distasteful, as calculated to raise against him a storm of prejudice. His tact and judgment, however, overcame all obstacles, and the War Department commended his success. This was not the only instance in which his soldierly determination to obey orders, brought upon him much abuse. But whatever may have been said against him, this impartial verdict must be given: The unusually trying positions in which he was sometimes placed were not of his own seeking, and he exerted his best judgment in endeavoring to execute the behests of his lawful superiors. In his private relations General Thomas exhibited traits no less strong and marked than in his official career. From early manhood he was an earnest, active, and useful worker in the Church to which he was attached. Up to the time when he became absorbed in the stirring scenes of the war, he was Superintendent of the Sunday School. It was here, as in the circle of his own family, that the unbounded kindness of his heart steadfastly shone forth. He delighted in contriving means to contribute to the innocent pleasure and instruction of his young friends. Even when duty called him away from them for a season, he always returned with a store of anecdotes of his travels to amuse them, thus showing that he was engaged in a genuine labor of love.

One who knew him long and intimately, now bears testimony which hundreds will corroborate: That no man ever went further to oblige a friend or to return a favor received; and but few men in this world have ever done less to resent an injury or pursue an enemy. In everything but this last trait — resentment — this man was well characterized by his family motto, *"Jamais arriere"* [Never Behind].

Biographical Register[4]

342 .. (Born Del.) ..... LORENZO THOMAS ..... , (Ap'd Del.)

Military History. — Cadet at the Military Academy, Sep. 1, 1819, to July 1, 1823, when he was graduated and promoted: in the Army to

(SECOND LIEUT., 4TH INFANTRY, JULY 1, 1823)

Served: in garrison at Cantonment Clinch, Fla., 1824, — and at Ft. St. Marks, Fla., 1824 ; in constructing Military Road to St. Augustine, Fla., 1824–25; in garrison at Cantonment Clinch, Fla. 1825; in Creek Nation, Ga., 1825–26; in garrison at Cantonment Clinch, Fla., 1826, 1827–28; as Adjutant, 4th Infantry, at Regimental headquarters, Mar. 1, 1828, to Feb. 15, 1831; on Recruiting service, 1831–33; in Adjutant-

(FIRST LIEUT., 4TH INFANTRY, Mar. 17, 1829)

General's Office at Washington, D.C., June 5, 1833, to Sep. 3, 1836; in the Florida War, 1836–37, doing Quartermaster duty; in the Quarter-

(CAPTAIN, 4TH INFANTRY, SEP. 23, 1836)

master-General's Office at Washington, D.C., Oct. 16, 1837, to July 7,

(ASST. QUARTERMASTER, SEP. 3, 1836, TO JULY 7, 1838)

1838; as Chief of Staff of the Army in Florida, Dec. 2, 1839, to May 10,

(BVT. MAJOR, STAFF — ASST. ADJUTANT-GEN.,
JULY 7, 1838)

1840; as Asst. Adjutant-General, at Washington, D.C., 1840–46; as Member of the Board of Visitors to the Military Academy, 1844; in the War with Mexico, as Chief of Staff of Major-General Butler, commanding Volunteer Division, Aug. 25, 1846, to Feb. 19, 1848, and the Army of Mexico, Feb. 19 to June 21, 1848, being engaged in the Battle of Monterey.

(BVT. LIEUT.-COL., SEP. 23, 1846, FOR GALLANT
AND MERITORIOUS CONDUCT IN THE SEVERAL
CONFLICTS AT MONTEREY, MEX.)

Sep. 21–23, 1846; as Asst. Adjutant-General at the Headquarters

(MAJOR, 4TH INFANTRY, JAN. 1, 1848:
VACATED, JAN. 1, 1848)

of the Army, Washington, D.C., July 10, 1848, to Mar. 15, 1853; and

(LIEUT.-COL., STAFF — ASST. ADJUTANT-GEN.,
JULY 18, 1852)

as Chief of Staff of Lieut.-General Scott (General-in-Chief), Mar. 15, 1853, to Mar. 7, 1861. Served during the Rebellion of the Seceding States, 1861–65: in charge of the Adjutant-General's Office, Washington, D.C., Mar. 7, 1861, to

(COL., STAFF — ASST. ADJUTANT-GENERAL, MAR. 7, 1861)
(BVT. BRIG.-GENERAL, U.S. ARMY, MAY 7, 1861)
(BRIG.-GEN., STAFF — ADJUTANT-GENERAL
OF THE U.S. ARMY, AUG. 3, 1861)

Mar. 23, 1863; in organizing Colored Troops, Mar. 23, 1863, to Aug. 18, 1865; on Military Commission at Washington, D.C., Aug. 18 to Nov. 6.

(BVT. MAJ.-GENERAL, U.S. ARMY, MAR. 13, 1865,
FOR FAITHFUL AND MERITORIOUS SERVICES
DURING THE REBELLION)

1865; and in waiting orders, Nov. 6, 1865, to Sep. 3, 1866. Served: on tour of inspection of the business relating to the Provost. Marshal General's Office, Sep. 3 to Nov. 19, 1866; in waiting orders. Nov. 19, 1866, to May 6, 1867; on tour of inspection of the National Cemeteries, May 6, 1867, to Feb. 22, 1869.

RETIRED FROM ACTIVE SERVICE, FEB. 22, 1869,
UNDER THE LAW OF JULY 17, 1862, "HAVING
BEEN BORNE ON THE ARMY REGISTER
MORE THAN 45 YEARS."

DIED, MAR. 2, 1875, AT WASHINGTON, D.C.: AGED 70.
OBITUARY ORDER

Upon the death of General Thomas, the War Department issued the following order: "The Secretary of War with regret announces to the Army the death of BRIG-GEN. LORENZO THOMAS, Brevet Major-General, U.S. Army, on the retired list, and late Adjutant-General. He died at his residence in this city the 2d instant.

"But few officers have served so actively and continuously through so long a period as General Thomas. Energetic of character and vigorous of constitution, he was enabled to be in the field throughout much of both the Florida and Mexican wars. His training as Adjutant of the 4th Infantry developed his fitness for duties in the Staff, which he performed zealously and efficiently, first in the Quartermaster's and then in the Adjutant-General's Department. In the latter Department, at its first organization, he was commissioned Major and Assistant Adjutant General, July 7, 1838. In the War with Mexico he was Adjutant-General and Chief of Staff' to Major-General Butler, both while commander of a Division of Volunteers and commander of the Army. His experience and systematic administrative powers were conspicuous in the final movements and the withdrawal of the Army in Mexico.

"Early in the War of the Rebellion he became Adjutant-General of the Army by succession, and was afterwards specially assigned to the duty of organizing Volunteer troops, particularly the colored regiments. He was brevetted Major-General, 13th March, 1865. Having passed beyond the age of sixty-two years, he was placed on the retired list of the Army 11 February, 1869.

"General Thomas was a man of generous and kindly disposition, who in his day has done much good in the communities where he lived.

"In respect to his memory the officers of the Adjutant-General's Department will wear the usual badge of mourning for thirty days."

General Order 143, issued May 22, 1863, established the United States Colored Troops (USCT).

GENERAL ORDERS,
No. 143 WAR DEPARTMENT,
ADJUTANT GENERAL'S OFFICE,
Washington, May 22, 1863.

I — A Bureau is established in the Adjutant General's Office for the record of all matters relating to the organization of Colored Troops. An officer will be assigned to the charge of the Bureau, with such number of clerks as may be designated by the Adjutant General.

II — Three or more field officers will be detailed as Inspectors to supervise the organization of colored troops at such points as may be indicated by the War Department in the Northern and Western States.

III — Boards will be convened at such posts as may be decided upon by the War Department to examine applicants for commissions to command colored troops, who, on Application to the Adjutant General, may receive authority to present themselves to the board for examination.

IV — No persons shall be allowed to recruit for colored troops except specially authorized by the War Department; and no such authority will be given to persons who have not been examined and passed by a board; nor will such authority be given any one person to raise more than one regiment.

V — The reports of Boards will specify the grade of commission for which each candidate is fit, and authority to recruit will be given in accordance. Commissions will be issued from the Adjutant General's Office when the prescribed number of men is ready for muster into service.

VI — Colored troops may be accepted by companies, to be afterward consolidated in battalions and regiments by the Adjutant General. The regiments will be numbered seriatim, in the order in which they are raised, the numbers to be determined by the Adjutant General. They will be designated: "— Regiment of U.S. Colored Troops."

VII — Recruiting stations and depots will be established by the Adjutant General as circumstances shall require, and officers will be detailed to muster and inspect the troops.

VIII — The non-commissioned officers of colored troops may be selected and appointed from the best men of their number in the usual mode of appointing non-commissioned officers. Meritorious commissioned officers will be entitled to promotion to higher rank if they prove themselves equal to it.

IX — All personal applications for appointments in colored regiments, or for information concerning them, must be made to the Chief of the Bureau; all written communications should be addressed to the Chief of the Bureau, to the care of the Adjutant General.

BY ORDER OF THE SECRETARY OF WAR:
E. D. TOWNSEND,
Assistant Adjutant General.

APPENDIX F

Significant Battles Fought by U.S. Colored Troops

African Americans fought in many battles during the Civil War. The African American participation in battles for the Union is easily tracked since the African Americans were organized into segregated regiments. Not so in the South — African Americans who joined the Confederate Army were integrated into regular units and there was no great battle won for the Confederacy by African Americans: their participation in key battles is not visible. They fought in white units alongside their white fellow soldiers. The listing of battles below is not a complete list of Union African American battles — only those that were significant and had a major impact on how the whites viewed African Americans as soldiers. The total list of all battles in which African Americans fought for the Union is impressive: 39 major battles and 449 engagements.

Port Hudson, 27 May 1863

The Battle of Port Hudson, Louisiana, occurred on 27 May 1863. In cooperation with General Grant's attack on Vicksburg, General Banks moved against Port Hudson on the Mississippi. Two regiments of African American troops, the 1st and 3rd Louisiana Regiments, led the assault on the Confederate stronghold. At least six charges were made against Port Hudson and the regiments sustained heavy losses. After the attack failed, the Union Army settled into a siege that ended on 9 July when the Confederates surrendered the fort. The attack by the African American regiments proved their effectiveness and courage.[1] As Banks wrote to Halleck, Lincoln's general-in-chief, "Whatever doubt may have existed heretofore as to the efficiency [of the African American regiments] the history of this day proves conclusively ... no doubt of their ultimate success."[2]

The *Christian Recorder*, however, was not pleased with the battle: "It is reported that the 2nd Louisiana native guard, a regiment of blacks which lost six hundred in the gloriously bloody charge at Port Hudson, were placed in front, while veteran white troops brought up the rear. Great God, why is this? We care not so much for the loss of men, however bravely they may die, but we damn to everlasting infamy, those who will thus, pass by *veteran troops of any color*, and place a regiment of raw recruits in the front of a terrible battle."[3]

There were many other battles during this period that proved that African Americans could fight just as well as, if not better than, their white counterparts. Battles such as Honey Springs in Indian Territory and Milliken's Bend in Louisiana displayed African Americans' courage and determination to the Union Army.[4]

Battle of Milliken's Bend, 7 June 1863

Milliken's Bend was a Union outpost on the Mississippi River above Vicksburg defended by white units and African Americans of the Ninth Regiment of the Louisiana Volunteers. Rushing upon and over the entrenchments and flanking the fort, the rebels closed in on the defenders of Milliken's Bend. What ensued was a bloody hand-to-hand fight that ranked as one of the most bitter knock-down-and-drag-out struggles of a war famous for its hard-fought actions. It was a contest between enraged men fighting with bayonets and musket butts. Both sides freely used the bayonet — a rare occurrence in warfare, (General Lorenzo Thomas, in commenting on the battle, stated that usually "one of the party gives up before coming in contact with steel"). In one instance two men lay side by side, each having the other's bayonet in his body. A new recruit to whom young Captain Matthew M. Miller of Company I, Ninth Louisiana, had issued a gun the day before was "found dead with a firm grasp on his gun, the bayonet of which was broken in three places." A teenage cook, who had begged for a gun when the enemy was seen approaching, was badly injured with one gunshot and two bayonet wounds. In one Negro company there were six broken bayonets.[5] Captain M. M. Miller of the Ninth described the battle in a letter home to his aunt:

> Dear Aunt: We were attacked here on 7 June, about 3 o'clock in the morning, by a brigade of Texas troops about 2,500 in number. We had about 600 men to withstand them — 500 of the negroes.... Our regiment had about 300 in the fight.... We had about 50 men killed in the regiment and 80 wounded; so you can judge of what part of the fight my company sustained ... I never more wish to hear the expression, "the niggers won't fight." ... The enemy charged us so close that we fought with our bayonets, hand to hand.... It was a horrible fight, the worst I was ever engaged in — not even Shiloh. The enemy cried "No quarter!" but some of them were very glad to take it when made prisoners.[6]

The Confederate commander General Henry McCulloch wrote, "This charge was resisted by the negro portion of the enemy's force with considerable obstinacy while the white or true Yankee portion ran like whipped curs almost as soon as the charge was ordered."[7] No African American soldier taken prisoner by the rebels during that fight was found alive.[8]

Battle of Honey Springs, 17 July 1863

In Indian Territory (now Oklahoma), General Blunt's Union command attacked and defeated Confederate General Cooper. It was the largest engagement in the territory and the African American regiments were instrumental in handing the Confederates a defeat.[9]

Battle of Fort Wagner, 18 July 1863

The 54th Massachusetts Regiment, commanded by Colonel Robert Gould Shaw, moved south for operations against Charleston, South Carolina. Fort Wagner was among the forts guarding Charleston and the 54th was given the task of leading the assault on the fort. Wagner had been under artillery fire for most of the day, which did little good. The approach to the fort was a narrow sandy beach that forced the troops to bunch up and the Confederates opened fire with devastating effect.[10] The Union lost the battle, but the valor of the 54th was recognized by all.

Baxter Springs, 6 October 1863

The Battle of Baxter Springs was fought in Kansas when Southern raider William Clark Quantrill attacked a Union column on a road near Baxter Springs. After some members of the column were captured and murdered, the rest fled to the nearby fort. The African Americans fought off the Quantrill attack.

Battle of Olustree, 20 February 1864

The Eighth Regiment USCT and Seventh New Hampshire Regiment fought under General Truman Seymour near Ocean Pond in Florida. This was the only major battle of the war in Florida. The Union was defeated by an equal force of Confederates under General Joseph Finegan. Both Union regiments suffered heavy casualties.[11]

The Fort Pillow Massacre, 12 April 1864

Nathan Bedford Forrest reported after the battle that of 500 African Americans and 200 white soldiers, 500 were killed in the battle.[12] A later investigation stated that 300 of the men were murdered in cold blood after they had surrendered. There were many examples of the murder of African American Union soldiers (and usually their white leaders as well) by the Confederate Army. The Confederacy viewed African American Union soldiers as traitors and, as such, believed they should be killed while, white officers of African American regiments were executed for "fermenting slave insurrection."[13] General Grant informed the Confederacy that for every African American murdered by the South, one white Confederate prisoner would be executed.[14] It was not an idle threat for, some of the white Confederate prisoners were indeed shot in retaliation for the murders committed by the Confederacy. Unfortunately, Southern generals such as Pickett and Forrest were not charged for their war crimes after the war as they should have been. Grant's order stopped the wholesale murder of Union African American soldiers by the Confederacy, but they were still mistreated.[15]

Battle of Petersburg, 15 June 1864

The Federals attacked the Confederate position but a courageous Confederate defense saved Petersburg, although a gallant charge by the 22nd Regiment USCT carried the first Confederate line.[16]

Battle of the Crater, 30 July 1864

The concept was to dig a mine under the Confederate line, load it with explosives and blow the mine thus breaking the Confederate defenses. It was a risky plan. Two African American brigades were chosen to lead the attack after the mine was blown, but Grant changed that at the last minute. He later said that if the African American brigades were slaughtered, it would be said that they had been sacrificed to save white soldiers.[17] Therefore, white troops were put in first. They were untrained for this operation and battle weary. As a result, when the mine blew, the white troops spent time milling around in the crater, accomplishing nothing for two hours, and the two African American brigades were then ordered in. By that time the Confederates had recovered from the shock of the blast and had reformed their line. The African American brigades sustained heavy casualties.[18] The white troops broke and ran back to federal lines, shortly followed by the African American troops. The total killed in the African American brigades was 195. By chance or Confederate design,

The 22nd USCT at Petersburg (Library of Congress).

many of the white officers in the African American regiments were killed or wounded, adding to the chaos in the crater.[19]

Athens, Alabama, 23–24 September 1864

The 106th, 110th and 111th USCT held the Union fort at Athens while Confederate General Nathan Bedford Forrest was destroying railroad tracks and bridges nearby. When Forrest moved against the fort, he demanded that the Union commander, Colonel Wallace Campbell, surrender the fort. After a parley, Campbell surrendered the fort and all three regiments of USCT. Wallace's surrender was condemned by both his subordinates and his superiors. Forrest captured thirteen hundred officers and enlisted soldiers, as well as a large amount of supplies.[20] This episode highlighted the fact that in nearly every engagement in the Civil War the USCT fought well — in many cases, better than white regiments. When a battle in which the USCT fought was lost, it was usually because of poor white leadership.

Battle of Chaffin's Farm (Also Called the Battle of New Market Heights), 29–30 September 1864

Chaffin's Farm was part of the defense system surrounding Richmond. Thirteen regiments of the USCT participated in the battle and fourteen Medals

The Battle of the Crater (Library of Congress).

of Honor were awarded to African Americans (see Appendix G for details).[21] In total, 870 African Americans were killed or wounded in the battle.[22]

Battle of Nashville, 15–16 December 1864

In December 1864, Confederate General John Bell Hood attacked a Union force under General John Schofield at Franklin, Tennessee, in an effort to defeat the Union Army in the west. Hood's army was decimated by the entrenched Yankee force. After the battle, Schofield withdrew to Nashville while Hood followed. The Union Army at Nashville under General George Thomas consisted of a superior force of Union corps that included two brigades of USCT commanded by General James Steedman. By 1864, USCT had proven their valor in a series of earlier battles, as seen above, but at Nashville the same question remained: Would USCT fight? Earlier, Sherman had thought not and refused to take USCT in his march to the sea. At Nashville, Steedman had 7,500 troops, most of which were black. His problem was that he had a hybrid of one white brigade and two brigades of USCT. It was known as the Provisional Detachment (District of Etowah) — not an awe-inspiring name. Francis McKinney, a biographer of General George Thomas described the command as follows:

Significant Battles Fought by U.S. Colored Troops 163

A hybrid ... made up of fragments from ... ill-provided regiments. A large portion were unfit for duty.... Some of these troops were not armed until the evening of the fourteenth [December 1864]. Some of the recruits were untrained. Many were unable to speak or understand English. Whatever their shortcomings, Steedman's brigades would not be lacking in numbers, for each brigade was about the size of a Confederate division.

Colonel Henry Stone on Thomas's staff described the subsequent Union attack on Hood's left and its result:

It was more like a scene in a spectacular drama than a real incident in war. The hillside in front, still green, dotted with the boys in blue swarming up the slope; the dark background of high hills beyond; the lowering clouds; the waving flags; the smoke slowly rising through the leafless tree-tops and drifting across the valleys; the wonderful outburst of musketry; the ecstatic cheers; the multitude racing for life down into the valley below — so exciting was it all that the lookers-on instinctively clapped their hands as at a brilliant and successful transformation scene, as indeed it was. For in those few minutes an

The USCT breakthrough at Nashville (Library of Congress).

army was changed into a mob, and the whole structure of the rebellion in the southwest, with all its possibilities, was utterly overthrown.

Steedman's brigades of USCT again attacked Hood's right flank while Steedman's white regiments were driven back. The flight of the white regiments under Steedman enabled the Confederates to concentrate their fire on the two African American brigades, with devastating results. Corporal Jones of the 18th Alabama described the advance of the USCT: "Just before the negroes entered the open we turned loose a volley. They fell like wheat before a mowing machine. They wavered, staggered and in confusion they fled.... The ground was literally blue with dead and wounded.... In no time we heard the confusion and noise and cursing and urging forward again, and we discovered they were coming for a second dose of lead pills and blue whistlers. Again we held our fire until they approached the open."[23] The USCT had lost 552 casualties in two days, but this time their charge seized the objective.[24]

The USCT attack persuaded Hood to reinforce his right flank, since he thought that this was the main attack.[25] This was a decisive error. By reinforcing his right with troops from his left, he allowed the Yankee main attack to pour through the left and attack his rear while the USCT broke through on the right, defeating the Confederate Army. The valor of USCT was a key factor in winning the battle, and perhaps the war.

As Thomas rode across the battlefield after Hood had been beaten, he saw Union soldiers, both black and white, lying where they had fallen in battle. To his staff he said, "Gentlemen, the issue has been settled! Negroes will fight!" As the U.S. Colored Regiments marched past him in pursuit of Hood, Thomas turned his horse, removed his hat in a mark of respect and watched as they filed past.[26]

Battle of Spanish Fort, 27 March–8 April 1865

The Battle of Spanish Fort in Alabama took place from 27 March through 8 April 1865, with the 68th USCT as a participant.[27] After the Union naval victory at the Battle of Mobile Bay, the city of Mobile, Alabama, remained in the hands of the Confederate Army. As a major port and railroad hub, it was necessary to take Mobile and Union forces (including A. J. Smith's XVI Corps under General Canby[28]) advanced to take Spanish Fort, a major stronghold defending Mobile. While Grant was trapping Robert E. Lee in Virginia, General Canby was preparing for the attack on Mobile, Alabama. This would be trench warfare, with the Union troops slowly digging their way to the Confederate Spanish Fort defenses. This was a formidable defensive position but the Union regiments reduced casualties by digging at night and throwing up dirt and logs to protect them from the enemy fire that followed each morning.

The trench followed a zigzag pattern toward the fort that afforded an opportunity to bring in Union artillery, but these guns were unable to penetrate the fort's defenses. By 7 April, the Union troops had dug their way to the stronghold of Spanish Fort and were now ready for the final assault. That night a heavy bombardment was started by several hundred Union guns, which continued the next day and into the evening of 8 April. In the end, the Union troops rushed in and overwhelmed the Spanish Fort defenders only to find that the Confederates had spiked their guns and fled to nearby Fort Blakely, seven miles away. One soldier, on entering the fort, described the scene: "Our shells had converted the ground into a striking resemblance to a hog yard that had been rooted over and over. We had avoided the torpedoes by having gotten our trench higher than they were. Spanish Fort with its heavy armaments was ours."[29]

Battle of Fort Blakely, 9 April 1865

Fort Blakely was a smaller fort and not well defended. While Lee was surrendering to Grant at Appomattox on Palm Sunday, 9 April 1865, the Union Army was assembling before Fort Blakely. By that afternoon, the troops surrounding Fort Blakely launched their attack. Nine regiments of USCT fought there.[30] Fort Blakely and two thousand Confederate prisoners were taken. Total cost in Union casualties for this two-week campaign was about fifteen hundred dead and wounded, or about one in ten of those engaged.[31]

Battle of Palmetto Ranch, 15 May 1865

Palmetto Ranch was the last battle of the Civil War and occurred after the Confederate surrender and Lincoln's assassination.[32]

APPENDIX G

Medal of Honor

A spectacular naval exploit was performed in May 1862 by Robert Smalls, a slave living in Charleston, South Carolina. The following account is taken from a book about the Negro in the Civil War, Camp-Fires of the Afro-American, *published in 1889:*

When Fort Sumter was attacked, [Smalls] and his brother John, with their families, resided in Charleston, and saw with sorrow the lowering of its flag, but they were wise enough to think much, while saying little, except among themselves, and hoped for a time to come when they might again live under its Government. The high-pressure side-wheel steamer *Planter*, on board which they were employed, Robert as an assistant pilot, and John as a sailor and assistant engineer, was a light-draught vessel, drawing only five feet when heavily ladened [*sic*], and was very useful to the Confederates in plying around the harbor and among the islands near Charleston. ... On Monday evening, May 12, 1862, the *Planter* was lying at her wharf, the Southern, and her officers having finished their duties for the day, went ashore, first giving the usual instructions to Robert Smalls, to see that everything should be in readiness for their trip next morning. They had a valuable lot of freight for Fort Ripley and Fort Sumter, which was to be delivered the next day, but Robert thought to himself that perhaps these forts would not receive the articles after all, except as some of them might be delivered by the propulsion of powder out of Union guns. He did not betray his thoughts by his demeanor, and when the officers left the vessel he appeared to be in his usual respectful, attentive, efficient and obedient state of mind. He busied himself immediately to have the fires banked, and everything put shipshape for the night, according to orders. A little after eight o'clock the wives and children of Robert and John Smalls came on board. As they had sometimes visited the vessel, carrying meals, nothing was thought of this circumstance by the wharf guard, who saw them.

Somewhat later a Colored man from the steamer *Etowah* stepped past him, and joined the crew. Robert Smalls, for some time, had been contemplating the move which he was now about to make. He had heard that Colored men were being enlisted in the United States service at his old home [Beaufort], and that General Hunter was foreshadowing the mancipatory [*sic*] policy, giving kindly treatment to all contraband refugees. Now he was more anxious to get within the Union lines, and to join its forces. He had seen from the pilothouse, at a long distance, the blockading vessels, and thought over a plan to reach them with the *Planter*, and his desire was to run her away from the Confederates when she would have a valuable cargo. He had to proceed cautiously in the unfolding of his designs. First his brother was taken into confidence, and he at once approved the project. He, of course, could be trusted to keep the secret. Then the others were approached, gradually, after sounding with various lines the depths of their patriotism.... The brave men knew what would be their fate in the event of failure, and so, in talking over the matter together, just before cutting loose, they decided not to be captured alive, but to go down with the ship if the batteries of Castle Pinckney, Forts Moultrie and Sumter, and other guns should be opened upon them.

They also determined to use the *Planter's* guns to repel pursuit and attack, if necessary ... after midnight, when the officers ashore were in their soundest and sweetest slumbers, the fires were stirred up and steam raised to a high pressure, and between 3 and 4 o'clock Robert Smalls, the conceiver, leader and manager of this daring scheme, gave orders to "cast off," which was done quietly. To guard against a suspicion of anything being wrong in the movements of the *Planter*, he backed slowly from the wharf, blew her signal whistles, and seemed to be in no hurry to get away. He proceeded down the harbor, as if making towards Fort Sumter, and about quarter past 4 o'clock passed the frowning fortress, saluting it with loud signals, and then putting on all steam. Her appearance was duly reported to the officer of the day, but as her plying around the harbor, often at early hours, was not a strange occurrence, and she had become a familiar floating figure to the forts, she was not molested; and the heavy guns that easily could have sunk her, remained silent.

Passing the lower batteries, also, without molestation, the happy crew, with the greater part of the strain removed from their minds, now jubilantly rigged a white flag that they had prepared for the next emergency, and steered straight on to the Union ships. They were yet in great danger, this time from the hands of friends, who, not knowing anything concerning their escape, and on the lookout to sink at sight torpedo-boats and "rebel-rams," might blow them out of the water before discovering their peaceful flag. An eye-witness of the *Planter's* arrival, a member of the *Onward's* crew, and a war correspondent, gave a good account of it; and with some alterations it is here introduced: "We have been anchored in the ship channel for some days, and have frequently seen a secesh [*sic*] steamer plying in and around the harbor. Well, this morning, about sunrise, I was awakened by the cry of 'All hands to quarters!' and before I could get out, the steward knocked vigorously on my door and called: 'All hands to quarter, sah! de ram am a comin', sah!' I don't recollect of ever dressing myself any quicker, and got out on deck in a hurry. Sure enough, we could see, through the mist and fog, a great black object moving rapidly, and steadily, right at our port quarter.... Springs were bent on, and the *Onward* was rapidly warping around so as to bring her broadside to bear on the steamer that was still rapidly approaching us; and when the guns were brought to bear, some of the men looked at the Stars and Stripes, and then at the steamer, and muttered 'You! if you run into us we will go down with colors flying!' Just as No.3 port gun was being elevated, someone cried out, 'I see something that looks like a white flag'; and true enough there was something flying on the steamer that would have been *white* by application of soap and water. As she neared us, we looked in vain for the face of a white man. When they discovered that we would not fire on them, there was a rush of contrabands out on her deck, some dancing, some singing, whistling, jumping; and others stood looking towards Fort Sumter, and muttering all sorts of maledictions against it, and '*de heart of de Soul,*' generally. As the steamer came near, and under the stern of the *Onward*, one of the Colored men stepped forward, and taking off his hat, shouted, 'Good morning, sir! I've brought you some of the old United States guns, sir!'"

Congress granted half of the prize money for the *Planter* to Smalls and his men. Smalls became one of the most valuable assets of the Union blockade fleet in the South Atlantic.[1]

The Medal of Honor (MOH) was established in 1862 by President Lincoln as the nation's highest award for bravery, then and now. At first it was abused. For example, all members of the 27th Maine Infantry Regiment (864 troops) were awarded the MOH on the eve of Gettysburg. They were entitled to be discharged because their enlistment had expired, but they agreed to stay and fight the battle. A later review board chaired by General Nelson Miles rescinded hundreds of MOH awards as unworthy, including those of 27th Maine.[2] None of the rescinded awards were for African Americans. (As of 2011) only 3,464 MOH have been awarded. Of these, twenty-five African Americans in the Civil War were approved for the award, as were many others in the wars that followed.[3] Nineteen servicemen have received two MOH, including the African American Robert Augustus Sweeny, who served in conflicts after the Civil War. In perhaps the final chapter of the Civil War, Andrew Jackson Smith, discussed below, was awarded the MOH in 2001, *137 years after the fact*. The reason for the delay was a missing battle report. President Clinton pushed a bit to get this done.[4]

Robert Smalls, who seized the Confederate ship *Planter* (*Harper's Weekly*).

Listed below are Union African Americans who were awarded the Medal of Honor for bravery in the Civil War.[5] In many cases, as with white recipients, the citations mention seizing or defending flags. Today, this may appear trivial to some, but at the time, performing this act was fraught with danger and many who attempted this did not survive. Capturing or defending the colors was a rallying point for the battle and in many cases determined its outcome. Most of these medals for African Americans were a result of the Battle of New Market Heights (also called Chaffin's Farm). These awards were based upon recommendations of General Butler (see Chapter 3 for discussion of Butler).

The Civil War Union Medal of Honor (Library of Congress).

Aaron Anderson (AKA Sanderson). Served on board the U.S.S. *Wyandank* during a boat expedition up Mattox Creek, 17 March 1865. Participating with a boat crew in the clearing of Mattox Creek, Anderson carried out his duties courageously in the face of a devastating fire that cut away half the oars, pierced the launch in many places and cut the barrel off a musket being fired at the enemy.

Private **Bruce Anderson** (Company K, 142nd New York Infantry). At Fort Fisher, North Carolina, 15 January 1865. Entered service at Ephratah, New York. Born: Mexico, Oswego County, New York, 9 June 1845. Voluntarily advanced with the head of the column and cut down the palisading.

Private **William H. Barnes** (Company C, 38th U.S. Colored Troops). At Chapin's Farm, Virginia, 29 September 1864. Born: St. Mary's County, Maryland. Date of issue: 6 April 1865. Among the first to enter the enemy's works, although wounded.

First Sergeant Powhatan Beaty (Company G, 5th USC Infantry, September 29, 1864). All his company officers being killed or wounded, he took control of his company, leading them gallantly throughout the battle at New Market Heights.

Robert Blake (Contraband, U.S. Navy). Entered service at Virginia. G.O. No.: 32, 16 April 1864. Accredited to Virginia. On board the U.S. steam gunboat *Marblehead* off Legareville, Stono River, 25 December 1863, in an engagement with the enemy on John's Island. Serving the rifle gun, Blake, an escaped slave, carried out his duties bravely throughout the engagement, which resulted in the enemy's abandonment of positions, leaving a caisson and one gun behind.

First Sergeant James H. Bronson (Company D, 5th USC Infantry, September 29, 1864). At New Market Heights, he took command of his company after all its officers were killed or wounded, and led them on to victory.

William H. Brown (Landsman, U.S. Navy). Born: 1836, Baltimore, Maryland. Accredited to Maryland. G.O. No.: 45, 31 December 1864. On board the U.S.S. *Brooklyn* during successful attacks against Fort Morgan, rebel gunboats and the ram *Tennessee* in Mobile Bay on 5 August 1864. Stationed in an area that was twice cleared of men by bursting shells, Brown remained steadfast at his post and performed his duties in the powder division throughout

Powhatan Beaty (Library of Congress).

William H. Carney (Library of Congress).

the furious action, which resulted in the surrender of the prize rebel ram *Tennessee* and in the damaging and destruction of batteries at Fort Morgan.

Wilson Brown (Landsman, U.S. Navy). Born: 1841, Natchez, Mississippi. Accredited to Mississippi. G.O. No.: 45, 31 December 1864. On board the flagship U.S.S. *Hartford* during successful attacks against Fort Morgan, rebel gunboats and the ram *Tennessee* in Mobile Bay on 5 August 1864.

Christian A. Fleetwood (Library of Congress).

Knocked unconscious into the hold of the ship when an enemy shell burst, fatally wounding a man on the ladder above him, Brown, upon regaining consciousness, promptly returned to the shell whip on the berth deck and zealously continued to perform his duties although 4 of the 6 men at this station had been either killed or wounded by the enemy's terrific fire.

Sergeant William H. Carney (Company C, 54th Massachusetts, Colored Infantry, July 18, 1863). While storming the ramparts at Fort Wagner, the standard bearer was shot down. Sergeant Carney caught the banner and held it high throughout the battle. Though seriously wounded, he carried the colors to the rear when retreat was ordered, saying, "The old flag never touched the ground, boys."

Sergeant Decatur Dorsey (Company B, 39th USC Infantry, July 30, 1864). Planted his colors on the Confederate works in advance of his regiment, at Petersburg; when the regiment was driven back to the Union works, he carried the colors there and bravely rallied the men.

Sergeant-Major Christian A. Fleetwood (4th USC Infantry, September 19, 1864). At New Market Heights, he seized the colors after two color bearers had been shot down, and bore them "nobly" through the fight.

Private James Gardiner (Company I, 36th USC Infantry, September 29, 1864). At New Market Heights, he rushed in advance of his brigade, shot a rebel officer who was on the parapet rallying his men, then ran him through with his bayonet.

James H. Harris (Company B, 38th USC Infantry, September 29, 1864). Fought with great skill and courage in the assault at New Market Heights.

Sergeant-Major Thomas R. Hawkins (6th USC Infantry, July 21, 1864). At the battle of Deep Bottom, Virginia, at the

James Gardiner (Library of Congress).

risk of his life, he rescued the colors from the enemy.

Sergeant Alfred B. Hilton (Company H, 4th USC Infantry, September 29, 1864). He carried the national colors at New Market Heights; when the regimental standard bearer fell, he caught the banner, struggled forward carrying both flags until badly wounded, and fell. While on the ground and in great pain, he continued to hold the colors aloft.

Sergeant-Major Milton M. Holland (5th USC Infantry, September 29, 1864). Took command of Company C, at the Battle of Chaffin's Farm, after all its officers had been killed or wounded and led it through the battle.

Corporal Miles James (Company B, USC Infantry, September 30, 1864). Having had his arm so badly mutilated that immediate amputation was necessary, he loaded and discharged his piece with one hand and urged his men forward — all within 30 yards of the enemy's works.

James H. Harris (Library of Congress).

First Sergeant Alexander Kelly (Company F, 6th USC Infantry, September 29, 1864). At New Market Heights, he seized the colors, which had fallen near the ramparts, raised them, and rallied his men at a time of confusion and a place of the greatest possible danger.

John Lawson (Landsman, U.S. Navy). Born: 1837, Pennsylvania. Accredited to Pennsylvania. G.O. No.: 45, 31 December 1864. On board the flagship U.S.S. *Hartford* during successful attacks against Fort Morgan, rebel gunboats and the ram *Tennessee* in Mobile Bay on 5 August 1864. Wounded in the leg and thrown violently against the side of the ship when an enemy shell killed or wounded the 6-man crew as the shell whipped on the berth deck, Lawson, upon regaining his composure, promptly returned to his station and, although urged to go below for treatment, steadfastly continued his duties throughout the remainder of the action.

Left: Thomas R. Hawkins. *Right:* Milton M. Holland (Library of Congress).

James Mifflin (Engineer's Cook, U.S. Navy). Born: 1839, Richmond, Virginia. Accredited to Virginia. G.O. No.: 45, 31 December 1864. On board the U.S.S. *Brooklyn* during successful attacks against Fort Morgan, rebel gunboats and the ram *Tennessee* in Mobile Bay on 5 August 1864. Stationed in the immediate vicinity of the shell whips, which were twice cleared of men by bursting shells, Mifflin remained steadfast at his post and performed his duties in the powder division throughout the furious action, which resulted in the surrender of the prize rebel ram *Tennessee* and in the damaging and destruction of batteries at Fort Morgan.

Joachim Pease (Seaman, U.S. Navy). Born: Long Island, New York. Accredited to New York. G.O. No.: 45, 31 December 1864. Served as seaman on board the U.S.S. *Kearsarge* when she destroyed the *Alabama* off Cherbourg, France, 19 June 1864. Acting as loader on the No. 2 gun during this bitter engagement, Pease exhibited marked coolness and good conduct and was highly recommended by the divisional officer for gallantry under fire.

First Sergeant Robert Pinn (Company I, 5th USC Infantry, September 29, 1864). After all company officers had been killed or wounded, he took command and led the company through the entire battle.

First Sergeant Edward Ratcliff (Company C, 38th USC Infantry, September 29, 1864). Thrown into command of his company by the death of his commanding officer, he was the first enlisted man in the enemy's works, leading his company with great gallantry.

Corporal Andrew Jackson Smith, of Clinton, Illinois, 55th Massachusetts Voluntary Infantry, distinguished himself on 30 November 1864 by saving his regimental colors, after the color bearer was killed during a bloody charge called the Battle of Honey Hill, South Carolina. In the late afternoon, as the 55th Regiment pursued enemy skirmishers and conducted a running fight, they ran into a swampy area backed by a rise where the Confederate Army awaited. The surrounding woods and thick underbrush impeded infantry movement and artillery support. The 55th and 54th Regiments formed columns to advance on the enemy position in a flanking movement. As the Confederates repelled other units, the 55th and 54th Regiments continued to move into flanking positions. Forced into a narrow gorge crossing a swamp in the face of the enemy position, the 55th's color-sergeant was killed by an exploding shell, and Corporal Smith took the regimental colors from his hand and carried them through heavy grape

Left: Alexander Kelly. *Right:* John Lawson (Library of Congress).

and canister fire. Although half of the officers and a third of the enlisted men engaged in the fight were killed or wounded, Corporal Smith continued to expose himself to enemy fire by carrying the colors throughout the battle. Through his actions, the regimental colors of the 55th Infantry Regiment were not lost to the enemy. Corporal Andrew Jackson Smith's extraordinary valor in the face of deadly enemy fire is in keeping with the highest traditions of military service and reflect great credit upon him, the 55th Regiment, and the United States Army. The award was made in 2001. Smith's descendents received the award from President Clinton.

Robert Pinn (Library of Congress).

Private Charles Veal (Company D, 4th USC Infantry, September 29, 1864). After two color bearers had been shot down with the regimental colors, Private Veal seized them and bore them through the battle.

Chapter Notes

Preface

1. Michael A. Eggleston, *10th Minnesota Volunteers, 1862–1865: A History of the Action in the Sioux Uprising and the Civil War with a Regimental Roster* (Jefferson, NC: McFarland, 2012).

2. Letter, Lorenzo Thomas to A. Lincoln, 30 March 1864.

3. U.S. War Department, *The War of Rebellion: A Compilation of the Official Records of the Union and Confederate Armies* (Washington, D.C., 1880–1901).

4. David R. Logsdon, *Eyewitnesses at the Battle of Nashville* (Nashville: Kettle Mill Press, 2004), 70.

5. National Park Service, *Civil War Soldiers & Sailors System*, http://www.civilwar.nps.gov/cwss/.

6. H. H. Cunningham, *Doctors in Gray: The Confedereate Medical Service* (Baton Rouge: Louisiana State University Press, 1958), 27.

7. William A. Gladstone, *United States Colored Troops, 1863–1867* (Gettysburg: Thomas Publications, 1990), 120.

8. James M. McPherson, *The Negro's Civil War: How American Blacks Felt and Acted during the Civil War* (New York: Vintage Books, 1965), 160.

9. Joseph T. Wilson, *The Black Phalanx: African American Soldiers in the War of Independence, the War of 1812 and the Civil War* (Memphis: General Books, 2010), 80.

10. McPherson, *The Negro's Civil War*, Appendix A.

11. Hondon B. Hargrove, *Black Union Soldiers in the Civil War* (Jefferson, NC: McFarland, 1988), 3.

12. McPherson, *The Negro's Civil War*, Appendix A.

13. Wilson, *The Black Phalanx*, 60.

14. *Ibid.*, 70.

Introduction

1. Chester G. Hearn, *The Impeachment of Andrew Johnson* (Jefferson, NC: McFarland, 2000), 147–148.

2. Benjamin P. Thomas and Harold M. Hyman, *Stanton: The Life and Times of Lincoln's Secretary of War* (New York: Alfred A. Knopf, 1962), 163.

3. Dudley Taylor Cornish, *The Sable Arm: Negro Troops in the Union Army, 1861–1865* (New York: W. W. Norton, 1956), 114.

4. McPherson, *The Negro's Civil War*, 3.

5. *Ibid.*, 12.

6. Hargrove, *Black Union Soldiers in the Civil War*, 17.

7. McPherson, *The Negro's Civil War*, 19.

8. *Ibid.*, 22.

9. *Ibid.*, 31.

10. *Ibid.*, 34.

11. *Ibid.*, xvi.

12. *Ibid.*, 40.

13. Richard Rollins, ed., *Black Southerners in Gray: Essays on Afro-Americans in Confederate Armies* (Murfreesboro, TN: Southern Heritage Press, 1994), 76.

14. Hargrove, *Black Union Soldiers in the Civil War*, x.
15. McPherson, *The Negro's Civil War*, 243.
16. Wilson, *The Black Phalanx*, 80.
17. McPherson, *The Negro's Civil War*, 241.
18. *Ibid.*, 160.
19. Wilson, *The Black Phalanx*, 84.

Chapter 1

1. In 1969, Dave Richard Palmer wrote a book about West Point and its history during the American Revolution. He titled his book *The River and the Rock*. This chapter follows the book title since it tells the story of Lorenzo Thomas and his time at the U.S. Military Academy at West Point.
2. Constance J. Cooper, *350 Years of New Castle, Delaware: Chapters in a Town's History* (Wilmington, DE: Cedar Tree Books, 2001), xv.
3. *Ibid.*, 71.
4. United States Military Academy, *Sixth Annual Reunion of the Association of Graduates of the United States Military Academy at West Point, New York June 17, 1875* (New York: A. S. Barnes, 1875), 74.
5. Letter, James Tilton to the President of the United States, 2 June 1819.
6. Letter, Caesar A. Rodney to John C. Calhoun, 31 May 1819.
7. United States Military Academy, *Sixth Annual Reunion of the Association of Graduates*, 74–75.
8. Stephen E. Ambrose, *Duty, Honor, Country: A History of West Point* (Baltimore: Johns Hopkins University Press, 1966), 22.
9. Robert Cowley and Thomas Guinzburg, *West Point: Two Centuries of Honor and Tradition* (New York: Warner Books, 2002), 26–30.
10. *Ibid.*, 30–31.
11. Ambrose, *Duty, Honor, Country*, 112.
12. *Ibid.*, 75.
13. John David Smith, *Black Soldiers in Blue: African American Troops in the Civil War Era* (Chapel Hill: University of North Carolina Press, 2002), 253.
14. Major Alexander Macomb to Brevet Major William Jenkins Worth, 31 January 1823, Miscellaneous Military Academy Papers (F-77), 1813–1825, RG 77, NA.
15. Court Martial file number Z29, Proceedings of Courts Martial, 1808–1940, RG 153, 34–59, Records of the Judge Adjutant General, NA.
16. United States Military Academy, *Sixth Annual Reunion of the Association of Graduates*, 75.
17. William Henry Powell, *A History of the Organization and Movements of the Fourth Regiment of Infantry, United States Army* (Washington City: McGill & Witherow, 1871), 193.

Chapter 2

1. Powell, *A History of the Organization and Movements of the Fourth Regiment of Infantry*, 74–78.
2. *Ibid.*, 9–12.
3. *Ibid.*, 17.
4. Thomas would join the ranks of many Civil War generals who served with the Fourth before the Civil War. These included Ulysses S. Grant, John Bell Hood, James Longstreet, and Philip Sheridan, among others.
5. John K. Mahon, *History of the Seminole War* (Gainesville: University of Florida Press, 1967), 19.
6. Powell, *A History of the Organization and Movements of the Fourth Regiment of Infantry*, 16.
7. *Ibid.*, 17.
8. *Ibid.*
9. United States Military Academy, *Sixth Annual Reunion of the Association of Graduates*, 308.
10. *Ibid.*, 309.
11. Delaware Public Archives, *Marriage: Lorenzo Thomas to Elizabeth Colesberry*, V. 11, p. 181, 12/4/1832, 120.
12. Delaware Public Archives, *Baptism:*

Lorenzo Thomas (Adult), V. 87, p. 130, 9/25/1836, 130.

13. Mahon, *History of the Seminole War*, 104–106.

14. Association of Graduates, United States Military Academy, *The Register of Graduates and Former Cadets of the United States Military, 2010* (West Point: Association of Graduates, 2010), 360.

15. Powell, *A History of the Organization and Movements of the Fourth Regiment of Infantry*, 35–37.

16. Felice Flanery Lewis, *Trailing Clouds of Glory: Zachary Taylor's Mexican War Campaign and His Emerging Civil War Leaders* (Tuscaloosa: University of Alabama Press, 2010), 18

17. Christopher D. Dishman, *A Perfect Gibraltar: The Battle of Monterry, Mexico, 1846* (Norman: University of Oklahoma Press, 2010), xv.

18. Lewis, *Trailing Clouds of Glory*, 60–62.

19. *Ibid.*, 64–65.

20. Michael Hogan, *The Irish Soldiers of Mexico* (Guadalajara: Intercambio Press, 1997), 35.

21. Samuel E. Chamberlain, *My Confession* (New York: Harper & Brothers, 1956), 140–141.

22. Dishman, *A Perfect Gibraltar*, xv.

23. Frank P. Blair, *The Life and Public Services of Gen. William O. Butler* (Baltimore: N. Hickman, 1848), 26.

24. Dishman, *A Perfect Gibraltar*, 107.

25. *Ibid.*, 186.

26. *Ibid.*, xvii.

27. For the complete Thomas report, see Appendix E of this book.

28. Lewis, *Trailing Clouds of Glory*, 156–157.

29. *Ibid.*, 150.

30. Hogan, *The Irish Soldiers of Mexico*, 69.

31. Peter F. Stevens, *The Rogue's March: John Riley and the St. Patrick's Battalion, 1846–1848* (Washington, D.C.: Potomac Books, 1999), 59–96.

32. *Ibid.*, 41.

33. Dishman, *A Perfect Gibraltar*, 104.

34. Hogan, *The Irish Soldiers of Mexico*, 83.

35. *Ibid.*, 174.

36. *Ibid.*, 188–190.

37. Powell, *A History of the Organization and Movements of the Fourth Regiment of Infantry*, 39.

38. *Ibid.*, 40.

39. John S. D. Eisenhower, *So Far from God: The U.S. War With Mexico, 1846–1848* (New York: Random House, 1989), 259–260.

40. Samuel Chamberlain was a veteran of the war, but some say that his narrative was composed of hearsay; however, his account tracks with others and Chamberlain's version is undoubtedly the most entertaining.

41. Chamberlain, *My Confession*, 226–228.

42. William S. McFeely, *Grant* (New York: W. W. Norton, 1981), 39.

43. *Ibid.*

44. CONGRESSIONAL GLOBE, 30th Cong., 1st Sess. 64 (1847) (emphasis in original). The text of these resolutions is available at http://www.sewanee.edu/faculty/Willis/Civil_War/documents/LincolnSpot.html.

Chapter 3

1. Association of Graduates, United States Military Academy, *The Register of Graduates and Former Cadets of the United States Military, 2010*, 360.

2. U.S. War Department, *The War of Rebellion*, LXII, page 464.

3. Thomas MacCurdy Vincent, *Abraham Lincoln and Edwin M. Stanton* (Washington, D.C.: Commandery of the District of Columbia, 1892), 9.

4. Roswell Marsh, *Defence of Edwin Stanton* (Steubenville, OH: W. R. Allison's Printing Establishment, 1873), 10.

5. *Ibid.*, 114.

6. *Ibid.*, 113.

7. U.S. War Department, *The War of Rebellion*, IV, Pt II, page 302.

8. Cornish, *The Sable Arm*, 113.
9. *Ibid.*, 114.
10. *Ibid.*
11. U.S. War Department, *The War of Rebellion*, III, Pt 3, pages 100–101.
12. Smith, *Black Soldiers in Blue*, 252.
13. Benjamin Quarles, *The Negro in the Civil War* (Boston: Little, Brown, 1953), 195.
14. Cornish, *The Sable Arm*, 124.
15. U.S. War Department, *The War of Rebellion*, XXXVII, Pt V, page 347.
16. *Ibid.*, XXXIX, page 613.
17. *Ibid.*
18. *Ibid.*
19. Martin H. Greenberg and Charles G. Waugh, *The Price of Freedom: Slavery and the Civil War* (Nashville: Cumberland House, 2000), 62.
20. Cornish, *The Sable Arm*, 114.
21. Smith, *Black Soldiers in Blue*, 257.
22. Cornish, *The Sable Arm*, 116.
23. *Ibid.*, 117.
24. *Ibid.*, 123.
25. Smith, *Black Soldiers in Blue*, 259.
26. Cornish, *The Sable Arm*, 117.
27. *Ibid.*, 232–233.
28. Quarles, *The Negro in the Civil War*, 197.
29. *Ibid.*
30. *Ibid.*
31. McPherson, *The Negro's Civil War*, 172–173.
32. Cornish, *The Sable Arm*, 118.
33. *Ibid.*
34. William O. Stoddard, *Inside the White House in War Times: Memoirs and Reports of Lincoln's Secretary* [1890] (Lincoln: University of Nebraska Press, 2000), 174.
35. Cornish, *The Sable Arm*, 114.
36. Mark Lardas, *African American Soldier in the Civil War: USCT 1862–1866* (Oxford: Osprey, 2006), 7.
37. Richard M. Reid, *Freedom for Themselves: North Carolina's Black Soldiers in the Civil War Era* (Chapel Hill: University of North Carolina Press, 2008), 8.
38. Lardas, *African American Soldier in the Civil War*, 7.
39. Cornish, *The Sable Arm*, 138.
40. *Ibid.*, 139.
41. *Ibid.*, 140.
42. *Ibid.*, 124.
43. *Ibid.*
44. Lardas, *African American Soldier in the Civil War*, 11.
45. *Ibid.*, 6.
46. U.S. War Department, *The War of Rebellion*, page 132, XXXIV, 441.
47. Cornish, *The Sable Arm*, 251.
48. *Ibid.*, 288.
49. U.S. War Department, *The War of Rebellion*, LI, 132.
50. Greenberg and Waugh, *The Price of Freedom*, 138.
51. *Ibid.*, 149.
52. Hargrove, *Black Union Soldiers in the Civil War*, 4.
53. *Ibid.*
54. *Ibid.*
55. *Ibid.*
56. *Ibid.*, 45.
57. *Ibid.*, 147.
58. *Ibid.*, 198.
59. Lardas, *African American Soldier in the Civil War*, 27.
60. Cornish, *The Sable Arm*, 240.
61. *Ibid.*, 246.
62. Bell Irvin Wiley, *Southern Negroes, 1861–1865* (Baton Rouge: Louisiana State University, 1938), 322.
63. Joseph T. Glatthaar, *Forged in Battle: The Civil War Alliance of Black Soldiers and White Officers* (New York: The Free Press, 1990), 185.
64. *Ibid.*
65. McPherson, *The Negro's Civil War*, 200.
66. *Ibid.*, 241.
67. Lardas, *African American Soldier in the Civil War*, 28.
68. *Ibid.*, 29.
69. The Lieber Code, General Order Number 100, allows "summary execution of ... guerilla forces if caught in the act of carrying out their missions."
70. Wilson, *The Black Phalanx*, 73.
71. Lardas, *African American Soldier in the Civil War*, 30–31.
72. Cornish, *The Sable Arm*, 187.

73. *Ibid.*
74. *Ibid.*, 188.
75. McPherson, *The Negro's Civil War*, 200–201.
76. Wilson, *The Black Phalanx*, 78.
77. McPherson, *The Negro's Civil War*, 204.
78. Cornish, *The Sable Arm*, 184.
79. Wilson, *The Black Phalanx*, 84.
80. Glatthaar, *Forged in Battle*, 174–175.
81. Lardas, *African American Soldier in the Civil War*, 13.
82. *Ibid.*
83. *Ibid.*, 12.
84. *Ibid.*, 9.
85. *Ibid.*
86. *Ibid.*, 43.
87. *Ibid.*, 44.
88. George Washington Adams, *Doctors in Blue: The Medical History of the Union Army in the Civil War* (New York: Henry Schulman, 1952), 43.
89. *Ibid.*, 45.
90. Margaret Humphreys, *Intensely Human: The Health of the Black Soldiers in the American Civil War* (Baltimore: Johns Hopkins University Press, 2008), 46.
91. *Ibid.*, 11.
92. *Ibid.*, 48.
93. *Ibid.*
94. *Ibid.*, 49.
95. Adams, *Doctors in Blue*, 16.
96. *Ibid.*, 206.
97. *Ibid.*, 207.
98. *Ibid.*, 208.
99. *Ibid.*
100. *Ibid.*, 211.
101. *Ibid.*, 213.
102. *Ibid.*
103. *Ibid.*
104. McPherson, *The Negro's Civil War*, 174.
105. Humphreys, *Intensely Human*, 6–7.
106. Wilson, *The Black Phalanx*, 80.
107. Humphreys, *Intensely Human*, 10.
108. Charles Kelly Barrow, *Black Confederates* (Gretna, LA: Pelican, 1995), 17.
109. Humphreys, *Intensely Human*, 11.
110. *Ibid.*, 11–12.
111. *Ibid.*
112. *Ibid.*
113. *Ibid.*, 57.
114. *Ibid.*
115. U.S. War Department, *Official Army Register of the Volunteer Force of the United States Army for the Years 1861, 1862, 1863, 1864; Volume 8* (Washington, D.C.: Adjutant General's Office, 1867).
116. Humphreys, *Intensely Human*, 59.
117. *Ibid.*, 60.
118. *Ibid.*, 61.
119. *Ibid.*, 69.
120. *Ibid.*, 71.
121. *Ibid.*, 105.
122. *Ibid.*, 117.
123. *Ibid.*, 108.
124. *Ibid.*, 137.
125. *Ibid.*, 131.
126. *Ibid.*, 126.
127. *Ibid.*, 142–143.
128. *Ibid.*, 159.
129. Cornish, *The Sable Arm*, 38.
130. Greenberg and Waugh, *The Price of Freedom*, 116.
131. Humphreys, *Intensely Human*, 4–5.
132. Glatthaar, *Forged in Battle*, 5–6.
133. *Ibid.*, 75.
134. U.S. War Department, *The War of Rebellion*, Series III, Volume IV, 225.
135. Cornish, *The Sable Arm*, 115.
136. U.S. War Department, *The War of Rebellion*, Series III, Volume IV, 454–455.
137. *Ibid.*, 453.
138. Wiley, *Southern Negroes*, 226–227.
139. *Ibid.*, 225.
140. *Ibid.*, 226.
141. It is not clear how the Treasury Department could write a lease for an abandoned plantation.
142. Cornish, *The Sable Arm*, 118.
143. *Ibid.*, 111.
144. *Ibid.*, 206.
145. *Ibid.*, 213.
146. *Ibid.*, 218.

147. Lardas, *African American Soldier in the Civil War*, 15.
148. Cornish, *The Sable Arm*, 217.
149. *Ibid.*, 207.
150. *Ibid.*, 214.
151. *Ibid.*, 206.
152. *Ibid.*, 206–207.
153. Lardas, *African American Soldier in the Civil War*, 15.
154. Cornish, *The Sable Arm*, 203.
155. McPherson, *The Negro's Civil War*, 176–177.
156. U.S. War Department, *The War of Rebellion*, XXXIX, page 496.
157. *Ibid.*, 526.
158. McPherson, *The Negro's Civil War*, 176.
159. Humphreys, *Intensely Human*, 58.
160. Adams, *Doctors in Blue*, 46.
161. Humphreys, *Intensely Human*, 63.
162. Gladstone, *United States Colored Troops*, 24.
163. Humphreys, *Intensely Human*, 59.
164. *Ibid.*, 60–61.
165. Glatthaar, *Forged in Battle*, 190.
166. Cunningham, *Doctors in Gray*, 37.
167. Thomas Jefferson Hunt, *Observations of T. J. Hunt in the Civil War: A Narrative of the Military Life of T. J. Hunt in the Sioux Indian and Civil Wars of 1862–1865*, 19.
168. *Ibid.*
169. Benjamin Quarles, *The Negro in the Civil War* (Boston: Little, Brown, 1953), 204–205.
170. Adams, *Doctors in Blue*, 215.
171. Eggleston, *10th Minnesota Volunteers*, 86.
172. Adams, *Doctors in Blue*, 16.
173. *Ibid.*, 224–225.
174. Eggleston, *10th Minnesota Volunteers*, 60.
175. Lardas, *African American Soldier in the Civil War*, 25.
176. *Ibid.*
177. *Ibid.*, 14.
178. Wiley, *Southern Negroes*, 269.
179. *Ibid.*, 15.
180. Lardas, *African American Soldier in the Civil War*, 15.
181. *Ibid.*, 17.
182. McPherson, *The Negro's Civil War*, 134.
183. Cornish, *The Sable Arm*, 240–241.
184. McPherson, *The Negro's Civil War*, 215.
185. *Ibid.*, 216.
186. Glatthaar, *Forged in Battle*, 178.
187. Greenberg and Waugh, *The Price of Freedom*, 124.
188. *Ibid.*
189. McPherson, *The Negro's Civil War*, 176.
190. Wilson, *The Black Phalanx*, 139–140.
191. Cornish, *The Sable Arm*, 159–160.
192. *Ibid.*, 160.
193. Wilson, *The Black Phalanx*, 95.
194. Cornish, *The Sable Arm*, 161.
195. *Ibid.*, 158.
196. *Ibid.*, 166–167.
197. *Ibid.*, 168.
198. Lardas, *African American Soldier in the Civil War*, 44.
199. Cornish, *The Sable Arm*, 172.
200. *Ibid.*
201. Greenberg and Waugh, *The Price of Freedom*, 124.
202. Quarles, *The Negro in the Civil War*, 207.
203. *Ibid.*, 207–208.
204. Smith, *Black Soldiers in Blue*, 268.

Chapter 4

1. David O. Stewart, *Impeached: The Trial of President Andrew Johnson and the Fight for Lincoln's Legacy* (New York: Simon & Schuster Paperbacks, 2009), 18.
2. *Ibid.*, 16.
3. *Ibid.*, 31.
4. *Ibid.*, 50.
5. *Ibid.*
6. *Ibid.*, 53.
7. Logsdon, *Eyewitnesses at the Battle of Nashville*, 5.

8. Stewart, *Impeached*, 62.
9. *Ibid.*, 17.
10. *Ibid.*, 68.
11. Fletcher Pratt, *Stanton: Lincoln's Secretary of War* (New York: W. W. Norton, 1953), 447.
12. Stewart, *Impeached*, 69.
13. *Ibid.*, 251.
14. *Ibid.*, 69.
15. Pratt, *Stanton*, 447.
16. Stewart, *Impeached*, 43.
17. *Ibid.*, 69.
18. *Ibid.*, 77.
19. *Ibid.*, 96.
20. *New York Independent*, December 12, 1867.
21. Stewart, *Impeached*, 57.
22. *Ibid.*, 70.
23. *Ibid.*, 259.
24. *Ibid.*, 101.
25. *Ibid.*, 106.
26. *Ibid.*, 316.
27. *Ibid.*, 123.
28. *Ibid.*, 125.
29. *Ibid.*, 143–144.
30. *Ibid.*, 129.
31. *Ibid.*, 136.
32. Hearn, *The Impeachment of Andrew Johnson*, 149.
33. Stewart, *Impeached*, 42.
34. *Ibid.*, 136.
35. *Ibid.*, 138.
36. *Ibid.*, 155.
37. E. D. Townsend, *Anecdotes of the Civil War in the United States* (New York: D Appleton, 1883), 126–127.
38. Stewart, *Impeached*, 139–140.
39. *Ibid.*, 210.
40. *Ibid.*, 142.
41. *Ibid.*, 140–141.
42. *Ibid.*, 233.
43. *Ibid.*, 252.
44. *Ibid.*, 149.
45. *Ibid.*, 190.
46. *Ibid.*, 249.
47. *The Great Impeachment and Trial of Andrew Johnson, President of the United States* (Philadelphia: T. B. Peterson & Brothers, 1868), 115.
48. *Ibid.*, 117–118.
49. Stewart, *Impeached*, 203.
50. *The Great Impeachment and Trial of Andrew Johnson*, 134.
51. Michael Les Benedict, *The Impeachment and Trial of Andrew Johnson* (New York: W. W. Norton, 1973), 168.
52. *Ibid.*.
53. This was the same Georges Clemenceau who was prime minister of France during World War I. Clemenceau, at the time of the impeachment, was a New York news correspondent.
54. Stewart, *Impeached*, 206.
55. *Ibid.*, 317.
56. John F. Kennedy, *Profiles in Courage* (New York: HarperCollins, 1955), 128–129.
57. Stewart, *Impeached*, 185.
58. Benedict, *The Impeachment and Trial of Andrew Johnson*, 179.
59. Most historians agree that Kennedy wrote the first and last chapters and Sorensen wrote the rest. The problem was that Kennedy gave Sorensen very little credit for anything.
60. Kennedy, *Profiles in Courage*, xxii.
61. Stewart, *Impeached*, 308–309.
62. Benedict, *The Impeachment and Trial of Andrew Johnson*, 182–183.
63. Kennedy, *Profiles in Courage*, 116.
64. United States Military Academy, *Sixth Annual Reunion of the Association of Graduates*, 74–77.
65. Henry Greenleaf Pearson, *The Life of John A. Andrew, Governor of Massachusetts, 1861–1865*, vol. 2 (Ann Arbor: University of Michigan Library, 1904), 90.
66. Cornish, *The Sable Arm*, 124.
67. Smith, *Black Soldiers in Blue*, 268–269.
68. United States Military Academy, *Sixth Annual Reunion of the Association of Graduates*, 74–77.

Biographical Dictionary

1. Tyrone Sanders, *The New Book of U.S. Presidents*, 7.
2. Ezra J. Warner, *Generals in Blue: Lives of the Union Commanders* (Baton

Rouge: Louisiana State University Press, 1964), 17–18.
3. *Ibid.*, 60–61.
4. Association of Graduates, United States Military Academy, *The Register of Graduates and Former Cadets of the United States Military, 2010*, 4–25.
5. Chamberlain, *My Confession*, 301–302.
6. Association of Graduates, United States Military Academy, *The Register of Graduates and Former Cadets of the United States Military, 2010*, 540.
7. Warner, *Generals in Blue*, 160–161.
8. *Ibid.*, 183–186.
9. Association of Graduates, United States Military Academy, *The Register of Graduates and Former Cadets of the United States Military, 2010*, 1630.
10. Sung to the tune of "The Yellow Rose of Texas."
11. *Collections of the Minnesota Historical Society, Volume XIV, Minnesota Biographies, 1655–1912*, 356.
12. Warner, *Generals in Blue*, 243–244.
13. Sanders, *The New Book of U.S. Presidents*, 8.
14. Association of Graduates, United States Military Academy, *The Register of Graduates and Former Cadets of the United States Military, 2010*, 541.
15. *Ibid.*
16. Warner, *Generals in Blue*, 288–289.
17. Sanders, *The New Book of U.S. Presidents*, 6.
18. Association of Graduates, United States Military Academy, *The Register of Graduates and Former Cadets of the United States Military, 2010*, 36.
19. *Ibid.*, 368–369.
20. Stevens, *The Rogue's March*, 51.
21. *Ibid.*, 293.
22. Warner, *Generals in Blue*, 420–421.
23. *Ibid.*, 425–426.
24. Hargrove, *Black Union Soldiers in the Civil War*, 17.
25. Warner, *Generals in Blue*, 441–444.
26. Association of Graduates, United States Military Academy, *The Register of Graduates and Former Cadets of the United States Military, 2010*, 1231.
27. Warner, *Generals in Blue*, 473–474.
28. Sanders, *The New Book of U.S. Presidents*, 13.
29. Association of Graduates, United States Military Academy, *The Register of Graduates and Former Cadets of the United States Military, 2010*, 36.
30. Edwin B. Coddington, *The Gettysburg Campaign: A Study in Command* (New York: Touchstone, 1997), 423.
31. *Army and Navy Journal*, May 3, p. 602, and June 14, 1873, p. 697 (Kingsbury); Don Rickey Jr., *Forty Miles a Day on Beans and Hay: The Enlisted Soldier Fighting the Indian Wars* (Norman: University of Oklahoma Press, 1963), 279.
32. Warner, *Generals in Blue*, 517–518.
33. *Ibid.*, 557–558.
34. Association of Graduates, United States Military Academy, *The Register of Graduates and Former Cadets of the United States Military, 2010*, 1825.

Appendix A

1. Family history is based upon U.S. Census Records of 1850, 1860, and 1870 as well as family records found on Ancestry.com.

Appendix B

1. This statue was completed in 1997. A major feature is the inscribed panel that surrounds the statue and contains the names of over two hundred thousand African Americans who fought for the Union. The inscription on the memorial reads, "Civil War to Civil Rights and Beyond. This memorial is dedicated to those who served in the African American units of the Union Army in the Civil War.

The 209,145 names inscribed on these walls commemorate those fighters for freedom."
2. McPherson, *The Negro's Civil War*, 34–35.
3. *Ibid.*, 10.
4. *Ibid.*, 8.
5. *Ibid.*, 9.
6. Barrow, *Black Confederates*, 10.
7. *Ibid.*
8. *Ibid.*, 47–48.
9. Robert Franklin Durden, *The Gray and the Black: The Confederate Debate on Emancipation* (Baton Rouge: Louisiana State University Press, 1972), 277.
10. Wilson, *The Black Phalanx*, 62.
11. *Ibid.*, 60.
12. Rollins, *Black Southerners in Gray*, 76.
13. Ibid.
14. Barrow, *Black Confederates*, 111.
15. Wilson, *The Black Phalanx*, 59.
16. *Ibid.*
17. *Ibid.*, 317.
18. Barrow, *Black Confederates*, 62.
19. Wilson, *The Black Phalanx*, 318.
20. Cornish, *The Sable Arm*, 16.
21. *Ibid.*, 57.
22. Barrow, *Black Confederates*, 15.
23. *Ibid.*, 17.
24. *Ibid.*, 18.
25. *Ibid.*, 25.
26. *Ibid.*, 47–48.
27. *Ibid.*, 48.
28. Wilson, *The Black Phalanx*, 322.
29. Barrow, *Black Confederates*, 48.
30. *Ibid.*
31. *Ibid.*, 51–54.
32. McPherson, *The Negro's Civil War*, 67.
33. *Ibid.*, 163.
34. Cornish, *The Sable Arm*, 5.
35. *Ibid.*, 7.
36. *Ibid.*, 10.
37. *Ibid.*, 13.
38. McPherson, *The Negro's Civil War*, 41.
39. Cornish, *The Sable Arm*, 11.
40. McPherson, *The Negro's Civil War*, 47.
41. Hargrove, *Black Union Soldiers in the Civil War*, 15.
42. Cornish, *The Sable Arm*, 17–18.
43. *Ibid.*, 18.
44. *Ibid.*, 19.
45. *Ibid.*, 20.
46. *Ibid.*, 24.
47. McPherson, *The Negro's Civil War*, 23.
48. Lardas, *African American Soldier in the Civil War*, 4.
49. *Ibid.*, 5.
50. *Ibid.*, 64–65.
51. Edward A. Miller Jr., *Lincoln's Abolitionist General: The Biography of David Hunter* (Columbia: University of South Carolina Press, 1997), 102.
52. Cornish, *The Sable Arm*, 120.
53. *Ibid.*, 53.
54. Wilson, *The Black Phalanx*, 94.
55. Miller, *Lincoln's Abolitionist General*, 122.
56. Wilson, *The Black Phalanx*, 94.
57. McPherson, *The Negro's Civil War*, 48.
58. Cornish, *The Sable Arm*, 46.
59. *Ibid.*, 51.
60. McPherson, *The Negro's Civil War*, 300.
61. Miller, *Lincoln's Abolitionist General*, 111.
62. Melvin Claxton and Mark Puls, *Uncommon Valor: A Story of Race, Patriotism, and Glory in the Final Battles of the Civil War* (Hoboken, NJ: John Wiley and Sons, 2006), 1–2.
63. Stewart, *Impeached*, 160.
64. Wilson, *The Black Phalanx*, 115.
65. Cornish, *The Sable Arm*, 60–61.
66. *Ibid.*, 65.
67. Lardas, *African American Soldier in the Civil War*, 5.
68. Cornish, *The Sable Arm*, 65.
69. McPherson, *The Negro's Civil War*, 167.
70. Cornish, *The Sable Arm*, 70.
71. *Ibid.*, 73.
72. *Ibid.*, 75.
73. *Ibid.*, 77.
74. *Ibid.*, 86.

75. *Ibid.*, 93.
76. Civil War Society, *Civil War Society's Encyclopedia of the Civil War: The Complete and Comprehensive Guide to the American Civil War* (Princeton, NJ: Wing Books, 1997), 405–406.
77. Cornish, *The Sable Arm*, 96.
78. McPherson, *The Negro's Civil War*, 51.
79. Cornish, *The Sable Arm*, 99.
80. McPherson, *The Negro's Civil War*, 49–50.
81. *Ibid.*, 52.
82. Cornish, *The Sable Arm*, 101.
83. *Ibid.*, 102.
84. *Ibid.*, 107.
85. *Ibid.*, 105.
86. McPherson, *The Negro's Civil War*, 176.
87. *Ibid.*, 181.
88. *Ibid.*, 185.
89. *Ibid.*, 130.
90. *Ibid.*, 130–131.
91. *Ibid.*, 132.
92. Wilson, *The Black Phalanx*, 69.
93. Cornish, *The Sable Arm*, 128.
94. McPherson, *The Negro's Civil War*, 171.
95. Cornish, *The Sable Arm*, 129.
96. McPherson, *The Negro's Civil War*, 173.
97. Greenberg and Waugh, *The Price of Freedom*, 89.
98. Cornish, *The Sable Arm*, 244.
99. Lardas, *African American Soldier in the Civil War*, 6.
100. *Ibid.*, 9.
101. Some historians identify the border slave states as including West Virginia, removing Delaware.
102. Lardas, *African American Soldier in the Civil War*, 13.

Appendix C

1. Stewart, *Impeached*, 331.

Appendix D

1. Stewart, *Impeached*, 343.

Appendix E

1. Powell, *A History of the Organization and Movements of the Fourth Regiment of Infantry*, 193.
2. Blair, *The Life and Public Services of Gen. William O. Butler*, 24–26.
3. United States Military Academy, *Sixth Annual Reunion of the Association of Graduates*, 74–77.
4. Biographical Register USMA 1891, 308–310.

Appendix F

1. Cornish, *The Sable Arm*, 142.
2. *Ibid.*, 143.
3. Greenberg and Waugh, *The Price of Freedom*, 122.
4. *Ibid.*, 145–146.
5. Quarles, *The Negro in the Civil War*, 222.
6. McPherson, *The Negro's Civil War*, 190.
7. *Ibid.*, 190–191.
8. Wilson, *The Black Phalanx*, 126.
9. E. B. Long, *The Civil War Day by Day: An Almanac, 1861–1865* (New York: Doubleday, 1971), 387.
10. Cornish, *The Sable Arm*, 153–156.
11. Long, *The Civil War Day by Day*, 466.
12. Cornish, *The Sable Arm*, 173.
13. Lardas, *African American Soldier in the Civil War*, 53.
14. *Ibid.*, 6.
15. *Ibid.*
16. Wilson, *The Black Phalanx*, 259.
17. Cornish, *The Sable Arm*, 274.
18. *Ibid.*, 275.
19. Wilson, *The Black Phalanx*, 264.
20. Jack Hurst, *Nathan Bedford Forrest: A Biography* (New York: Vintage Books, 1994), 218–219.
21. McPherson, *The Negro's Civil War*, 229–231.
22. Claxton and Puls, *Uncommon Valor*, 2.
23. Logsdon, *Eyewitnesses at the Battle of Nashville*, 87.

24. Hargrove, *Black Union Soldiers in the Civil War*, 193.
25. Cornish, *The Sable Arm*, 284.
26. Benson Bobrick, *The Battle of Nashville* (New York: Alfred A. Knopf, 2010), 100–101.
27. Gladstone, *United States Colored Troops*, 117.
28. Hunt, *Observations of T. J. Hunt in the Civil War*, 11–13.
29. *Ibid.*
30. Gladstone, *United States Colored Troops*, 114.
31. Hunt, *Observations of T. J. Hunt in the Civil War*, 11–13.
32. Long, *The Civil War Day by Day*, 688.

Appendix G

1. McPherson, *The Negro's Civil War*, 157–161.

2. The government asked that the medals be returned; however, this occurred fifty years after the Civil War. Most veterans were dead by then and those still alive were not interested in returning the medals even if they understood the request.
3. U.S. Army, http://www.history.army.mil/moh.html.
4. The issue started with claims that African Americans in World War II were denied the MOH due to racism. The result was that some of their awards were upgraded to the MOH after a Pentagon review. Smith's file was included in this review, although many years after the Civil War: a long journey and an amazing story.
5. Hargrove, *Black Union Soldiers in the Civil War*, Appendix H.

Bibliography

Primary Sources

Athearn, Robert G. *Soldier in the West: The Civil War Letters of Alfred Lacey Hough*. Philadelphia: University of Pennsylvania Press, 1957.

Blair, Frank P. *The Life and Public Services of Gen. William O. Butler*. Baltimore: N. Hickman, 1848.

Brown, William Wells. *Narrative of William W. Brown, an American Slave*. Memphis: General Books, 2009.

Chamberlain, Samuel E. *My Confession*. New York: Harper & Brothers, 1956.

Christie, Thomas, and William. *Brother of Mine*. St. Paul: Minnesota Historical Society Press, 2010.

Cox, Jacob D. *The March to the Sea: Franklin and Nashville*. New York: Charles Scribner's Sons, 1882.

Cullum, George Washington. *Biographical Register of the Officers and Graduates of the U.S. Military Academy at West Point from its Establishment, in 1802, to 1890 with the Early History of the United States Military Academy*. Boston: Houghton, Mifflin, 1891.

Douglass, Frederick. *The Life and Times of Frederick Douglass*. Mineola: Dover, 2003.

Dyer, Frederick H. *A Compendium of the War of the Rebellion*. 3 vols. New York: Thomas Yoseloff, 1959.

Eggleston, George Cary. *A Rebel's Recollections*. Baton Rouge: Louisiana University Press, 1966.

Grant, Ulysses S. *Memoirs and Selected Letters: Personal Memoirs of U.S. Grant, Selected Letters 1839–1865*. New York: Literary Classics of the United States, 1990.

The Great Impeachment and Trial of Andrew Johnson, President of the United States. Philadelphia: T. B. Peterson & Brothers, 1868.

Harpers Weekly. 14 June 1862, 372, March–June 1868.

Hunt, Thomas Jefferson. *Observations of T. J. Hunt in the Civil War: A Narrative of the Military Life Minnesota in the Civil War*. Minneapolis: 1862–1865. St. Paul: Minnesota Historical Society Collections. N.d.

Johnston, Joseph E. *Narrative of Military Operations during the Civil War*. New York: Da Capo Press, 1959.

A Journal of an Excursion Made by the Corps of Cadets of the American Literary, Scientific and Military Academy Under Capt. Alden Partridge June 1822. Concord: Hill and Moore, 1822.

Long, A. L. *Memoirs of Robert E. Lee*. Secaucus, NJ: The Blue and Grey Press, 1983.

Marsh, Roswell. *Defence of Edwin Stanton*. Steubenville, OH: W. R. Allison's Printing Establishment, 1873.

Post, Lydia Minturn. *Soldiers' Letters, from Camp, Battle-field and Prison*. New York: Bunce & Huntington, 1865.

Reynolds, Thomas C. *General Sterling Price and the Confederacy*. St. Louis: University of Missouri Press, 2009.

Ross, Edmund G. *History of the Impeachment of Andrew Johnson, President of the United States*. Teddington, UK: The Echo Library, 2007.

Sherman, William Tecumseh. *Memoirs of General W. T. Sherman*. New York: Literary Classics of the United States, 1990.

Stoddard, William O. *Inside the White House in War Times: Memoirs and Reports of Lincoln's Secretary* [1890]. Lincoln: University of Nebraska Press, 2000.

Townsend, E. D. *Anecdotes of the Civil War in the United States*. New York: D. Appleton, 1883.

United States Military Academy. *Register of the Officers and Cadets of the U.S. Military Academy, June 1820*. West Point: Headquarters, U.S. Military Academy, 1884.

_____. *Register of the Officers and Cadets of the U.S. Military Academy, June 1821*. West Point: Headquarters, U.S. Military Academy, 1884.

_____. *Register of the Officers and Cadets of the U.S. Military Academy, June 1822*. West Point: Headquarters, U.S. Military Academy, 1884.

_____. *Register of the Officers and Cadets of the U.S. Military Academy, June 1823*. West Point: Headquarters, U.S. Military Academy, 1884.

_____. *Sixth Annual Reunion of the Association of Graduates of the United States Military Academy at West Point, New York June 17, 1875*. New York: A. S. Barnes, 1875.

Upham, Warren, and Rose Barteau Dunlap. *Collections of the Minnesota Historical Society. Volume XIV, Minnesota Biographies, 1655–1912*. St. Paul, Minn: The Society, 1912.

Articles

Army and Navy Journal, May 3, p. 602, and June 14, 1873, p. 697 (Kingsbury).

New York Independent, December 12, 1867.

Washington Daily Morning Chronicle, June 23, 1863.

Public Documents

Delaware Public Archives. *Baptism: Lorenzo Thomas (Adult)*. V. 87, p. 130, 9/25/1836.

Delaware Public Archives. *Marriage: Lorenzo Thomas to Elizabeth Colesberry*. V. 11, p. 181, 12/4/1832.

U.S. War Department. *Official Army Register of the Volunteer Force of the United States Army for the Years 1861, 1862, 1863, 1864; Volume 8*. Washington, D.C.: Adjutant General's Office, 1867.

_____. *The War of Rebellion: A Compilation of the Official Records of the Union and Confederate Armies*. Washington, D.C., 1880–1901.

Online Databases

Ancestry.com. http://www.ancestry.com.

CONGRESSIONAL GLOBE, 30th Cong., 1st Sess. 64 (1847). http://www.sewanee.edu/faculty/Willis/Civil_War/documents/LincolnSpot.html.

National Park Service. *Civil War Soldiers & Sailors System*. http://www.civilwar.nps.gov/cwss/.

Slave Narratives, Federal Writers' Project Multiformat 1936–1938, United States Library of Congress. http://memory.loc.gov/ammem/snhtml/snhome.html

U.S. Army. http://www.history.army.mil/moh.html.

Unpublished Sources

Court Martial file number Z29, Proceedings of Courts Martial, 1808–1940, RG 153, 34–59, Records of the Judge Adjutant General, NA.

Curran, John A. *The Civil War Diary of an Iowa Soldier July 1864–February 1865*. Undated.

Letter, L. M. Lane to Hon John C. Calhoun, 29 May 1819.

Letter, Caesar A. Rodney to John C. Calhoun, 31 May 1819.

Letter, J. Dorsey to John C. Calhoun, 31 May 1819.
Letter, Nicholas Van Dyke to John C. Calhoun, Secretary of War, 1 June 1819.
Letter, Evan Thomas to John C. Calhoun, Secretary of War, 2 June 1819.
Letter, Evan Thomas to the President of the United States, 2 June 1819.
Letter, James Tilton to the President of the United States, 2 June 1819.
Letter, Evan Thomas to John C. Calhoun, 29 July 1819.
Letter, Lorenzo Thomas to Irving McDowell, 14 January 1858.
Letter, Lorenzo Thomas to A. S. Johnston, 18 February 1858.
Letter, Lorenzo Thomas to A. Lincoln, 30 March 1864.
Major Alexander Macomb to Brevet Major William Jenkins Worth, 31 January 1823, Miscellaneous Military Academy Papers (F-77), 1813–1825, RG 77, NA.

Secondary Sources

Adams, George Worthington. *Doctors in Blue: The Medical History of the Union Army in the Civil War*. New York: Henry Schulman, 1952.
Alotta, Robert I. *Civil War Justice: Union Army Executions under Lincoln*. Shippensburg, PA: White Mane, 1989.
Ambrose, Stephen E. *Duty, Honor, Country: A History of West Point*. Baltimore: Johns Hopkins University Press, 1966.
Association of Graduates, United States Military Academy. *The Register of Graduates and Former Cadets of the United States Military, 2010*. West Point: Association of Graduates, 2010.
Barrow, Charles Kelly. *Black Confederates*. Gretna, LA: Pelican, 1995.
Barrow, Charles Kelly, J. H. Sefars, and R. B. Rosenburg. *Forgotten Confederates: An Anthology about Black Southerners*. Atlanta: Southern Heritage Press, 1995.
Bell, Andrew McIlwaine. *Mosquito Soldiers: Malaria, Yellow Fever, and the Course of the American Civil War*. Baton Rouge: Louisiana State University Press, 2010.
Benedict, Michael Les. *The Impeachment and Trial of Andrew Johnson*. New York: W. W. Norton, 1973.
Bessler, John D. *Legacy of Violence: Lynch Mobs and Executions in Minnesota*. Minneapolis: University of Minnesota Press, 2003.
Blackmon, Douglas A. *Slavery by Another Name: The Re-enslavement of Black Americans from the Civil War to World War II*. New York: Doubleday, 2008.
Boatner, Mark M., III. *The Civil War Dictionary*. New York: Vintage Books, 1991.
Bobrick, Benson. *The Battle of Nashville*. New York: Alfred A. Knopf, 2010.
Bonner, Robert E. *Mastering America: Southern Slaveholders and the Crisis of American Nationhood*. Cambridge: Cambridge University Press, 2009.
Boritt, Gabor S. *Lincoln's Generals*. Lincoln: University of Nebraska Press, 1994.
Burchard, Peter. *One Gallant Rush: Robert Gould Shaw and His Brave Black Regiment*. New York: St. Martin's Press, 1965.
Carnegie, Andrew. *Edwin M. Stanton: An Address by Andrew Carnegie on Stanton Memorial Day at Kenyon College*. New York: Doubleday, 1906.
Carnes, Mark C., and John A. Garraty. *American Destiny: Narrative of a Nation*. Vol. I, *To 1877*. 2nd ed. New York: Pearson Longman, 2006.
Castel, Albert. *General Sterling Price and the Civil War in the West*. Baton Rouge: Louisiana State University Press, 1996.
Catton, Bruce. *The Civil War*. New York: Fairfax Press, 1980.
_____. *A Stillness at Appomattox: The Fateful Last Chapter of the Army of the Potomac's Dramatic Saga*. New York: Doubleday, 1957.
Channing, Steven A. *Crisis of Fear: Seces-*

sion in South Carolina. New York: W. W. Norton, 1974.

Cimprich, John. *Fort Pillow: A Civil War Massacre and Public Memory*. Baton Rouge: Louisiana State University Press, 2005.

Civil War Society. *Civil War Society's Encyclopedia of the Civil War: The Complete and Comprehensive Guide to the American Civil War*. Princeton, NJ: Wing Books, 1997.

Claxton, Melvin, and Mark Puls. *Uncommon Valor: A Story of Race, Patriotism, and Glory in the Final Battles of the Civil War*. Hoboken, NJ: John Wiley and Sons, 2006.

Clinton, Catherine, and Nina Silber. *Divided Houses: Gender and the Civil War*. New York: Oxford Press, 1992.

Coddington, Edwin B. *The Gettysburg Campaign: A Study in Command*. New York: Touchstone, 1997.

Collins, Donald E. *The Death and Resurrection of Jefferson Davis*. New York: Rowman & Littlefield, 2005.

Cooper, Constance J. *350 Years of New Castle, Delaware: Chapters in a Town's History*. Wilmington, DE: Cedar Tree Books, 2001.

Cornish, Dudley Taylor. *The Sable Arm: Negro Troops in the Union Army, 1861–1865*. New York: W. W. Norton, 1956.

Cowley, Robert, and Thomas Guinzburg. *West Point: Two Centuries of Honor and Tradition*. New York: Warner Books, 2002.

Cunningham, H. H. *Doctors in Gray: The Confedereate Medical Service*. Baton Rouge: Louisiana State University Press, 1958.

Current, Richard Nelson. *Lincoln's Loyalists: Union Soldiers from the Confederacy*. New York: Oxford University Press, 1992.

Davis, Burke. *Sherman's March*. New York: Random House, 1980.

Davis, William C. *The Image of War, 1861–1865*. 6 vols. New York: Doubleday, 1983.

Dishman, Christopher D. *A Perfect Gibraltar: The Battle of Monterry, Mexico, 1846*. Norman: University of Oklahoma Press, 2010.

Dobak, William A. *Freedom by the Sword: The U.S. Colored Troops, 1862–1867*. Washington, D.C.: Center for Military History United States Army, 2010.

Durden, Robert Franklin. *The Gray and the Black: The Confederate Debate on Emancipation*. Baton Rouge: Louisiana State University Press, 1972.

Eggleston, Larry G. *Women in the Civil War: Extraordinary Stories of Soldiers, Spies, Nurses, Doctors, Crusaders, and Others*. Jefferson, NC: McFarland, 2003.

Eggleston, Michael A. *10th Minnesota Volunteers, 1862–1865: A History of the Action in the Sioux Uprising and the Civil War with a Regimental Roster*. Jefferson, NC: McFarland, 2012.

_____. *The White Man's Fight*. Bloomington, IN: Author House, 2012.

Eicher, John H., and David J. Eicher. *Civil War High Commands*. Stanford, CA: Stanford University Press, 2001.

Eisenhower, John S. D. *Agent of Destiny: The Life and Times of Genral Winfield Scott*. Norman: University of Oklahoma Press, 1997.

_____. *So Far from God: The U.S. War With Mexico, 1846–1848*. New York: Random House, 1989.

Eliot, George Fielding. *Sylvanus Thayer of West Point*. New York: Julian Messner, 1959.

Ellis, Richard N. *General Pope and U.S. Indian Policy*. Albuqerque: University of New Mexico Press, 1970.

Faust, Drew Gilpin. *This Republic of Suffering: Death and the American Civil War*. New York: Alfred A. Knopf, 2008.

Field, Ron. *The Seminole Wars, 1818–1858*. New York: Osprey, 2009.

Field, Ron, and Alexander Bielakowski. *Buffalo Soldiers: African American Troops in the U.S. Forces, 1866–1945*. Oxford:Osprey, 2008.

Flower, Frank Abial. *Edwin McMasters Stanton: The Autocrat of Rebellion,*

Emancipation and Reconstruction. Boston: George M. Smith, 1905.

Foner, Eric. *Free Soil, Free Labor, Free Men: The Ideology of the Republican Party before the Civil War.* Oxford: Oxford University Press, 1995.

———. *Reconstruction: America's Unfinished Revolution, 1863–1877.* New York: Perennial Classics, 2002.

Foreman, Amanda. *A World on Fire.* New York: Random House, 2010.

Foster, Gaines M. *Ghosts of the Confederacy: Defeat, the Lost Cause, and the Emergence of the New South.* New York: Oxford University Press, 1987.

Frassanito, William A. *Grant and Lee: The Virginia Campaigns of 1864–1865.* New York: Charles Scribner's Sons, 1983.

Freehling, William W. *The South vs. the South: How Anti-Confederate Southerns Shaped the Course of the Civil War.* New York: Oxford University Press, 2001.

Gallagher, Gary W., and Alan T. Nolan. *The Myth of the Lost Cause and Civil War History.* Bloomington: Indiana University Press, 2000.

Garrison, Webb, Jr. *Strange Battles of the Civil War.* Nashville: Cumberland House, 2001.

Gladstone, William A. *United States Colored Troops, 1863–1867.* Gettysburg: Thomas Publications, 1990.

Glatthaar, Joseph T. *Forged in Battle: The Civil War Alliance of Black Soldiers and White Officers.* New York: The Free Press, 1990.

Greenberg, Martin H., and Charles G. Waugh. *The Price of Freedom: Slavery and the Civil War.* Nashville: Cumberland House, 2000.

Greene, Jerome A. *Indian War Veterans: Memories of Army Life and Campaigns in the West, 1864–1898.* New York: Savas Beatie, 2007.

Grimsley, Mark. *The Hard Hand of War: Union Military Policy toward Southern Civilians, 1861–1865.* New York: Cambridge University Press, 1995.

Hafendorfer, Kenneth A. *Nathan Bedford Forrest: A Distant Storm: The Murfreesboro Raid, July 13, 1862.* Louisville, KY: KH Press, 1997.

Hargrove, Hondon B. *Black Union Soldiers in the Civil War.* Jefferson, NC: McFarland, 1988.

Harrington, Arthur Elliot. *Edmund G. Ross: A Man of Courage.* Franklin, TN: Providence House, 1997.

Hattaway, Herman, and Archer Jones. *How the North Won: A Military History of the Civil War.* Urbana: University of Illinois Press, 1991.

Hearn, Chester G. *The Impeachment of Andrew Johnson.* Jefferson, NC: McFarland, 2000.

Higginson, Thomas Wentworth. *Army Life in a Black Regiment.* Boston: Fields, Osgood, 1870.

Hogan, Michael. *The Irish Soldiers of Mexico.* Guadalajara: Intercambio Press, 1997.

Horn, Stanley F. *The Decisive Battle of Nashville.* Knoxville: University of Tennessee Press, 1978.

Humphreys, Margaret. *Intensely Human: The Health of the Black Soldiers in the American Civil War.* Baltimore: Johns Hopkins University Press, 2008.

Hurst, Jack. *Nathan Bedford Forrest: A Biography.* New York: Vintage Books, 1994.

Johnson, Timothy D. *Winfield Scott: The Quest for Military Glory.* Lawrence: University Press of Kansas, 1998.

Jones, Madison. *Nashville, 1864: The Dying of the Light.* Nashville: J. S. Sanders, 1997.

Jones, Robert Huhn. *The Civil War in the Northwest: Nebraska, Wisconsin, Iowa, Minnesota and the Dakotas.* Norman: University of Oklahoma Press, 1960.

Jordan, Ervin L., Jr. *Black Confederates and Afro-Yankees in Civil War Virginia.* Charlottesville: University Press of Virginia, 1995.

Jordan, General Thomas, and J. P. Pryor. *The Campaigns of Lieut.-Gen N. B. Forrest and of Forrest's Cavalry.* Dayton, OH: Morningside Bookshop, 1977.

Josephy, Alvin M., Jr. *The Civil War in the American West.* New York: Alfred A. Knopf, 1991.

Kennedy, John F. *Profiles in Courage.* New York: HarperCollins, 1955.

Lardas, Mark. *African American Soldier in the Civil War: USCT 1862–1866.* Oxford: Osprey, 2006.

Lemann, Nicholas. *Redemption: The Last Battle of the Civil War.* New York: Farrar, Straus and Giroux, 2006.

Levine, Bruce. *Confederate Emancipation: Southern Plans to Free and Arm Slaves during the Civil War.* New York: Oxford University Press, 2006.

Lewis, Felice Flanery. *Trailing Clouds of Glory: Zachary Taylor's Mexican War Campaign and His Emerging Civil War Leaders.* Tuscaloosa: University of Alabama Press, 2010.

Logsdon, David R. *Eyewitnesses at the Battle of Nashville.* Nashville: Kettle Mill Press, 2004.

Long, E. B. *The Civil War Day by Day: An Almanac, 1861–1865.* New York: Doubleday, 1971.

Lounsberry, Colonel Clement A. *Early History of North Dakota: Essential Outlines of American History.* Washington, D.C.: Liberty Press, 1919.

Mahon, John K. *History of the Seminole War.* Gainesville: University of Florida Press, 1967.

Manning, Chandra. *What This Cruel War Was Over: Soldiers, Slavery, and the Civil War.* New York: Vintage Books, 2007.

McDonough, James Lee. *Chattanooga—Death Grip on the Confederacy.* Knoxville: University of Tennessee Press, 1984.

_____. *Nashville: The Confederacy's Last Gamble.* Knoxville: University of Tennessee Press, 2004.

McFeely, William S. *Grant.* New York: W. W. Norton, 1981.

McMurry, Richard M. *John Bell Hood and the War for Southern Independence.* Lincoln: University of Nebraska Press, 1982.

McPherson, James M. *For Cause and Comrades: Why Men Fought in the Civil War.* New York: Oxford University Press, 1997.

_____. *The Negro's Civil War: How American Blacks Felt and Acted during the Civil War.* New York: Vintage Books, 1965.

McWhitney, Grady, and Perry D. Jamieson. *Attack and Die: Civil War Military Tactics and the Southern Heritage.* Tuscaloosa: University of Alabama Press, 1982.

Merry, Robert W. *A Country of Vast Designs.* New York: Simon & Schuster, 2009.

Miller, Edward A., Jr. *Lincoln's Abolitionist General: The Biography of David Hunter.* Columbia: University of South Carolina Press, 1997.

Moe, Richard. *The Last Full Measure.* New York: Henry Holt, 1993.

Monaghan, Jay. *Civil War on the Western Border, 1854–1865.* Boston: Little, Brown, 1955.

Nagel, Paul C. *John Quincy Adams: A Public Life, a Private Life.* New York: Alfred A. Knopf, 1957.

Nolan, Alan T. *Lee Considered: General Robert E. Lee and Civil War History.* Chapel Hill: University of North Carolina Press, 1991.

Nolan, Dick. *Benjamin Franklin Butler: The Damnedest Yankee.* Novato, CA: Presidio Press, 1991.

Oates, Stephen B. *With Malice Toward None: The Life of Abraham Lincoln.* New York: Harper & Row, 1977.

Oates, Stephen B., and Charles J. Errico. *Portrait of America.* Vol. 1, *From the European Discovery of America to the End of Reconstruction.* 9th edition. Boston: Houghton Mifflin, 2007.

_____. *Portrait of America.* Vol. 2, *From Reconstruction to the Present.* 9th edition. Boston: Houghton Mifflin, 2007.

Packard, Randall M. *The Making of a Tropical Disease: A Short History of Malaria.* Baltimore: John Hopkins University Press, 2007.

Palmer, Dave Richard. *The River and the Rock: A History of Fortress West Point, 1775–1783.* New York: Hippocrene Books, 1969.

Pappas, George S. *To the Point: The United States Military Academy, 1802–1902.* Westport, CT: Praeger, 1993.

Paulsen, Gary. *Soldier's Heart: Being the Story of the Enlistment and Due Service of the Boy Charley Goddard in the First Minnesota Volunteers.* New York: Dell Laurel-Leaf, 1998.

Pearson, Henry Greenleaf. *The Life of John A. Andrew, Governor of Massachusetts, 1861–1865.* Vol. 2. Ann Arbor: University of Michigan Library, 1904.

Poland, Charles P., Jr. *The Glories of War: Small Battles and Early Heroes of 1861.* Bloomington, IN: Author House, 2004.

Powell, William Henry. *A History of the Organization and Movements of the Fourth Regiment of Infantry, United States Army.* Washington City: McGill & Witherow, 1871.

Pratt, Fletcher. *Stanton: Lincoln's Secretary of War.* New York: W. W. Norton, 1953.

Quarles, Benjamin. *The Negro in the Civil War.* Boston: Little, Brown, 1953.

Redkey, Edwin S. *Black Exodus: Black Nationalists and Back-to-Africa Movements, 1890–1910.* New Haven, CT: Yale University Press, 1969.

Reid, Richard M. *Freedom for Themselves: North Carolina's Black Soldiers in the Civil War Era.* Chapel Hill: University of North Carolina Press, 2008.

Reynolds, Thomas C. *General Sterling Price and the Confederacy.* St. Louis: University of Missouri Press, 2009.

Rickey, Don, Jr. *Forty Miles a Day on Beans and Hay: The Enlisted Soldier Fighting the Indian Wars.* Norman: University of Oklahoma Press, 1963.

Robertson, James. *The Untold Civil War: Exploring the Human Side.* Washington, D.C.: National Geographic, 2011.

Rodriguez, Ricardo J. *Black Confederates in the U.S. Civil War: A Compiled List of African-Americans Who Served the Confederacy.* Charleston, SC: Create Space, 2010.

Rollins, Richard, ed. *Black Southerners in Gray: Essays on Afro-Americans in Confederate Armies.* Murfreesboro, TN: Southern Heritage Press, 1994.

Russell, Andrew J. *Russell's Civil War Photographs.* New York: Dover, 1982.

Sandburg, Carl. *Abraham Lincoln: The War Years*, 4 vols. New York: Harcourt, Brace, 1939.

Sanders, Tyrone. *The New Book of U.S. Presidents.* CreateSpace Independent Publishing Platform, 2012.

Sateren, Shelley Swanson. *A Civil War Drummer Boy: The Diary of William Bircher, 1861–1865.* Mankato, MN: Blue Earth Books, 2000.

Schultz, Jane E. *Women at the Front: Hospital Workers in Civil War America.* Chapel Hill: University of North Carolina Press, 2004.

Segars, J. H. *Black Southerners in Confederate Armies: A Collection of Historical Accounts.* Gretna, LA: Pelican, 2007.

Shea, William L., and Earl J. Hess. *Pea Ridge: Civil War Campaign in the West.* Chapel Hill: University of North Carolina Press, 1992.

Smith, Derek. *In the Lion's Mouth: Hood's Tragic Retreat from Nashville, 1864.* Mechanicsburg, PA: Stackpole Books, 2011.

Smith, John David. *Black Soldiers in Blue: African American Troops in the Civil War Era.* Chapel Hill: University of North Carolina Press, 2002.

Speer, John. *Life of Gen. James H. Lane, " "The Liberator of Kansas": With Corroborative Incidents of Pioneer History.* Garden City, KS: John Speer, Printer, 1896.

Stern, Philip Van Doren. *Secret Missions of the Civil War.* New York: Wing Books, 1959.

Stevens, Peter F. *The Rogue's March: John Riley and the St. Patrick's Battalion, 1846–1848.* Washington, D.C.: Potomac Books, 1999.

Stewart, David O. *Impeached: The Trial of President Andrew Johnson and the Fight for Lincoln's Legacy.* New York: Simon & Schuster Paperbacks, 2009.

Stockdale, Paul H. *The Death of an Army: The Battle of Nashville & Hood's Retreat.* Murfreesboro, TN: Southern Heritage Press, 1992.

Stoker, Donald. *The Grand Design Strategy and the U.S. Civil War.* New York: Oxford University Press, 2010.

Stout, Harry S. *Upon the Altar of the Nation.* New York: Penguin Group, 2007.

Street, James, Jr. *The Struggle for Tennessee: Tupelo to Stones River.* Alexandria: Time-Life Books, 1985.

Sully, Langdon. *No Tears for the General: The Life of Alfred Sully, 1821–1879.* Palo Alto, CA: American West, 1974.

Sword, Wiley. *Embrace an Angry Wind: The Confederacy's Last Hurrah: Spring Hill, Franklin, & Nashville.* New York: HarperCollins, 1992.

Symonds, Craig L. *A Battlefield Atlas of the American Civil War.* London: Ian Allan, 1985.

Thomas, Benjamin P., and Harold M. Hyman. *Stanton: The Life and Times of Lincoln's Secretary of War.* New York: Alfred A. Knopf, 1962.

Thomas, Emory M. *The Confederate Nation, 1861–1865.* New York: Harper & Row, 1979.

Tindall, George Brown, and David Emory Shi. *America: A Narrative History.* Vol. 2. 7th edition. New York: W. W. Norton, 2007.

Trudeau, Noah Andre. *Southern Storm: Sherman's March to the Sea.* New York: Harper Perennial, 2009.

Vincent, Thomas MacCurdy. *Abraham Lincoln and Edwin M. Stanton.* Washington, D.C.: Commandery of the District of Columbia, 1892.

Wakefield, John F. *The Battle of Nashville, 1864.* Florence, AL: Honors Press, 2001.

Ward, Geoffrey C. *The Civil War: An Illustrated History.* New York: Alfred A. Knopf, 1990.

Warner, Ezra J. *Generals in Blue: Lives of the Union Commanders.* Baton Rouge: Louisiana State University Press, 1964.

Webb, Lester A. *Captain Alden Partridge and the United States Military Academy, 1806–1833.* Northport, AL: American Southern, 1965.

West, Nathaniel. *The Ancestry, Life, and Times of Hon. Henry Hastings Sibley, L.L.D.* St. Paul: Pioneer Press, 1889.

Wheeler, Richard. *Voices of the Civil War.* New York: Thomas Y. Crowell, 1976.

Wiley, Bell Irvin. *The Life of Billy Yank: The Common Soldier of the Union.* Baton Rouge: Louisiana State University Press, 1952.

_____. *The Life of Johnny Reb: The Common Soldier of the Confederacy.* Baton Rouge: Louisiana State University Press, 1943.

_____. *Southern Negroes, 1861–1865.* Baton Rouge: Louisiana State University, 1938.

Wills, Brian Steel. *The Confederacy's Greatest Cavalryman: Nathan Bedford Forrest.* Lawrence: University of Kansas, 1992.

Wilson, Joseph T. *The Black Phalanx: African American Soldiers in the War of Independence, the War of 1812 and the Civil War.* Memphis: General Books, 2010.

Woodworth, Steven E. *Civil War Generals in Defeat.* Lawrence: University Press of Kansas, 1999

_____. *Decision in the Heartland: The Civil War in the West.* Westport, CT: Praeger, 2008.

_____. *Jefferson Davis and His Generals: The Failure of Confederate Command in the West.* Lawrence: University of Kansas Press, 1990.

Wyatt-Brown, Bertram. *Honor and Violence in the Old South.* New York: Oxford University Press, 1986.

Wyeth, John Allan. *That Devil Forrest: The Life of General Nathan Bedford Forrest.* Baton Rouge: Louisiana State University, 1989.

Index

Adams, John 18, 20, 151, 181, 182, 191, 194
Adams, John Quincy 101
Anderson 169
Andrew, John 101, 133, 135, 195
Athens, Alabama 161
Augusta, Alexander 72, 101

Banks, Nathan 50, 72, 101, 102, 134, 157
Barnes, William 169
Baxter Springs 47, 79, 159
Beaty, Powhatan 169, 170
Beauregard, PGT 81, 107
Benton Barracks 58, 59, 62, 76, 111
Biddle, Nick 102
Blake, Robert 170
Blakely 165
Booth, John W. 83
Bronson, James 170
Brown, William 170
Brown, Wilson 171, 172
Buena Vista 27, 104, 112, 115, 150
Butler, Benjamin 48, 49, 62, 69, 77, 82, 93, 94, 103, 128, 130, 131, 133, 134, 148, 149, 150, 152, 154, 155, 169, 179, 186, 189, 194
Butler, William 22, 23, 25, 26, 27

Cameron, Simon 8, 31, 114, 127, 128, 147
Canby, Edward 103, 116, 164
Carney, William 170, 172
Chaffin's Farm 161, 169, 173
Chamberlain, Samuel 22, 28, 103, 104, 179, 184, 189
Chase, Samuel 94
Cleburne, Patrick 78, 104
Clemenceau, Georges 83, 97, 104, 183
Colesberry, Elizabeth 21
Colesberry, Henry 119
contraband 63, 67, 68, 105, 128, 135, 166
Crater 160, 162
Crockett, Davy 17

Davis, Jefferson 9, 27, 41, 60, 69, 78, 80, 81, 104, 105, 117, 125, 129, 147, 192, 196

Dixon, James 97, 147
Dorsey, Decatur 172
Douglass, Frederick 7, 8, 37, 49, 81, 105, 126, 127, 128, 134, 189

Evarts, William 94

Fleetwood, Christian 171, 172
Forrest, Nathan Bedford 3, 33, 79, 81, 105, 114, 160, 161, 186, 193, 196
Fort Pillow 105, 160, 192
Fort Wagner 31, 159, 172
Fourth Regiment 18, 19, 20, 21, 22, 27, 30, 35, 61, 148, 178, 179, 186, 195
Franklin 2, 3, 87, 104, 107, 112, 162, 189
Frémont, John 37, 105, 127, 134

Gardiner, James 172
Garrison, William Lloyd 106, 127, 193
Grant, U.S. 21, 22, 29, 30, 33, 42, 52, 77, 81, 82, 86, 87, 88, 89, 91, 92, 97, 103, 105, 106, 112, 117, 157, 160, 164, 165, 178, 179, 189, 193, 194
Greeley, Horace 38, 106

Harris, James 116, 172, 173
Hawkins, Thomas 172, 174
Hilton, Alfred 173
Honey Springs 158, 159
Hood, John Bell 2, 3, 105, 106, 107, 112, 115, 117, 118, 162, 163, 164, 178, 194, 195, 196
Horsford 55
Humphreys, Margaret 56, 57, 62, 181, 182, 193
Hunt, Thomas 73, 74, 107, 182, 187, 189
Hunter, David 40, 62, 80, 108, 125, 128, 129, 131, 132, 135, 166, 185, 194

Jackson, Andrew 20, 108, 176
James, Miles 173
Johnson, Andrew 1, 2, 7, 32, 65, 83, 84, 85, 86, 87, 88, 89, 90, 91, 92, 93, 94, 95, 96, 97, 98, 99, 100, 103, 104, 114, 115, 117, 118,

197

136, 137, 138, 139, 140, 141, 142, 143, 145, 146, 147, 177, 182, 183, 189, 190, 191, 193, 196
Johnston, Joseph 31, 60, 107, 189
Juarez, Benito 60, 108, 109, 112

Kelly, Alexander 173
Kirby Smith, Edmund 28, 59, 60, 114

Lane, James 43, 108, 109, 131, 190, 195
Lawson, John 173, 175
Lee, Robert E. 3, 32, 33, 34, 35, 60, 65, 104, 105, 107, 109, 122, 125, 129, 164, 165, 189, 193, 194
Lincoln, Abraham 1, 3, 6, 7, 9, 30, 31, 32, 34, 35, 37, 39, 42, 46, 49, 68, 71, 72, 77, 81, 83, 84, 85, 102, 105, 108, 112, 114, 117, 122, 124, 125, 127, 128, 129, 131, 132, 134, 135, 157, 165, 168, 177, 179, 180, 182, 183, 185, 190, 191, 192, 194, 195, 196

malaria 53, 59
Maximilian 60, 108, 109, 111
McArthur, John 3, 109, 110
McClellan, George 32, 127, 134
Milliken's Bend 33, 158
Monroe, James 13, 16, 101, 109, 110, 128
Monterreyn 23, 25, 26, 27, 103, 148, 149, 150

Nashville 1, 2, 3, 6, 64, 66, 76, 81, 85, 97, 105, 106, 107, 108, 109, 110, 111, 112, 113, 114, 115, 117, 118, 162, 163, 177, 180, 182, 186, 187, 189, 191, 193, 194, 195, 196

Olustree 159

Palmetto 165
Partridge, Alden 15, 16, 17, 110, 116, 189, 196
Pease, Joachim 174
Petersburg, 160, 161, 172
Phelps, John 110, 130, 131
Pinn, Robert 174, 176
Polk, James 22, 27, 30, 110
Port Hudson, 157, 158
Price, Sterling 61, 73, 76, 109, 111, 180, 181, 182, 186, 189, 191, 193, 195

Quantrill, William 47, 159

Radical Republicans 83, 84, 86, 87, 90, 94, 114, 115
Ratcliff, Edward 175
Riley, John 26, 27, 111, 179, 195
Ross, Edmund 64, 94, 96, 97, 98, 99, 147, 190, 193
Russell, Ira 62, 111, 195

Sanderson, Aron 169
San Patricio Battalion 26, 27, 28, 111
Santa Anna, 21, 22, 27, 28, 29, 111, 115, 150
Saxton, Rufus 112, 132
Schofield, John 42, 112
Schurz, Carl 83, 84, 87, 112, 113
Scott, Winfield 8, 9, 27, 28, 30, 113, 148, 152, 154, 192, 193
Seminole 1, 18, 19, 20, 21, 115, 178, 179, 192, 194
Seward, Secretay of State 85
Shaw, Robert 49, 113, 159, 191
Sheridan, Philip 87, 112, 178
Sherman, William T. 33, 34, 42, 43, 45, 62, 64, 65, 66, 70, 77, 88, 95, 96, 113, 117, 126, 128, 147, 162, 190, 192, 196
Smalls, Robert 113, 114, 166, 167, 168
Smith, A.J. 24, 114, 164, 168, 175, 176
Spanish Fort 103, 107, 114, 164, 165
Stanberry, Henry 94
Stanton, Edwin 1, 2, 6, 7, 8, 31, 32, 33, 34, 35, 41, 43, 65, 66, 67, 68, 71, 75, 82, 85, 86, 87, 88, 89, 90, 91, 92, 93, 94, 95, 96, 99, 100, 114, 117, 131, 132, 133, 136, 137, 138, 139, 140, 141, 145, 146, 177, 179, 183, 191, 192, 195, 196
Steedman, James 3, 114, 115, 162, 163, 164
Stevens, Thaddeus 84, 88, 89, 92, 97, 111, 115, 144, 179, 184, 195
Sumner, Charles 84, 115, 144, 147

Taylor, Zachary 22, 23, 27, 99, 103, 111, 115, 116, 125, 149, 150, 177, 179, 192, 194
Tenure of Office Act 86, 88, 89, 90, 94, 95, 96, 99
Thayer, Sylvanus 15, 16, 17, 116, 147, 192
Townsend, E.D. 72, 117, 156, 183, 190
Turner, Nat 117, 121

Ullmann, Daniel 46, 70, 75, 117, 132, 133, 134
USCT 3, 6, 9, 10, 38, 40, 45, 46, 47, 48, 51, 57, 58, 63, 68, 69, 70, 71, 72, 73, 74, 76, 81, 101, 109, 123, 155, 159, 160, 161, 162, 163, 164, 165, 180, 194

Veal, Charles 176

Wade, Benjamin 83, 92, 93, 97, 117, 118, 147
Wells, Gideon 127, 189
Wendell, Cornelius 93, 94, 144
West Point 1, 3, 13, 14, 15, 16, 17, 18, 20, 21, 107, 110, 114, 116, 118, 128, 151, 178, 179, 189, 190, 191, 192, 195
Whiskey Ring 93
Wild, Edward 51, 118, 135

yellow fever 20, 53

www.ingramcontent.com/pod-product-compliance
Ingram Content Group UK Ltd.
Pitfield, Milton Keynes, MK11 3LW, UK
UKHW042007140426
5217IPUK00015B/1029